Highways and Hedges

Highways and Hedges

Anglicanism and the Universal Church

John Howe

Published for the Anglican Consultative Council
CIO Publishing
Church House, Dean's Yard, London SW1P 3NZ

ISBN 0 7151 4756 0

Published 1985 for the Anglican Consultative Council
by CIO Publishing
and in Canada by Anglican Book Centre, 600 Jarvis Street,
Toronto, Ontario, Canada M4Y 2J6

Contents

Foreword

In the lives of individual persons and of institutions, there are times when one event follows so closely upon another that there is little time for reflection. If persons and institutions do not reflect upon the things that happen, they miss the learnings that such reflection makes possible, and they become less able to focus future development with clarity. There is a growing conviction in many parts of the world that this is the situation of the world-wide family of autonomous Provinces which make up the Anglican Communion, and that it is vital for us to make time for such reflection.

If people in different parts of the world, living in different cultural contexts, are to be able to reflect responsibly, there is a primary task of gathering together data about what has been happening in the Communion. Bishop John Howe, as the first Fellow of the Anglican Consultative Council's Research Trust, has made a very important first contribution to the gathering and organizing of such data in *Highways and Hedges.* There is found in this volume information gathered from many sources, and it has been organized in such a way that the reader is not only furnished with much useful factual information but is also made aware of many of the issues and tensions that confront the Communion, and is encouraged to think about them. The book will be of great interest to anyone who is concerned about the Anglican Church and its contribution both to the wider Christian community and to the world the Church is called to serve. It will be of special importance to those in each Province and in pan-Anglican and ecumenical gatherings who are called upon, under God, to help shape the future of our Communion. It should be made widely known and should be widely circulated.

In this volume Bishop Howe, who has been so intimately connected with many of the developments about which he writes, shares some personal reflections upon them. I say "some of his reflections" because I am sure he was faced with two limiting factors. The first was his close involvement with the events and the limited time available to him to draw back from his involvement to be able to reflect in a wider context. The second was his obligation to submit this study to the Anglican Consultative Council before it could be published. I am sure that, at the sub-conscious as well as the conscious level, these factors would influence the extent of the personal reflections that Bishop Howe might have included.

Approval has now been given for the volume to be published. I know that it is the hope of many that, as Bishop Howe continues to reflect upon the developments in the family of Churches to which he has made such a great contribution, he will do further writing to share his thoughts about central issues of concern which he believes confront the Church. We will profit from his vision if he indicates the direction in which he feels the Anglican Communion should move and, from his wide experience, suggests the steps that might be taken to help the Communion grow and change, so that it may become a more faithful instrument of the Lord it is called to love and to serve. Such an additional volume would make *Highways and Hedges* even more valuable in enabling the Anglican Communion to learn from its experience.

Edward W. Scott
Primate
Anglican Church of Canada
19 November 1984

Preface

In September 1981 the Anglican Consultative Council set up a Research Trust. The Council's kind invitation to me to be the first Research Fellow I accepted gladly. I was requested during 1983 (later extended to mid-1984) "to make a study of developments in the Anglican Communion during the last twenty to twenty-five years" (*ACC-5 Report*, Resolution 37b).

My principal qualification for this Fellowship was that I had been appointed Anglican Executive Officer from 1969. The office of Anglican Executive Officer was succeeded by the Anglican Consultative Council in 1971 of which I was then elected the first Secretary General, an appointment which I held until the end of 1982. By that appointment I belonged to all the Provinces of the Anglican Communion, and I visited them all, some several times. Their ecumenical activities were also an involvement of mine.

The pages which follow are the study of developments in the Anglican Communion (1958–82) which I have made as the ACC's Research Fellow.

This is not a history or a report, but a study, which is what I was asked to do. Several histories have been written, and while some of the more recent are referred to and quoted, there is no attempt to repeat what their writers have done. The only exception has been when the events referred to are of too recent occurrence for objective historical accounts to be easily available.

This, then, is a study of developments. The views expressed, and any analyses made, are the responsibility of the writer alone.

I wish to express my gratitude to Miss Pamela Bird, Executive Assistant to Archbishop E.W. Scott of Canada, for typing the master copy of this study.

John Howe
Research Fellow
Anglican Consultative Council

Acknowledgements

I am especially grateful to the Seabury-Western Theological Seminary of Evanston, Illinois, for inviting me to give the M. Dwight Johnson lectures for 1984, and for agreeing that the lectures should include a significant measure of the material that is incorporated and printed in this book.

I am grateful also to Bishop Jabez Bryce of Polynesia for asking me to give the Floyd Memorial Lecture for 1984 in Suva, Fiji. Some of the material used appears in this text.

Also I wish to thank the following authors and publishers who have allowed me to quote passages for which they hold the copyright:

Abingdon, Nashville, Tennessee; and John S. Pobee *Towards an African Theology* by John S. Pobee

A.R. Mowbray & Co. Ltd., publishers; and Bishop Stephen Neill *Anglicanism* by Stephen Neill

Secretary-General, General Synod of the Church of England *Agreed Statement*, 1975

The Historical Society of the Episcopal Church, USA *An Anglican Turning Point* by Bishop Stephen F. Bayne, Jr.

The Society for Promoting Christian Knowledge
1. *Anglican-Orthodox Dialogue* by Archimandrite Kallistos Ware and the Reverend Colin Davey
2. *Preparatory Essays, Lambeth Conference 1968: Essay "Women and the Priesthood"* by the Very Reverend Alan Richardson

The Reverend Dr A.M.G. Stephenson
  The First Lambeth Conference 1867

Times Newspapers Ltd.; article in the issue of 17th September,
1983, by Monsignor Ralph Brown
  Insight into Catholic Canon Law

I

Of Change and Development

a. Change

The last twenty-five years have seen changes in the Anglican Communion. To the Anglican Christian who, with suitable humility, tries to see the world as God may see it, the picture of world change is not wholly discouraging. This applies not only to the Anglican Communion but also to other widespread Christian Churches. However, the present study relates to the Anglican Communion and that will be the principal subject of our attention.

'Change' and 'development' are not the same. Change can include all the alterations that go to the making of history. And change can be for the worse. There need be no development in the sense of getting better and better.

By the end of this study a picture should have built up which also provides some record of developments, and which also portrays something of what in the present is halt or maimed or blind.

Here, then, are several changes which can reasonably be assessed in terms of progress and development in the Anglican Communion.

The Bishops from Africa

The Lambeth Conferences since World War II have taken place every ten years, from 1948 to 1978, that is four Conferences in the period of thirty years. The Conferences are of bishops only, coming from every Anglican diocese throughout the world. Until well into our period many bishops in Third World countries were expatriate whites, which, given the way that Christianity had spread in the 19th and 20th centuries, was not surprising. But in the recent decades the speed at which the Church at all levels has become indigenous has been notable.

Here for the last four Lambeth Conferences is the proportion of bishops from Africa who were black bishops:

1948	approximately	6%
1958		30%
1968		55%
1978		80%

Relevant to these figures is the number of all bishops from Africa, and the percentage these were of the whole Conference:

Total of all bishops from Africa		Percentage of the Lambeth Conference from Africa
1948	37	11%
1958	50	16%
1968*	74	16%
1978	102	25%

This Conference included many assistant bishops, of which Africa has few.

New Provinces

The understanding of the Anglican Communion as a family of regional Churches was given expression in the Encyclical Letter of the 1930 Lambeth Conference:

> This Communion is a commonwealth of Churches without a central Constitution: it is a federation without a federal government. (*Report*, p. 28)

And a committee of that Conference wrote:

> There are two prevailing types of ecclesiastical organization: that of centralized government, and that of regional autonomy within one fellowship. Of the former, the Church of Rome is the great historical example. The latter type, which we share with the Orthodox Churches of the East and others, was that upon which the Church of the first centuries was developing. . . . The Provinces and Patriarchates of the first four centuries were bound together by no administrative bond: the real nexus was a common life resting upon a common faith, common Sacraments, and a common allegiance to an Unseen Head. (p. 153/3)

(There has been some variety in the meanings given to the word 'Province.' In common Anglican use now a Province is not subsidiary, but regional and autonomous. Provinces are major constituents of a body, in this case the Anglican Communion. Each Province has its own Constitution which no other Province can interfere with. Some of the Provinces are themselves composed of smaller areas which, while having a standing of their own, come under the main Constitution of the whole Province or Central Synod: these for convenience, and to accord with local terminology, may also be termed provinces, but are frequently distinguished, as here, by the spelling of province with a small 'p.'

(This may be the convenient point at which to indicate something of the varied use of the word 'Church'. A Province may be called a Church, and so may the whole Anglican Communion. 'Church' is used for every other denomination, as well as for the whole body of Christian believers, however that is conceived. But with a small 'c,' a church is usually a particular congregation or building. The context in which the word is used has to provide the meaning — and fortunately usually does.)

As Anglican activity spread in the world, the earlier tendency was to attach the newer church areas in some way or other to the Church of England: thus the American colonies were part of the Diocese of London. The inadequacies of the method became especially apparent with the American Revolutionary War, and American independence. The upshot was that the Episcopal Church in America in 1789 declared itself autonomous and independent, with its own Constitution; but it remained in voluntary and unique relationship with the See of Canterbury. It had become an autonomous Province.

In the 19th century somewhat similar Provinces came into being in the larger units of the British Empire, where British power and sense of responsibility might be strong — such as Canada, India, Australia.

Meanwhile in many parts of the world the Church was spreading through missionaries, the majority from England. Dioceses were being formed usually in connection with Canterbury, or occasionally with the Protestant Episcopal Church in the United States of America. For a time there were no more Provinces: but there was a Communion, a family of a sort. The Anglican Communion was perhaps a little surprised, as well as pleased, to find the ancient pattern of Church organization re-appearing in its own membership.

The next major event in this process starts in the 1950s when Geoffrey Fisher had become Archbishop of Canterbury. For a long time the importance of the universality of the Church had been recognized as transcending other considerations in the structuring of the Anglican Communion. The Church belonged to the countries and regions where it had developed: many Anglicans were neither white nor culturally of Britain or the North Atlantic, and most were far from the See of Canterbury. But their deliberate allegiance was to the world Church they knew. The good and growing pressure was eased by Archbishop Fisher's initiative in establishing further Anglican Provinces. These were the Province of West Africa in 1951, the Province of Central Africa in 1955, the Province of East Africa in 1960.

It is true that by that time the majority of the countries involved were moving towards political independence, but it will not do to limit Archbishop Fisher's accomplishment to a following of the political trend. The new Anglican Provinces of his time came before political independence. The order of events is as follows:

Country	In the Anglican Province of	Province founded	Political Independence
Nigeria	West Africa	1951	1960
Sierra Leone	West Africa	1951	1961
Zambia	Central Africa	1955	1964
Kenya	East Africa	1960	1963

These Provinces of the 1950s had theological reasons for their formation, having their instigation in the universality of God's redemption and his lack of respect for persons. Wherever the Church is it belongs, and belongs to the people of that place. And because God is one and universal, the brotherhood of a world family is its proper expression.

The number of Provinces in the Anglican Communion has grown fairly rapidly to twenty-seven so far. All are indigenous, equal in standing within the Communion, and each with its own Constitution. Thus the past twenty-five years has seen the most significant stage in that process whereby the Anglican Communion has changed from consisting of a head office and branch offices to being a world-wide family of equals, held together by a common faith and affection.

Two Watersheds

In its pilgrimage in this world the Church is faced periodically with passes that must be climbed and summits to be crossed. From the top of a pass streams flow in a new and forward direction. This summit is the watershed. Often it is reached only by a long struggle; and one has to hope also that the pass is the right one.

In the past quarter of a century the Anglican world has been climbing towards two separate watersheds. One it has crossed, though not everywhere simultaneously. Nevertheless the achievement is notable. That is the change we have just noticed which occurs by the establishment of new Provinces. It is the passage from occupation with missionary outreach to existence everywhere as part of the universal catholic Church: the transition from what we have described as head office and branch offices to being a world-wide family. The centre of attention is shifted from the expatriate missionary to the indigenous Church in the country to which he went. The expatriate missionary may be St. Paul, or St. Augustine of Canterbury, or Bishop Hannington, or a multitude of others, mostly quite recent: all have wished that the gospel message of salvation should not be a foreign faith, but should become a faith that was indigenous and autonomous — which belonged to the people of the land. That watershed has been crossed.

With that watershed goes another, which has not yet been crossed. The indigenous sharing of a faith requires an adequate universal agreement on the acceptable limits of faith and practice in the Anglican Communion. The need is not for acceptance of a universal, total, and therefore imposed, canon law. In peoples and situations so different, there will always be diversity, and a measure of diversity is welcome. The norm does not require the same details everywhere. The Anglican norm, as was observable at the Lambeth Conference in 1978, is not the historical or present decrees of one Church, however apt they may have been once upon a time for a contemporary local situation; it lies in the kind of broader sweep that is the basis of the Chicago/Lambeth Quadrilateral focussing on Scripture, Creeds, Sacraments and Ministry.

The emphasis here is on the need to agree the limits of interpretation, and consequently of practice. The need concerns not only the member Provinces in a world-wide Church, which holds together by common faith and affection, but also the need of other Churches to know more clearly where the Anglican Communion stands. It is difficult to know, for example, what are the acceptable Anglican limits in matters of marriage and divorce, or of ministry and eucharist. This assertion is made not to provide an opportunity for the confident to attribute blame but to emphasize the need to agree limits to diversity.

On many matters agreement on the limits is sufficient and causes no real difficulty. Reasons for a contrary situation may arise from a lingering fear of excessive diversity, or because national synods and the like can become so responsibly engrossed with their own current situation that they find it difficult to remember that all the world is not the same. There is a case for more universal appreciation of the limits. That is a watershed that has not been crossed. One may doubt whether it has been attempted very energetically.

An Anglican Procession

The contribution of the Anglican Consultative Council to the more recent years of the Anglican story will be recorded later in this study. At present we are concentrating on change. In the months before the first meeting of the Council, its "diminutive" staff in London became very familiar with the list of names of those whom the Anglican Churches were choosing for membership of this pan-Anglican body. At the wish of all the Churches, they would constitute a powerful advisory voice for the whole Communion in the affairs it chose to discuss.

The first meeting took place in 1971 in Limuru, Kenya, and included a special Evensong on February 28th in All Saints' Cathedral, Nairobi. The procession at the end of the Service was different from any we had known previously. The Council members from the Church of each Province or region walked together in little clusters — a bishop, a priest, a lay person (man or woman). The membership represented, in however small a way, the whole people of God. Because even in equality there has to be an order, the order was alphabetical. The clusters were: Australia, Brazil and Latin America, Burma, Canada, Central Africa, Ceylon, England . . . and so on to Uganda, United States of America, Wales, West Africa, West Indies. At the end was the Council's President and preacher, the Archbishop of Canterbury, Michael Ramsey.

It was, perhaps, the first time since before the Council of Nicaea that a world Council had met without a white majority.

A note of that day in my log-book reads: "As we proceeded out of the cathedral, with the groups of members in order of country, suddenly the list of members, for so long familiar on paper in the office in London, repeated itself in multi-racial flesh and blood. A moving moment."

Superseding Overseas Missionaries

Today one can travel half-way round the world in 24 hours. If there is an urgent crisis or a tragedy at home, and your home happens to be on the other side of the globe, it is usually possible to be there within a couple of days. Not so very long ago, from the time the news reached you it might be nearer a couple of months or more before you could expect to be home. There is a tendency still to think of 'missionaries overseas' as men and women who are rather heroic people who might not see their homes again for much of a lifetime. But now, in many aspects, the style of the missionary life has changed. Unless it is by choice, one need not anywhere be seriously out of touch, or live a life characterized by remoteness. Indeed, the response of much of the Third World may constitute a less difficult environment than the apathy or secularism with which many may have to contend who stay in their own country in the western world. One is not denigrating either. One is noting a change.

Another change which works in the opposite direction is that the 'overseas missionary' is much less likely to be in a position of leadership. The Church to which he goes will be autonomous, and one reason for his going is that the autonomous Church has asked for his services.

Non-Western Theology

During its first century the Christian faith was moving into the Greek world. The language, thought patterns, the style of logic and the assumptions of the subsequent centuries when the faith was acquiring theological forms were characteristically Platonic and European rather than Judaean. Until our own times the Christian culture has been European, and for most the norm has been western European, Reformation and all. This was understandable. The Christianity one taught was Christianity as one had learned it, and the thinking done — often profound thinking — was in accordance with the education, method and procedure that had been received.

Occasionally the identification of Christianity with the assumptions of western culture has been questioned — as by some Jesuit missionaries of the 16th century in China. They encountered systems of thought, language and culture that were not of the western manner, but which they felt certainly did not by nature exclude the Christian faith — rather, they were capable of adding to its light and qualities. Such an outlook received little sympathy from the west.

The story is a long one, and begins to move a little faster in the last hundred years as more Christians of the west lived abroad. Some began to consider that the culture, customs, social relationships and assumptions of those among whom they lived were not to be banned in the name of Christianity, but had a rightful place in the world of a catholic Creator and Father.

The great change in the last quarter century has been not merely the increase in momentum but the passage of much initiative to non-western people. Having acquired Christianity from the west, they are turning to examine their own cultures and traditional assumptions to consider what Christ and the gospel may be saying to them, and possibly through them, to the world.

In the west, so great a change after so long a time does not make for easy acceptance — or even recognition. Some go so far as to assign its manifestations to ways of currying favour for local political ends.

Particularly since the renaissance, the significance of the individual has, in the west, been at the centre of much thought and deliberation. Even when, as now, there is emphasis on the community, the thought concerns the desirability of a community that is composed of individuals. In a number of parts of the world, however, the *sensus communis* is inseparable from that concept of the 'wider family', which is rare in the west. Descartes' classical description of human existence — "I think *(cogito)* therefore I exist" — is not uncongenial in the west even when it is not accepted precisely. But in many parts elsewhere it is scarcely comprehensible. Writing of his own West Africa, Professor John Pobee has said that for him and the assumptions of his people the word *cogito* needs to be replaced by *cognatus* — "I am known," with the necessary implication that individual existence is impossible. Of the *cognatus* Pobee expands the ontology thus:

> I am related by blood, therefore I exist, or I exist because I belong to a family. And a family, which is the basic unit, consists of the living, the dead, and the yet-to-be-born. The family relationships determine the view of man. The unit is the extended family, i.e. grandparents, blood relatives, in-laws, constituting a dynamic unity, or togetherness, with parents and children, according to prevalent mores. (J.S. Pobee: *Towards an African Theology* 1979, p. 49. For similar important studies, see the writings of Bishop John V. Taylor, particularly *The Primal Vision.*)

Assumptions of existence in the wider family are not only normal to many civilizations, they are also common to much of Scripture itself. It is not unfair to propose that much of the Old Testament, and not a little of the New, can only be understood in its fullness by those who share the concept of the wider family, because for them it is the natural understanding of life and of human beings. There are factors in the gospel which the west cannot understand unless other civilizations and cultures teach them.

Once in Africa, when I was discussing this aspect of Christian faith, I was firmly reminded that Africa detected and understood matters in the Christian faith about liberation, for example, about Israel and Egypt, to which the west has become less sensitive. This too may be true: certainly it is widely thought to be true. It is not casual chance that in Latin America there have rapidly developed not one but several Christian theologies in which liberation has a prominence that most western Christian thought has not been used to.

My point here is not to argue a particular case, but to indicate another area of recent change. Western thought and assumptions may no longer be regarded as the norm for hearing the Christian faith and Scriptures — even though many are still unaware that the old order has changed. The point is made in this way by Canon John Macquarrie:

> Everyone wants to claim that his arguments are theological but every theology comes out of a particular historical situation and is therefore culturally and socially conditioned. (*1978 Lambeth Conference Report*, Appendix I, p. 117)

Most Christians

In 1900 the percentage of all Christians who were white by colour was 81.1. "By 1980, massive church growth in the Third World had reduced these proportions to 50.5% white. By 1981 non-whites formed a majority of all Christians." (D.B. Barrett: *World Christian Encyclopedia* 1982, p. 9)

b. Development

This study is about developments. We have started with brief descriptions of a number of changes in recent years which have affected the Anglican Communion. They are changes most of which appear to contain at least an element of development, but before such an inference may be drawn it is necessary to discern what, in the Anglican Communion, constitutes development, what is the basic factor against which any change must be measured.

The basic factor is the purposes of Jesus Christ — the gospel and what he said. Development is to progress in fulfilling the Father's intention of salvation through Jesus. The Church, and any part of it, through the ages exists for that reason.

The description 'development' can reasonably be applied — with or without degrees of qualification — to manifold and sundry aspects of the performance of any Christian Communion, but however important the aspects are, they are at best secondary, and acquire importance only in relation to the gospel of salvation.

For example, a significant increase in the number of members of a Church is often regarded as one of the main criteria of development. It is important, but secondary — and not essential. The Anglican Communion, through its great increase in the Third World, has undoubtedly grown in the last quarter of a century. Anything like exact figures are impossible to come by: the total now may be put at 60 million, or 70 million, or 80 million. So much depends on what you count, especially if figures for other Churches are taken into the calculation. Baptisms may be counted, but records are patchy, especially in some parts of the world; and infant baptism is not a universal practice, and some Communions do not have water-baptism at all. Some base their records on Easter communions, but where a priest has congregations scattered over a vast area, some may not have the opportunity of Easter communion until weeks after the festival; and also the emphasis put on communion, as well as the age of admission, varies. There is no expeditious road.

Nevertheless, a general impression of trends, of increase and decrease is known, particularly to the travellers and listeners and judicious statisticians. The Anglican Communion grows. Growth is not uniform. For those parts of the western world which for years have been aware of a decline, and therefore aware of all the problems and discouragements that go with that situation, there is encouragement in the knowledge that by lifting their eyes to the whole width of God's world they perceive that they are members of a Communion that grows.

But, as we have seen, the question that has to be asked about every increase in numbers is whether the increase is a kind that gives expectation of salvation through the fulfilling of the Father's intention in Jesus Christ. The gospel implies an enormous expansion, from the little company of disciples and witnesses of the resurrection to the commission to teach and convert "all the nations" (Matthew 28:19). On the other hand, not every kind of expansion is acceptable. Where the Father's good pleasure does not prevail, talk may be of a "little flock" and a remnant. The requirement is that according to a person's capacity and opportunity he should "know God," through response to Christ. And just what that means is a mystery. One encounters belief that is enmeshed in intelligent complexities or hesitant through contradictory experiences. These, surely, can be sympathetically, even admiringly, understood – not merely by people but by Christ the Son too. One encounters faith that is brave and uncomplicated but whose origins have a simplicity that is not available to a more searching mind. Such seems to be the contending of the woman of Canaan who believed Jesus could heal her daughter and would not be put off. And Jesus said to her "Woman, great is your faith" (Mat-

thew 15:22ff). Her faith, such as it was, was marvellously acceptable. No less acceptable was the profundity of thought and experience that made St. John's faith or, one may suppose, that of the
many Christian mystics and scholars. But there remains an element
of surprise and consolation to encounter Christ saying, in one of the
great revelations of the incarnation:

> I thank thee, Father, Lord of heaven and earth, for hiding these
> things from the learned and wise, and revealing them to the sim-
> ple. Yes, Father, such was thy choice. Everything is entrusted to
> me by my Father; and no one knows the Son but the Father, and
> no one knows the Father but the Son and those to whom the Son
> may choose to reveal him. (Matthew 11:25–27; Luke
> 10:21–22/NEB)

The faith that is not acceptable appears to be that which is superficial and artificial, that which is obscured by hypocrisy, pride, and
the like. The gospels, and not least St. Paul, warn against a faith built
on rules when the appropriate response for a free gift is thankfulness
and love.

This consideration, which could be much extended, is relevant
when one is faced with an increase in numbers in the Anglican Communion and therefore must ask whether this is a development. Old
questions recur in one's mind. How much faith qualifies for salvation? What measure of intelligence does the gospel require for effective faith? There is no quantitative answer. There is no way of
measuring sincerity or mercy. The most one can say is that the
average of faith today does not appear to differ much from the
average faith in other times. Only the Father and the Son will know
whether that is enough. For this study, if we are to have much hope
at all, it means that, yes, an increase in numbers may be reckoned a
development, but only because it is a response to Christ, not because
of numbers themselves.

Similarly at this stage in opening up our study it is suitable to consider whether the ethnic extension of the Anglican Communion, and
its growth into a universal family, is development or merely change.
The measure again is the Scriptures, and the Church that sprang
from what Jesus did and said. The Fatherhood of God is universal.
With the resurrection even the Jews have no special place. God is the

catholic Creator of heaven and earth. The cross is for all, not some. There is no respect of persons. So increase in the diversity of membership is according to the divine mind. It is development, not change.

One or two other fields where there might be development may be introduced here. With both the implication is that changes in the whole style of human life are not far away; and the question concerns what measures the Anglican Communion may be taking to make suitable witness to Christ in changes that seem to be coming on the earth. One of the fields for consideration concerns the population environment in which the work of salvation will have to be carried on. In Christ's day the population of the world was probably about 250 million. It was not until 1830 that the figure was approximately 1,000 million, but a rapid growth was already under way. A quarter of a century ago – the mark had reached 3,000 million. By the end of the century, which is now very near, the figure will reach 6,000 million, and it will continue increasing very rapidly thereafter.

It is estimated that the 6,000 million will be composed like this:

58%	Asian
13%	African
10%	Latin America
9%	European
5%	North American
5%	Russian

This is a different world. Generally, for the east as much as for the west, the proportions are almost too difficult to grasp. Changes in power and poverty, to name but two, are unavoidable. It seems unlikely that the Christian religion will dominate. Moreover, the considerable Christian growth falls ever further behind the population growth. The growth in the Anglican Communion which we have noticed is slower still, and in the vastness of Asia, is minute.

For any Christian, with his faith in the gospel, to see how this situation can be met is humanly speaking near to impossible. A big, old-style missionary activity could be more offensive than effective. A considerable redeployment of resources does have relevance and necessity. But really we are talking of a vastly altered world, yet which remains nevertheless a world created and redeemed by God through Jesus Christ, not talking just of percentages on paper. In relation to this the Anglican Communion has a profound part to play, but it is not immediately obvious that significant Anglican development is taking place in that direction.

The issue is complicated by other influences which are likely to be transforming the world before long. There is ample probability that by the end of the century the increased capacity and use of computers will have consequences which are revolutionary in nature. The smaller computer is likely to transform the way communities live and the distribution of homes in which they live. Much of the work and collaboration which brings people together will be done by virtually instantaneous communication from the home base. There seems no reason why such procedures should have a national limitation. Some of the main characteristics of what is coming are fairly widely known, although the trend of the consequences is less clear. But to be giving the matter thought is relevant, not least in the whole arena of Christian living.

A deeper significance attaches to the developments that are taking place in what may for convenience be called the large computers. From the initial instructions or questions they operate, of course, infinitely faster than the human mind. And there is no reason for the memory they contain to stop short at the million million 'bits' that are roughly the limits of a human memory. The capacity to process information at great speed, the vast memory, instructions about deriving its own rules from experience with previous samples, these and other capacities have already resulted in an ordinary – but very large – working computer producing rules in the field of organic chemistry which were previously unknown. Such capacity may be termed – not very accurately – 'intelligence.' The point seems to be that already it is within the compass of a big computer, mindless though it is, to do what the slower human brain cannot accomplish. Development of such procedures will no doubt continue. Some computer scientists expect – and one hesitates to doubt them – that in due course the 'Ultra-Intelligent Machine' (UIM) will emerge. The capacity to give opinions from known or deducible evidence, or to combine, say, climate forecasting, world crops and world economy, has great penetration and depth. One may assume that UIMs would participate in designing the next generation of UIMs.

Such computers would be able, at great speed, to give probable answers to major issues and problems such as are virtually impossible for human beings to formulate in the shape of questions, let alone to perceive an answer. Man becomes an observer and not a contributor. It is again a different world.

If this picture of the near future has much accuracy, then a great deal concerning human reasoning and behaviour with which we are familiar may soon be obsolete. And it is to a world of this kind that the Church has in part to give its attention. Compared with the consideration which is based on known population increase, in this case there are more unknown factors. What, in such a situation is conscience? What is the role of spiritual understanding? What is to constitute Christian fellowship for human beings? What has the Father in mind about his work of creation and redemption?

The question arises: Is this an area in which Anglican thinking has begun to develop? There is no evidence that it has done so yet, although individuals in this and other Churches are drawing attention to the shape of things that may be expected to come dramatically before long.

II

The Anglican Denomination

If we are to discern developments in the Anglican Communion in the past twenty-five years, it is necessary to see what Anglicanism is.

The Church exists solely to do and be what God wants of it, particularly as that purpose was revealed in Jesus Christ. The Christian Church has its roots in Christ and his gospel; and in the transmission through the apostles, and through the catholic tradition, particularly as this faith and tradition were expressed in the first centuries. The guiding power then, and through all the centuries, is God the Holy Spirit.

Of course, the gospel is not always fully and identically comprehended, and the activity of the Holy Spirit is not always clearly understood. People are human and situations diverse, but the source and the continuing grace are divine. Thus, the Anglican Church thinks in terms of one continuing Church – one, holy, catholic and apostolic.

Those four 'marks of the Church' derive through the creeds, and are often used in Anglicanism. They are a better description than the name 'Anglicanism' because Anglicans think in terms of one continuing and universal Church. There is no separate Anglican identity. To search for one, as some ecumenists feel they must, is an unprofitable exercise. Moreover, labels, however misleading, have a tendency to take root and possibly to become definitive. Even where they may reasonably exist, identity labels are always best handled with care.

Anglicanism, in the past, has had a lot to do with England, and indeed there are languages today where, to widespread Anglican dismay, the world translates as 'English.' Half the dioceses in the Anglican Communion now are not in the British Commonwealth. Regularly someone proposes that the name 'Anglican' be changed for some other name that carries a gospel connotation, not a national or political one. There is a good case, but the habit is too ingrained for alteration to be likely, at least yet awhile.

The most important point is that the Anglican Church lays its emphasis on continuity – continuity of the one universal Church with its origin in Christ and the gospels and the apostles.

That other Churches or denominations proclaim their foundation in the same apostolic and catholic Church is obvious, and therein lies a deep tragedy in which we share: the followers of Christ are divided, the Church is divided. And as years and generations go by, divisions become consolidated. The reunion of the Christian world is a great endeavour of these times, and to that subject we shall devote ourselves later on to consider what contribution the Anglican Communion may be making to the development which is the restoration of wholeness.

Sometimes it is appropriate to associate the Reformation with past division and present ecumenism. Most generally in Anglican thought, Reformation is seen not as a sort of re-birth, a new beginning, but as a procedure, when true faith and practice were being lost, of restoring the 'marks' and continuity of the Church. The procedure has almost always been well-meant, the actual consequences not always happy.

The Anglican Church's appeal to the gospel, the apostolic Church and the early centuries, has been the foundation of its faith and worship. A good expression of that general belief is to be found conveniently in a hymn. And it is good to realize this well-known 19th century hymn is sung lustily and with sincerity by all sorts of Anglicans (who sometimes think they are more diverse than they are) as well as by people of other Churches. The hymn – here abbreviated to three verses – is this:

> The Church's one foundation
> Is Jesus Christ, her Lord:
> She is his new creation
> By water and the Word:
> From heaven he came and sought her
> To be his holy Bride,
> With his own Blood he bought her,
> And for her life he died.

Elect from every nation,
Yet one o'er all the earth,
Her charter of salvation
One Lord, one Faith, one Birth;
One holy name she blesses,
Partakes one holy Food,
And to one hope she presses
With every grace endued.

Yet she on earth hath union
With God the Three in One,
And mystic sweet communion
With those whose rest is won:
O happy ones and holy!
Lord, give us grace that we
Like them, the meek and lowly,
On high may dwell with thee.

(*Hymns Ancient and Modern, No. 255*
The English Hymnal, No. 489
by S.J. Stone, 1839–1901)

The basic tenets, as formulated for the purposes of Christian unity, and in brief compass, can be located in the Chicago/Lambeth Quadrilateral (1886/1888) as follows:

A.   The Holy Scriptures of the Old and New Testaments "as containing all things necessary for salvation," and as being the rule and ultimate standard of faith.

B.   The Apostles' Creed as the Baptismal Symbol; and The Nicene Creed as the sufficient statement of the Christian Faith.

C.   The two Sacraments ordained by Christ Himself – Baptism and the Supper of the Lord – ministered with unfailing use of Christ's Words of Institution, and the elements ordained by Him.

D.   The Historic Episcopate, locally adapted in the methods of its administration to the varying needs of the nations and peoples called of God into the Unity of His Church.

That is the original form of the Quadrilateral, but the fourth clause concerning the historic ministry has undergone alterations since (cf p. 119f). Some passages concerning the Chicago/Lambeth Quadrilateral are:

Lambeth Conference of 1930 Report, page 114
Lambeth Conference of 1948 Resolution 59
Lambeth Conference of 1978 Resolution 28/3 and page 99
A.M. Ramsey, *From Gore to Temple*, 1960, page 119 (American edition called *An Era in Anglican Theology*)

Two points are particularly to be noticed. One is how short the list is. Among Christians there is in fact a lot of diversity, but experience of many years of travelling about the Anglican world fosters a conviction that the number of essentials is comparatively few. There are many differences of one sort or another, but however deep-rooted these are, they are never more than secondary. It was illuminating, if not surprising, to find that Bishop Stephen Bayne, the first Executive Officer of the Anglican Communion, told of this as a fruit of his experience in an address he gave to the Anglican Communion at a Congress in Canada in 1963. He said:

A second great condition of Anglican action is that we shall travel light – that we shall remember that we are a pilgrim people, and that a pilgrim carries with him only those things that are essential for his life. It is a characteristic mark of the Anglican tradition, at our best, that we recognize how few and how important the essentials are.

One of the vivid examples of this is what we call the 'Chicago/Lambeth Quadrilateral.' It is not necessary to think of the Quadrilateral as either imperishable prose or an unfailing symbol of the Christian faith. It is no more than it pretends to be – a bare statement of those elements which we regard as essential to the full life of the Church. And it is instructive to meditate on the fact that there are only four of those elements, and that they are the barest of bones. We can imagine churches without most of the things we take for granted. We can imagine them without many of the opinions we share, the vestments we wear, the prayers we say, the traditional forms and instruments of Church life as we know them. None of these seems to us essential. Only the four sparse elements are needed, in our view, and they are indispensable. *(Anglican Congress 1963 Report,* p. 187)

This view is increasingly held in the Anglican world, so that there is a convergence based on a decrease in contentious fervour about particular varieties which, even if they are thought to be commendable, are not claimed as indispensable. This is a development, but the change that is taking place is fairly slow, and must not be exaggerated.

The second point to be noticed about the brevity of the list in the Lambeth Quadrilateral is that by giving the barest of outlines it seems to exclude a great many subjects that are reasonably discussable. The supreme status rightly given to Scripture, together with the presentation and expounding of Scripture indicated by the Creeds, leaves much that is important in Scripture short of a necessary interpretation. Increasingly, the urge meticulously to define everything is diminishing. Uniformity in interpretation of secondary matters, if it is serious and responsible, is respected even when it is not accepted. Inflexibility of view is less admired than once it was. One result is to make a place for a measure of comprehensiveness without deliberately setting out to do so.

Comprehensiveness is a criticism that is often laid against Anglicanism. How far it is good or bad may depend on what in the particular instance is meant by comprehensiveness. If it means scooping up diversities and contradictions and letting the one pot contain them all, it is a bad thing. If it means regretting that other Anglicans are still not 'like us' (whatever that may be) and generally avoiding them, there is little that is commendable. But comprehensiveness, while seldom, if ever, an end in itself, can have respectable origins. So, too, can pluralism, which is often seen as a relation: "The liberty of pluralism is possible only because there are wide areas of agreement" (Macquarrie: Appendix I to *Lambeth Conference Report 1978,* page 117). They can facilitate serious progress, and so development.

The impression gained from travelling extensively in the Anglican Communion is that whereas obviously diversities continue, they are decreasing, although remaining excessive.

The Church in England has a special place in the Anglican Communion. While the Communion sees itself as part of Christ's universal Church, it sees itself also as that part which, in the course of history, was funnelled through Britain – a fact which it sees as interesting but not fundamental.

When Christianity spread to Britain in the early centuries it made its entrance from all directions. Most prominent in the early days was the Celtic Church of the western and northern parts of Britain. The principal figure of the second wave of Christian growth in Scotland, St. Columba, died in 597, the year in which St. Augustine arrived in southern England and set up his base at Canterbury. Undoubtedly there were Christians in the south before that but not a great deal is known about them. Unlike the Celtic Church, the south, and certainly St. Augustine, looked to Rome as the centre of ecclesiastical organization and authority, and this became the general British pattern. Thus Britain was an area in the medieval Church in Europe, with Canterbury as its own principal see.

There is no shortage of studies of church history, and an account of some of the events of the last two or three decades does not require another. To this glance at the beginning of the Anglican Church, a note about some of the effects of the Reformation may be added as necessary background for this consideration of the Anglican Communion's present activity.

The motives which underlay reform in the Church of western Europe in the 16th century were excellent when witness to the gospel itself appeared as distorted and clouded. So were many of the achievements of reform in both the Protestant and Catholic allegiances (as they came to be known). Left to itself the Reformation had an enormous capacity for one-ness in Christ and Christlikeness everywhere. But it was not left to itself: it is not possible that the great movements of history should be. It had to contend with the capacity of free man for diversity, and of individuals with the upper hand for energetic self-righteousness. It had to contend with the fears of politicians and churchmen, and the power-politics of States and newly self-conscious nations. In the turmoil of those centuries much happened that was excellent, but there might have been much more. Perhaps it is time we had all got over the struggles.

The dominance of the papacy, universal in the west in the Middle Ages, was broken at the Reformation. In England the unsatisfactoriness of the Roman style and political power was widely acknowledged, but it was not specifically on a theological issue that the break came. The immediate issue was of politics and sovereignty. To an extent which now it is almost impossible to realize, Church and State were inseparable in a Christian land. Underlying the violence and hatred that was soon being meted out in England and elsewhere to adherents to Rome was the fact that they were adherents to an alien power and therefore to be classed as traitors.

However, the fracture with Rome rapidly widened to varying degrees of theological condemnation and distrust. The tensions released by engagement in reform were many, deep and diverse. Most affected England to a greater or lesser degree, sometimes for good, sometimes not, and often with a violence that at the time was thought appropriate for matters concerning the gospel and the salvation of souls.

At the heart of most reform was the desire to recover the gospel, and the outlook of the early and apostolic Church. Even here there could be conflict. The gospel proclaims salvation through faith in Jesus Christ who is the Son of God. The early Church which established the Canon of the New Testament and formulated the Creeds paid particular attention to the incarnation. Following the theology and insights of Martin Luther, the reforming churches laid stress on God's free and gracious gift in the unique work of justification, forgiveness and salvation. For Christian response to Jesus Christ there was a change at the centre which deeply affected the proclamation of faith and the gospel. Some may think that according to its time the early Church comprehended rightly both incarnation and salvation, and that the fusion of emphasis is not wholly apart from the origins of Anglican comprehensiveness.

Undoubtedly English participation in reform, and later in Reformation theologies, and its perennial appeal to the gospel and the early Church, brought about a measure of variety in the behaviour of the Anglican Communion. Of the 19th century in England Bishop Stephen Neill writes:

> We must sedulously avoid the temptation to simplify what was in reality a very complex scene. It will be convenient once again to work out a kind of spectrum of Anglican life and thought; and, as in the rainbow, we shall find it necessary to distinguish not less than seven colours. But, even when we have attempted to identify all these various strands in the Anglican complex, it will still re-

main true that the majority of Anglicans, then as now, cannot be identified wholly with any one of these tendencies. (*Anglicanism,* 4th (1977) edition, p. 232)

The Anglican foundation in the gospel, and the Church which flowed from it through the apostles and the tradition (παραδοσις) under the Holy Spirit, had its expression not in a code of canon law or a reformation 'confession' but in the Book of Common Prayer. Belief and worship are inseparable. The actual form of the book or the worship derived from it have not always been outwardly identical in all times and places, as present-day revisions, often provincially based, bear out. And there is still some — though a decreasing amount — of individual liturgizing where individuals or congregations, or even dioceses, (of whatever outlook) are happy in the belief that they know best; but the foundation is constant.

'Articles of Religion' do exist, and they are at times usefully referred to, but they are not a 'confession', they are not the foundation. The '39 Articles' are the most widely known and respected. In wide areas of the Anglican Communion they have never appeared in any constitutional document and no subscription to them is required. Their existence and content are, though, significant. They derive from the vigorous contentions of the 16th century, and state the position of a Church which in that tussle accepted neither the corruptions that were attributed to the later medieval Rome, nor the more particular and extreme contentions of some Reformation parties, such as the Anabaptists. The 39 Articles, whatever criticisms they may have been subjected to, were aimed to state evangelical and catholic principles as seemed proper at the time. The Anglican continues in the same principles. At the Lambeth Conference of 1968, where every part of the Anglican Communion was represented and 459 bishops were present, fewer than 40 dissented from Resolution 43 which:

a. suggests that each Church of our communion consider whether the [39] Articles need to be bound up with its Prayer Book;

b. suggests to the Churches of the Anglican Communion that assent to the Thirty-nine Articles be no longer required of ordinands;

c. suggests that, when subscription is required to the Articles or other elements in the Anglican tradition, it should be required and given only in the context of a statement which gives the full range of our inheritance of faith and sets the Articles in their historical context. (*1968 Lambeth Conference Report*, p. 41)

(It should be noted that 'suggesting' and not 'instructing' is the proper language of a Lambeth Conference.)

Appeal of the Anglican kind to the apostolic Church and its tradition has made Anglicanism hard to understand by those accustomed to a 'confession' or to listed beliefs that you can point to with your finger. This difficulty seems to be decreasing, perhaps as the concept of one apostolic Church is more generally emphasized. It is interesting that Bishop Stephen Bayne, the first Anglican Executive Officer, in the 1960s, a man not inclined to repeat himself, wrote repeatedly explaining and protesting that Anglicanism is not 'confessional,' and even declined to participate in meetings of his counterparts of many Churches which called itself a meeting of Secretaries of 'World Confessional Families.' Among informed people now, Bishop Bayne's point would hardly need to be made. And there was no particular excitement when, years later, Lutherans proposed the conference change its name to 'Christian World Communions.' So we did that.

We have noted that a very short but important account of the Anglican characteristics is given in the Chicago/Lambeth Quadrilateral, and the foundation on which that structure rests is the origins and tradition of the Church itself. Important in Anglicanism for the interpretation and application of these bases is the use of reason. The ability of reasoning is not only proper to understanding human dignity, but has its status as being consonant with the nature of God and of his action in creation. Human reasoning has its limits, and theological reasoning can be a vehicle of conflict as well as of insight. But without the mobility injected by the endeavours of responsible human reasoning, the Anglican faith — and that of many other Christians — cannot be understood. If, however, reason is taken in isolation or to excess the result is likely to be a dry, or even deistic, theology. But against this danger there is a natural protection in the inseparability of worship and faith in the Book of Common Prayer; and a demonstration such as that which in 18th century England showed that there could be among leading and highly influential churchmen both Bishop Joseph Butler, with his outstanding powers of reasoning, and John Wesley, with his magnetic powers of teaching and converting.

The action of God in creation is understood increasingly in its universal aspect. The tendency has been to think of the divine activity in creation in the terms of western theology and experience. That is understandable: for centuries no other course came naturally. Now humanity in all its diversity is much better known and its distinct voices are beginning to be more clearly heard. Mankind, we might propose, is beginning to be seen more as the Creator has always seen it. This is a development that gains momentum, and will continue to increase.

Anglicanism has a built-in capacity, within limits, for comprehensiveness. The limits are the bounds of Anglicanism, but within those there is no imposed rigidity. But there are dangers that comprehensiveness, developed for whatever reason, can produce excessive diversity which within the one Communion is a hindrance to witness to the gospel; and also hinders acceptance by other Christians that Anglicanism as a whole can be taken seriously. Diversity has to be viewed sympathetically. *It also prevents union with them.*

The seven strands listed by Stephen Neill (see quotation from *Anglicanism*, pages 34, 35 above) for the 19th century illustrate the capacity, and the seriousness and sincerity, with which the followers arrived at their respective positions. Various influences were and are at play. There are great factors which may well set their pattern on life and faith: emphasis on Christ's gospel of salvation and its proclamation in the Word; emphasis on the Church which is the Body of Christ; and other great patterns. Correlative with each there is usually emphasis on particular doctrines and interpretations which have become linked together in a style that is more partisan than necessary or objective. To know one or two positions often enables one to predict the rest, for a particular school of Anglican churchmanship. The patterns become fairly elaborate, and typical.

The capacity for diversity, and even individual variety, as we have seen, has contributory factors in history and in the life of communities. For example, the post-Reformation dislike of Rome varied between those who wanted to put Rome right and those who wanted to reject it. Without Pope, King or Parliament as the generally recognized authoritative power in ecclesiastical affairs, there was scope for diversity in bishops and everyone else, and the Anglican concentration on the pastoral and practical requirements of the faith, good as it was, engendered a degree of difference between parish and parish. While it is a cause for thankfulness that a literal interpretation of the Bible has never been imposed, the lack of this requirement has made diversity easier.

The effect on world-wide Anglicanism we shall come to shortly. The effect on the Secretary General of the Anglican Consultative Council, who is the property of every Province of the Anglican Communion, and visits them all and participates in the common life of faith and worship, has a relevance here. My experience is that those things that are essential to the faith are few (see page 31f). Also that differences that are obvious to the outward eye or ear seldom penetrate to the essentials.

It is appropriate to recall that a long time ago Archbishop Wake of Canterbury (1716–37), in his consideration of the Gallican Churches, gave it as his opinion that there is a distinction between fundamental articles of the faith and articles which are reasonably accounted secondary, and that it was proper to allow considerable liberty to individual Churches.

Evidence is showing that differences, including comprehensiveness, in the understanding of the Christian faith, are not necessarily unacceptable or essentially objectionable. In some measure they are inevitable, and a complete unanimity is more properly a cause of worry than a universal goal. This proposal applies not only within Anglicanism but in the relationship that exists or is to be sought among the different denominations.

Difference, however, cannot be allowed to rest when it approaches contradictions. In that situation there can be no delay or termination in seeking further into a proper grasp of the matter — a search preferably undertaken jointly, from established common ground, and in the light of the gospel. That increasingly a procedure such as this is replacing defence of one's own original standpoint in the contradiction is among the good tidings of our times.

Shifting the field of this consideration from the more general to the particularly Anglican – though it may have application elsewhere – the concept of reasonable difference becomes associated with the word churchmanship. The fact of the membership in the one Anglican Communion almost always means we are not here dealing with contradiction but difference. Churchmanship (catholic, evangelical, high, low) is awry when it concentrates on the difference. My impression is that thinking Christians of the various schools of thought are increasingly aware that for the most part their faith is the same, and that it is a sad thing if differences in the expression of it are given unnecessary weight. Greater mutual appreciation, and learning from one another, are possible, and both possible and desirable in a world that is impatient with a faith that seems to occupy much of its energy with internal discords.

It would be unreasonable to assume that the collaboration so many wish to see could be established overnight. Of course people have different ways, and have been thrown into different parts of the historical map. It is not easy to change from the way you were brought up, and in which you learned Christ, or from the style surrounding the conversion that brought you to Him. We are all human. Below, and often only just below, the styles and approaches is a common faith about Christ, and the Word, about justification and salvation, about love and humility. However a cause for concern may arise when one theological style or interpretation is credited with necessary orthodoxy to the virtual exclusion of the rest. The atonement wrought by Christ is of the essence, whereas different views can be held of the means of its achievement. The presence of Christ in the Eucharist is of the essence, but no one philosophy which offers an account of that sublime accomplishment can expect to be received universally and finally. Much is admirable which is not primary and obligatory. Also much that is outwardly diverse is not different at heart. To perceive and share the common joy is the constructive objective.

Outwardly, the diversity of forms, not least in regular worship and style of ceremonies, is enough to confuse people. The lack of an obvious and appreciated expression of the shared and universal faith has been an Anglican weakness for too long, and is a considerable factor in the comparatively slow growth of Anglicanism and to some measure of its decline in the west. Slowly, as many hope, difference is being replaced by convergence and by the realization that near the surface there is much more agreement than was thought; and that Anglicanism has been called to no small witness to the universality of Christ's Church.

To assess the present and recent development in the Anglican Communion it has been necessary so far to look a good deal at earlier times. In doing so a number of the more recent occurrences have come into the story, particularly in relation to growth and spread. These are now brought together, with some amplification.

III

The Anglican Family;
and the Church as the People of God

a. The Anglican Family

The traditional kind of 'mission activity' is a thing of the past. The missionaries travelled great distances and worked for long periods with the intention that the Church should take root in the lands to which they went. That has happened. The Church is indigenous. Of the transition Adrian Hastings has written:

> The 1950s could well be judged the last great missionary era in Africa's history. Through the greater part of it missionaries continued to hold the senior posts in all the larger churches. . . (*A History of African Christianity 1950–1975*, p. 108)

The leaders, the members, the teachers, the witnesses, are the people of the land and increasingly they express their faith in the manner of the land. Those expatriates who are still there are there at the request of the indigenous Church, and usually for special skills. These may include works of ministry and teaching, much as the missionaries of old, if that is the service the Province wants.

There is nothing new in the Anglican Communion seeing its future as part of the universal Church in this way. The Church of India, Burma and Ceylon, in its Constitution of 1930, says:

> As the Church of England, receiving Catholic Christianity from the undivided Church, has given characteristically English interpretation to it, so the Church of this Province aspires to give characteristically national interpretations of that same common faith and life. (Declaration 20)

We have noted how theology of a non-western provenance is adding to the understanding of the faith in a Church that is universal, and how the assumptions of different cultures within the Church are recognized where formerly alien assumptions, often strangely understood, were regarded as the Christian norm.

The regions which have received Provincial status in the Anglican Communion since 1950 are:

1951   West Africa
1955   Central Africa
1960   East Africa (see also 1970)
1961   Uganda, Rwanda, Burundi and (later) Boga Zaire (1961)
1965   Brazil
1970   Kenya (by division of the Province of East Africa: see 1960)
1970   Tanzania (by division of the Province of East Africa: see 1960)
1970   Burma
1973   Indian Ocean
1974   Consejo Anglicano Sud Americano (South America) (revised Constitution as Iglesia Americana del Cono Sur: see 1982; see also Appendix I)
1975   Melanesia
1976   Jerusalem and the Middle East
1976   Sudan
1977   Papua New Guinea
1979   Nigeria (by division of West Africa: see 1951)
1980   Burundi, Rwanda and Zaire (by division from Uganda: see 1961)
1982   Iglesia Americana del Cono Sur (Southern Cone, Latin America: see 1974)

The present number (1983) of Provinces which form the Anglican Communion is 27. Those formed before 1950 are:

Anglican Church of Australia
Anglican Church of Canada

Chung Hua Sheng Kung Hui (Holy Catholic Church in China) (For some time only the Diocese of Hong Kong has been in normal touch with the Anglican Communion. The revival of overt Christianity in The People's Republic of China is to be welcomed. The emphasis on its Chinese character needs to be understood sympathetically and the Anglican preparedness to serve the Christians there as at any time they may wish, and to avoid pressing any western initiative, is a sensitive attitude and doubtless to be commended. The future course of things is not yet clear.)

Church of England
Church of Ireland
Nippon Sei Ko Kai (Holy Catholic Church in Japan)
Church of the Province of New Zealand
Episcopal Church in Scotland
Church of the Province of Southern Africa
Episcopal Church in the United States of America
Church in Wales
Church in the Province of the West Indies

The Lusitanian Church of Portugal, and the Spanish Reformed Episcopal Church each joined the Anglican Communion as one diocese in 1980.

Of the remaining 13 dioceses which are not yet members of a Province, ways and means are being considered by some in East Asia.

The number of Anglicans around the world has certainly grown in the period but, as we have seen, precise figures are not possible. The total may now be about 70 million. In the early 1970s the total climbed but evidence indicates a distinct flattening of the graph thereafter, with, perhaps, the steeper climb resuming now.

As the Anglican Communion has grown from more than one base, occasionally a situation has arisen of two bishops or dioceses (usually one American and one English) operating in the same area. The situation has usually been referred to as 'parallel jurisdictions.' A natural dissatisfaction with this situation was expressed as long ago as 1853, and was also pressed in relation to the then overlapping jurisdictions in West Africa for discussion at the first Lambeth Conference in 1867, although nothing came of that (Stephenson: *The First Lambeth Conference*, pp. 203 and 248). The last trace of that state of affairs disappeared quite recently. In the final form the autonomous Province of West Africa, which spread through dioceses from Nigeria to Gambia, did not include the diocese of Liberia which was an American foundation. There was amiable discussion between America and the Province aimed at bringing an unsatisfactory situation to a suitable end. In 1982 Liberia became a diocese in the Province of West Africa, and, indeed, its bishop, George Browne, is now the Archbishop of the Province.

The situation that had slowly grown up in Europe occupied the Lambeth Conference of 1968. Resolution 63 begins:

> The Conference deplores the existence of parallel Anglican juris-dictions in Europe and in other areas, and recommends that the (Anglican Consultative Council) should give early attention to the problems involved. (*1968 Lambeth Conference Report*, p. 45)

The situation is complicated, and has undoubted difficulties, such as the chaplaincies of English connection in Europe being far more numerous than the half-dozen or so congregations of the American Convocation in Europe which operates under a suffragan bishop to the Presiding Bishop of the Episcopal Church of the U.S.A. The Americans are emphatic about getting things sorted out soon. The English connection, in the process of sorting out some of its own complications, expressed, in an 'Agreed Statement' (1975), which went to the General Synod of the Church of England over the signatures of the Archbishop of Canterbury, the Bishop of London, the Bishop of (then) Fulham and Gibraltar, and the Secretary General of the Anglican Consultative Council, the following:

> The meeting agreed further that it was important to maintain and develop close working links with the Convocation of American Churches in Europe and its Bishop, and had particularly in mind Resolution 63 of the 1968 Lambeth Conference which deplored parallel episcopal jurisdictions. But it felt that the most useful practical step which could be taken at the present juncture would be to resolve the future of the Bishop of London's Jurisdiction [viz: northern Europe] and the Diocese of Gibraltar before proceeding to consider a further formal integration of the Jurisdiction [nor-thern Europe] and the Diocese with the American Convocation. ("Agreed Statement," paragraph 4)

So far, the parallel episcopal jurisdiction in Europe remains.

Reference has been made to an Anglican Communion of autonomous units going back as far as 1789 and the formation by Anglican Christians in America of the autonomous Protestant Epis-copal Church in the United States of America, which was in full com-

Euro

munion with the See of Canterbury. Other Provinces with their own Primates and Constitutions came into being in the next century and a half, with full relationship with Canterbury and with one another. The last quarter of a century has seen this rapid growth of Anglican Provinces until now there are very few dioceses of the old order left. De-centralization is virtually complete, but there is not disintegration. The Provinces are of equal standing, autonomous and indigenous, but are aware of themselves as all parts of the one Anglican Communion within the one greater Church of Christ. The transition of recent years has manifested the Communion as a family. Slowly this family relationship, aided by modern ease of travel, is bringing about some changes in the Anglican Communion which have a potential for good.

While the Church of England has its fundamental appeal to the apostolic Church, it has, through the course of history, as we have seen, included a diversity of interpretations, theologies and practices. This diversity has in considerable measure been reproduced in the dioceses that have grown from it. In some regions this takes the form of a similarity in diversity; in other regions one type is exclusive or dominant. A major reason is that individuals or societies which engaged in the great work of mission overseas frequently reproduced their own thinking and churchmanship in a whole area where they were active: it was an opportunity not to be missed. The intention to bring as many as possible to salvation and holiness of life in the best and right way is commendable. Criticism must be that excessive diversity was possible, perhaps inevitable. The consequences are still very clear. For example, an evangelical emphasis is marked in the Anglican Communion in, say, Uganda or southern Latin America, an Anglo-Catholic one in Zambia or most of the West Indies.

A family holds together largely through affection. This affection, which following gospel terminology is suitably called Christian love, is a powerful bond throughout the Anglican family. Also people travel much more, and meet. The importance of having a common objective, and often common problems, tends slowly to develop common ground where before it was less apparent. One importance of affection is that when people meet they like one another. Of course different parts of the world, east and west, old and new, have their own problems arising from indigenous assumptions and contemporary situations: here the Anglican allowance for a reasonable flexibility has a cohesive effect. By younger people especially, some of the ingredients of division are seen as coming from a different history and a different place from theirs, and so are of diminished importance.

There is more than a passing significance in the way members met in 1971 for the first meeting of the Anglican Consultative Council. It was in Limuru, Kenya, and people came from every Province of the Anglican Communion. They were lay people and clergy and bishops. Probably to me as Secretary half of them were already known from my visits to their own countries, but few of them had ever met one another before. Arrivals took place over a day or two. Within half an hour of arrival each one of them appeared quite at home and relaxed. They were part of one family. It was an impressive experience.

Of particular interest in this consideration of the 'family' in its relation to society is a passage in an account which Kenneth Skelton, Bishop of Matabeleland 1962–70, gives of Africa as he came to know it:

> This conception of the family underlies all the African's ideas about life and society. . . . It is because decisions are arrived at by the whole family or group that it is quite erroneous to point the finger of scorn. . . at African 'one-party states.' There is no place in the African system for an 'opposition' after the western model. Anyone may disagree, question and argue: but an agreement must eventually be reached, however protracted is the process of arriving at it. . . . The African family comes into its own when it has to take care of the basic needs of its members. (Typescript: "Purulent Prelate," pp. 37–38)

In quoting this, the intention is not to propose that the Church should follow this or that political pattern, but that in the concept of family as it has developed in recent years in the Anglican Communion, there has come into clearer existence a characteristic which has not only a good theology but also a base that is natural to much of human society.

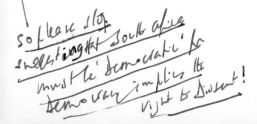

b. The Church as the People of God

There was significance, too, in the presence of lay people as well as clergy at meetings of the Anglican Consultative Council. This was not contrived but is of the true nature of the Church as the whole people of God. Within its one ministry there are special ministerial roles of clergy and laity, as well as of bishops. There has long been a tendency, among Anglicans as among others, for bishops particularly to be seen as a class apart who are the Church 'par excellence.' The membership of all baptized people in the one Christian Church has been re-stressed many times since the books of the New Testament were written. The steady re-assertion of this fundamental character of the Church, which has often been lost sight of, is perhaps the most important development in Anglicanism in this century. It is at the heart of much that has happened in the last twenty years or so, but it has always had an up-and-down career, and may not be so sharp in Anglican focus at the moment as it was just a few years ago. Problems about hierarchy are one cause of hesitations, and the quotations on page 54 from Resolutions by the Lambeth Conferences of 1968 and 1978 may serve as a symbol of how in this area good intentions can slip into a decline.

The intrinsic status of the laity was prominent in Cranmer's mind; and in the famous Assize Sermon of July 1833, John Keble said: "In speaking of the Church, I mean of course the laity, as well as the clergy in their three orders — the whole body of Christians, according to the will of Jesus Christ, under the successors of the Apostles." The involvement of the whole people of God is witnessed to in the structure of every Anglican general synod.

The importance of this theology of the Church and all its baptized members achieved an impressive dominance at the Second Vatican Council of the Roman Catholic Church. This is not confined to the Decree on the Apostolate of the Laity (*Apostolicam Actuositatem*); for example, an article by Cardinal (then Bishop) J.G.M. Willebrands in the book *Anglican/Roman Catholic Dialogue* by Clark and Davey, 1974, pages 31f, refers to the subject in *Constitutio De Ecclesia* and other Council documents. When the 1983 *Code of Canon Law* was published, Monsignor Ralph Brown (President of the Canon Law Society of Great Britain and Ireland) wrote in an article in *The Times* (17th September, 1983):

[handwritten note: + Puun's comment on the rôle of the laity are worth knowing too.]

If one were to single out one area of the 1983 code which expresses the 'new look' of Vatican II, one would have to choose the role of the laity in the Church. That was, of course, an area which was much explored and developed in the council. But the code, for the first time, gives expression to a whole series of rights which belong to all the people of God, which include, of course, the clergy and the laity; and then to further rights and obligations pertaining specially to the laity.

Book II of the Code is entitled *The People of God*. As if to underline Monsignor Brown's point, its first Canon (No. 204/1) is:

Christ's faithful are those who, since they are incorporated into Christ through baptism, are constituted the people of God. For this reason they participate in their own way in the priestly, prophetic and kingly office of Christ. They are called, each according to his or her particular condition, to exercise the mission which God entrusted to the Church to fulfil in the world.

In the Anglican family as it now exists, an essential part is that the members of the family consult together, and that they are moved to do so not only by the course things have taken, or particularly by theological theory, but through affection. The procedure goes further into development than the prospect of change. Differences that are not necessary, even if they are of long standing, begin to be queried, and possibilities of better — and maybe less local — response to Christ are heard.

Change does not come about by magic. It is probably hesitant, and slow. The Province of Tanzania has deliberately brought together two Anglican traditions in adjacent groups of dioceses. Some have an evangelical tradition associated with support from the Church Missionary Society and the Sydney district of Australia. The others have a history connected with the Anglo-Catholic style of the Universities Mission to Central Africa. They will tell you it is not easy, especially when any first delight with the rightness of it all has worn off. But it is right, and it illustrates the development in the Anglican Communion for which the universal family relationship has potential.

The nature of authority in the Church today is the subject of much study which is by no means confined to Anglicanism alone, though questions on this subject are often addressed to Anglicans. What is relevant here is to consider how one important aspect of authority operates in our world-wide community. There is no central authority; no equivalent to the Vatican, or, for example, any equivalent to a papal declaration that "we order that henceforth it (the Code) is to have the force of law for the whole latin Church" (*Apostolic Constitution of Pope John Paul II*, January 1983, to the *Code of Canon Law* of 1983). The independence of the Provinces is stated in their Constitutions. Their membership within the Anglican Communion is by their own choice. Some may occasionally turn to Lambeth and the Archbishop of Canterbury for advice — advice which will be respected — but the Archbishop may not give instructions. Each Province has within itself its own metropolitical authority and power of decision.

The procedure which binds the Provinces together is in two stages. Through their representatives the Anglican Churches confer together. In the light of that consultation, action is taken by each Province (member Church) through its law-making body (normally the Provincial Synod) as seems fitting to its own situation.

Power in an Anglican Province resides in the synod. The synod alone can, by the decision of its members, make canon law and alter Constitutions. Another factor common to all synods is that their membership includes bishops and clergy and laity. Many other things may differ, for example, how often a synod meets, what majorities are required for decisions to be passed, how the Orders relate to each other, how many members there are and how they are appointed. Such matters relate to circumstances and, perhaps, to history.

The fact that ultimate power resides with the synods means that where they are off balance they must be got right. For example, they must properly be composed in an appropriate proportion of all significant kinds and classes in the community, otherwise the concerns of all the people of God, or of all the nation, cannot be met. Synods can meet too often: some meet even several times a year. For laity, particularly, to have so much time available is unlikely, except for professional and middle classes. In this way a synod really representative of the people of God may be made impossible. Interestingly, the consequence of over-frequent synods is not that more business is accomplished but less: it becomes too easy, or even a convenient party strategem, to shelve or divert decisions on reports and serious business to a later meeting; and a consequence of that is a decline in a proper sense of urgency when, in the immediate interest of the gospel, the Church or the nation, action rather than delay is appropriate.

In England where history goes back a long way to times when there was much identity of Church and State, political power retains a lingering effect on some Church decisions, procedures and elections. Indeed, the present general synod is quite a recent growth from former less representative bodies. Many synods are older, with a differing measure of maturity, nevertheless their development typically belongs to the advent of autonomous Provinces. The creation of Provincial and diocesan synods is almost complete now in the Anglican world, but in many parts of the world — not always where the newest Provinces are — experience of how to use them has a long way to go.

It is said that I have attended (and, by courtesy, spoken at) more different Anglican Provincial synods than anybody else. That may well be true. Not only does the style in which a synod works differ from one part of the world to another, but interestingly the style is often inclined to imitate facets of the political ordering of the country. The General Synod (called General Convention) of the Episcopal Church in the USA has two Houses — one of bishops, and the other of clergy and laity — comparable to two houses in federal government — Senators and Representatives; and the procedure by which business is carried through is baffling at first to many Anglicans from elsewhere, but not to anyone familiar with the Capitol. Several synods reflect a parliamentary system of government and opposition, which may even include comparable manoeuvrings, whereas the very meaning of 'synod' is that people, perhaps of several differing views, set out to find how best, in Christ's cause, they can find a way forward together. It is with this concept in view that procedure by synod has its roots in the earliest centuries of the Church.

The element of representation on a synod is often nowadays valued as expressing democracy, a form of government more favoured in some parts of the world than others, and not universally characteristic of the gospels and the apostolic Church. One vital ingredient of synodical representation is that participation relates to the whole people of God. Concern is more with theology than democracy. Such participation must relate across to similar activity for similar purposes by other synods throughout the world. Synods, as yet, in older Provinces as in new, tend to be inward-looking to a disturbing degree. A visitor to a synod usually has little doubt as to which country he is in for he seldom hears of any other. Yet mention of the universality of Christ's Church, or of the internationalism of ecumenism, is warmly responded to on most occasions.

There is still a long way to go in learning how to use synods, but there should be no limit to thanksgiving that throughout the Anglican Communion they exist, and exist because Christian people wanted them.

The method of general consultation leading to Provincial decision and action, at which the Anglican Communion is arriving, is not new. It is fundamentally the same as that of the dioceses of the apostolic Church and the early centuries. It is not essentially different from that of the Orthodox Churches.

To speak of 'their representatives' conferring together is not precise, but to the Churches the meaning is clear enough. There tends to be some flexibility in any system that has come into existence more as a suitable way to meet a need than by deliberate planning. The conferring takes place by the fact of responsible and suitably appointed members of all the Provinces coming together with the purpose of consultation. In Anglican practice this is either a Lambeth Conference, or, more recently, a meeting of the Anglican Consultative Council.

'Their representatives' for Lambeth Conferences are all the Anglican diocesan bishops, and perhaps some other bishops, too — all are bishops so far. For the Anglican Consultative Council, which is a much newer and smaller body, every Province is again represented, but in this case the representation is not restricted to bishops but aims deliberately to consist of the whole people of God.

This means the membership includes laity and clergy (presbyters). By Constitution it must be so for the Council as a whole. By the limitation of numbers, it is not so for every one of the smaller Provinces.

Later consideration will be given to the performance in the last quarter century or so of the Lambeth Conferences, the Anglican Consultative Council, and also to Primates' Meetings. For this part of the study, the focus is on Anglicanism as a family of Churches.

No-one seems to know when the term 'Anglican Communion' originated, but it has been used for quite a long while for the whole spread of the Churches (dioceses) of the Anglican allegiance. The stress on 'family of equals' is recent, and its origins co-incide with the grouping of dioceses into autonomous Provinces and the consequent multiplication of Provinces — a process which we have seen is not yet quite complete.

Expression of the Church's catholicism, its universalism, is apt for the world-wide Anglican family with its involvement with the world's experiences, and with its appeal to the gospel and the early Church. There has been little time for maturity to have progressed far, and any impatience may be due to the close association with it that enables one to see potentials, and the vision.

One of the most profound shortcomings is the frequent failure to communicate, or adequately to consult. Conferences are inclined to rely excessively on their own thoughts at the time, and to make insufficient use of knowledge that could be available. They tend to become engrossed with affairs — often noble enough in themselves — within their own borders and synods. Representation requires both a bringing of information and an effective feed-back. Excellent work has been done on revision of liturgies and the re-shaping of occasional services, with valuable historical research, but often one part of the Communion has little idea, if any, of what others are doing, and more often duplicates than profits from their work. Not all liturgies, for example, can be — or should be — the same throughout the world, but Provinces can profit from one another. Moreover, even within a Province, a godly seeking of the common good can do more to unite the people of God in his service than was foreseen. There is an Anglican potential here in the ecumenical field which is seldom taken up.

One of the difficulties inadequate communication contributes in the field of ecumenism and the collaboration that leads toward Christian unity is that a carefully thought-out procedure in one part of the Communion may be generally unknown to another part. Worse, it may be thought unacceptable. One example is the American Episcopal Church's careful negotiations with Lutheran Churches, and the measure of con-celebration there achieved. Few Anglican Provinces, including the Church of England, know enough about this.

Approaching unity by 'covenanting' is not a new concept, but the form it can take, and the extent of permissibility it can imply, differ a lot. The 'covenant' relationship worked out in Wales is different from that in South Africa, and neither is the same as that attempted in England with member Churches of the British Council of Churches there. It is not even clear that the English formula would have been acceptable to the Anglican Province in South Africa. The sort of unhappy state of affairs that might be caused with other Churches, and also within the Anglican Communion, is easy to see. More ample communication in the Anglican Communion could and should reduce the dismal situations that could arise. For a world Communion ecumenical advances will always have their difficulties, and some process of universal vetting is hardly a total solution, but neither is a want of communication.

In the relationships of the Anglican family it is understandable that old habits die slowly. Among the newer Provinces there is a tendency to expect to be dominated by the Church of England despite their Constitutions. In fact when members visit England they are often surprised at being greeted as coming from some 'mission overseas.' Anglican visitors and returning expatriates are inclined to remark wryly "When will they catch up?" In the majority of English parishes the existence of all the equal Provinces of which the Church of England is one — the most prestigious one — is still news, or so it seems. The point in this little lament in to present another of the reasons for saying the Anglican Communion as it is at present is immature.

A shortcoming with some of the younger Provinces, which given its context is likewise understandable for the time being, is that while members do not wish to question their autonomy, and discuss abundantly and fruitfully when they are at home, they lack a proper confidence in the wider setting which would enable them to make a contribution which would be valuable and which they are capable of making. Their tendency then is to do nothing, or to wait for a more venerable Province to take a course they would like to follow. While this is sometimes a fair procedure, it is more often a kind of caution that should not linger too long.

An impediment to further establishment of the understanding of the Church as the whole people of God is the considerable emphasis in recent years on hierarchy. By hierarchy is not meant episcopacy but the idea that in the Church the places held by the ordained ministry, particularly by the bishops, are — by that fact — the top places. There has been a wide swing of the pendulum. No doubt it will move back to something less eccentric. Evidence of the swing is plain in the most recent Lambeth Conferences. The Conference of 1968 said (Resolution 24):

> The Conference recommends that no major issue in the life of the Church should be decided without the full participation of the laity in discussion and in decision.

The next (1978) Conference said (Resolution 11):

> The Conference advises member Churches not to take action regarding issues which are of concern to the whole Anglican Communion without consultation with a Lambeth Conference or with the episcopate through the Primates' Committee.

Of course there were reasons of a sort. Many bishops at the Conference of 1968 had just come from the Assembly of the World Council of Churches at Uppsala, and while the role of laity was not a specific subject of the studies there, the concentration on the 'whole man' in an unjust world, and — particularly in the west — on the appropriateness of renewal when confronted by secularization, affected the participants so that for some of them the role of laity was illuminated and emphasized. The 1978 Lambeth Conference was edgy over decisions about women priests, and the resolution (Resolution 11) then may have been thought by some bishops to be a safeguard. That is not certain. What is more certain is that the idea of episcopacy had become increasingly associated with an idea of 'leadership.' This idea is not Anglican only, it is still active and influential, and is generally a throwback.

Frequently a person who is becoming a bishop is said to be undertaking a position of 'leadership,' where leadership apears to be
closely allied to ideas of executive or commercial leadership. A more
cautious approach is made by Dean Edward Carpenter in the
summing up at the end of his book *Cantuar* (p. 521) where he says:
"Leadership is something indefinable; but whatever its character it
must bring out the best in others by fostering initiative."

A contemporary phrase is 'episcopal government,' and there is
thought to be difficulty about how this can combine with 'synodical
government'; but the difficulty of combination arises only if too
wide a distinction is made between episcopacy and 'the whole people
of God.' The ministries of bishops and priests are specialized within
the one ministry of the whole people of God. In the New Testament
the ministry, even in its highest reaches, seldom is spoken of in terms
of leadership as it is known today, but in terms of pastoral activity,
guiding, witnessing and serving. It belongs within the Body.
Apostleship relates to dying and rising with Christ, which finds
expression in Christ's assertion that following him requires that one
take up one's cross and follow. This utterance is addressed to
everyone, not only disciples or apostles (Mark 8:34. In this general
context of special interest is A.M. Ramsey's *The Gospel and the
Catholic Church* pp. 6–7).

The apostolic role of being a uniting person for all the Christians
of an area — of, as later terminology has it, representing the diocese
to the whole Church, and the Church to the diocese — has in mind
the Church that is all the people. There is surely no reason to object
to this understanding of episcopate: only that too often it is obscured
by emphasis on present ideas of leadership.

Not that all the confusions arising from hierarchical ideas derive
from the west. In many parts of the world people in top positions in a
social order receive and expect a deference that does not signify a
spirituality. Chieftainship can be of this order. One can be uncertain
whether the approach of a Mercedes-Benz with a flag signifies the
chief or a bishop. It may not be that the bishop wants this, but it may
well be that the people of his diocese want it: they want grandeur to
reflect on them. It is as though flags came fluttering on the
pentecostal wind.

A factor may be mentioned which slows the possible maturing
effect in the development of the Anglican family. The Third World
— where the majority of all Christians are today — is more aware of

poverty, oppression and injustice than most parts of humanity. Behind this lies the experience of a century, or perhaps of many centuries. The people of the Third World are also much more aware of Christ's condemnation by word and deed of these attitudes to one's fellow men and women. Part of the Christian ethic is an ethic of liberation and human justice.

In western parts of the world there has been and is a tendency to under-emphasize the place these have in the Christian faith, and in the Bible generally. The World Council of Churches, which has long ceased to have a predominantly western voice, does emphasize them. The difference underlies some western distaste for the Council. Let it be said both that the World Council gives a more fair presentation of the gospel than has always been the case and that it is disposed at times to over-emphasize and isolate. This in turn can lead to objections that political influence is too great in some members of the Council, and that, too, can be right. However, the west has more to learn here about the Bible than it supposed in days gone by. Convergence toward common understanding is happening, but the procedure is slow. In the Anglican Communion the greater realization of the universality of the Church, and the essential family relationship which builds up the unity of east and west, advances the convergence; the question is whether the speed of convergence is sufficiently outstanding to amount to development.

A reference to 'collegiality' is suitably placed here. This is not a study of the subject, which would be an extensive undertaking, but is a suggestion that a term frequently used nowadays has no very clear meaning, at least as it is used in Anglicanism. It comes as no surprise that Professor Stephen Sykes in his paper "Authority in the Anglican Communion" (p. 16) says of the concept of collegiality that "it deserves much more careful scrutiny within Anglicanism than its somewhat casual use in the Lambeth documents of 1968 and 1978 suggests."

The subject attracted a great deal of attention through the discussion at Vatican II of the relationship of the Pope and the bishops. Interesting as this was, it is not directly relevant to Churches without the papal office and function.

But the college or body of bishops has no authority unless it is simultaneously conceived of in terms of its head, the Roman Pontiff, Peter's successor, and without any lessening of his power of primacy over all, pastors as well as the general faithful. For in virtue of his office, that is, as Vicar of Christ and pastor of the whole Church, the Roman Pontiff has full, supreme, and universal power over the Church. (*Lumen Gentium III*, paragraph 22)

The Roman Church was at commendable pains to make its meaning clear, and to that end adds an Addendum and Explanation to the end of that Dogmatic Constitution, that states (in paragraph 3):

The Roman Pontiff proceeds according to his own discretion and in view of the welfare of the Church in structuring, promoting, and endorsing any exercise of collegiality.

This achieves clarity here, but not for others, including Anglicans. One Anglican use of collegiality is of bishops acting together. How many bishops is not clear: sometimes it seems to mean the House of Bishops in a Provincial Synod. Sometimes the interpretation seems to be simply that where two or three bishops are gathered together, there is collegiality.

But the use of the term in Anglicanism is not invariably confined to bishops: one can also find it used of the whole people of God, somewhat as 'family' is applicable to the Anglican Communion.

The purpose of this brief glance at an important subject is not to reject any particular point of view but to insist that Anglican thinking on the subject is as yet uncertain and incomplete. What is encouraging, and a sign of advance, is the general belief that collegiality has an honourable place in Christian thought, that at heart it is about action in co-operation, and to be spoken of as a good thing.

c. When the Spread of Anglicanism is Thin

The reference that has been made to the extension of Anglicanism requires that consideration be given to parts of the world where Anglicanism is thin on the ground, or does not exist at all, or where its advent is recent. Recent appearance in small numbers is not necessarily a development, especially where other Christian Churches are already established. Meagre existence may have come about through a belief that to fill empty places on the Anglican map is a good thing to do, but one may well question whether that is a good thing to do. Or it may come about through the zeal of a missionary to push ahead into new areas. A result of that tends to be that a vast region is nominally Anglican, and claims and appeals are made on its behalf; or, if the size is not necessarily vast, the shape of a diocese is extended in a haphazard way, and to minister to it, and to organize it, makes an excessive strain on manpower and other resources. Planning is sketchy, if it has existed at all. Once the devotee of pioneering departs or dies, then resources to keep the extension alive have got to be found from somewhere — and it is often a mission board or society. Once the church has been started, it is nearly impossible, however desirable, to close it down again or transfer it to another denomination. People are not like that. If they see themselves as belonging to this and or that denomination, however lonely they may feel, they are inclined to stay that way until they die, and maybe others — a few others — after them. Nowadays it is doubtful if the Spirit acts much through enthusiasm that is not closely associated with godly planning — which usually means with godly organization too.

Certainly people travel more than they used, and it is laudable that some of them wish to worship and to serve the community. If other Christian Churches exist in those parts then most people will attach themselves to one of them for the time being. If such a procedure is not acceptable, and one must recognize that to some it is a distasteful and individualist procedure, or if the expected stay should be for a long time and not temporary, then appropriate Anglican authority could surely authorize the abnormality of joining with another Christian Communion. That is better than confounding local Christianity by establishing what amounts to another little sect.

One may doubt if anywhere on the world map the Anglican responsibility is completely met. Development is more likely to be accomplished where the Communion builds up and consolidates its undertaking than where with foundations still being built, it goes pioneering off over someone else's horizon. It is difficult to know what that witnesses to.

IV

Anglican International Conferences

(Lambeth Conferences are a main subject in this section, but consideration of them is not confined to one part of it. Since the section was written, information has been given by the Archbishop of Canterbury about the future Conference in 1988. The report of this announcement was given in *Anglican Information*, No. 35 (December 1983) and is added here at the end of this section, on page 107f.)

Anglican conferences came into being because a need for them was felt. In the 19th century the universality of the Church had an increasing place in the minds of many Anglicans in different parts of the world, and their relationship to one another, and to one another's problems and prospects, indicated that clarification might best be achieved by some kind of conferring together. Already the growing need for communication was exerting pressure. The first Lambeth Conference took place in London in 1867. Later, and within our period of the past twenty-five years, came the appointment of the first Executive Officer who was a link person connected to all parts of the Anglican Communion, and this individual role developed rapidly into the Anglican Consultative Council. With this development were connected a few intermittent Anglican Congresses, the Advisory Council on Missionary Strategy, and the Lambeth Consultative Body consisting mainly of the Anglican Primates, which met occasionally between Lambeth Conferences. This last was also a precursor of the third of the present Anglican International Conferences, the Primates' Meetings, which first met as such in 1979.

The three regular Conferences that exist at the present time (Lambeth Conference, Anglican Consultative Council, and Primates' Meeting) are significant in the consideration of recent developments in the Anglican Communion, and they are now considered one by one. So also is their relationship together, which is important for Anglicans and also for our whole ecumenical relationship. For this I rely fairly heavily on a memorandum on the subject which I wrote at the request of the Lambeth Conference of 1978 (Resolution 12).

a. Beginnings of the Lambeth Conference

A brief look at how this Conference came into being is desirable because, although this takes us back to the last century, the Lambeth Conference is the largest, oldest and most prestigious of the three, and it has had much influence in shaping the Anglican Communion.

The autonomous Protestant Episcopal Churches in America and Scotland were closely associated in faith and order with the United Church of England and Ireland (as it then was) but they were not part of the establishment of Britain and its Colonies. In the early 1850s some proposals for a conference or synod of some kind were beginning to be suggested, principally by America (Bishop J.H. Hopkins of Vermont, Bishop W.R. Whittingham of Maryland) and Canada (Bishop F. Fulford of Montreal). While it is not difficult to discern various specific recommendations as to what such a conference might do – that it could accomplish a timely appraisal of Anglican missionary extension, of doctrine, of procedures for curbing Roman Catholicism, and even for promoting a common Canon Law for Anglicans – there is the general underlying thought that within one body consultation is necessary to harmony. In some minds the early councils of the universal Church provoked happy reflections.

In the 1860s the subject was again to the fore. Meanwhile in the Colonies church government had been developing on the American model with synods that included lay people. Approval by parliament in Westminster was not forthcoming, but before long the Colonies went ahead anyway, without Colonial or Imperial legislation. The fact that some advocates of an Anglican conference wanted laity included in one way or another caused hesitations and delays; the notion of such a manifestation of the Body of Christ provoked a sense of shock, and therefore of opposition, in many Christian minds. Indeed, the inclusion of laity in the councils of the whole Anglican Church had to wait a hundred years until the Anglican Consultative Council was formed.

More reasonably there was demur at a suggestion that came up from time to time in those first talks about such a conference that it should be a sort of supreme synod, the top of the pyramid, which made decisions and rules that all the Anglican Churches should obey. This, in the circumstances, was impossible, and, in the style of the growing Anglican universalism, undesirable. Archbishop Longley, who called the first Conference, in 1867, wisely avoided any action on that matter. In an opening address to that first Conference, he "reiterated that the assembly was not a general synod capable of enacting canons, but a conference to discuss practical questions, on which they could pass resolutions which would be a guide for future action." (Stephenson: *The First Lambeth Conference: 1867* p. 246)

By 1867 official recommendation of a conference had come from the Canadian Provincial Synod to Archbishop Longley of Canterbury and to the Canterbury and York Convocations. Major factors pressing on the Church were a revision by England alone of some of the Canons of 1604, and the form of subscription: the theology of certain parts of *Essays and Reviews*; and — with the Gray/Colenso dispute figuring prominently — the authority, if any, of the Privy Council in the Anglican Churches in the Colonies.

Prominent in bringing about the Canadian Church's action was Bishop John Travers Lewis of Ontario. Underlying his writing and speaking on the subject is a clear understanding that in a communion of autonomous Churches there must be such communication and consultation as makes possible common action on matters of universal importance. It is worth quoting a lengthy paragraph from a Charge he gave in 1865:

> But if there is much cause for thankfulness in the free and unfettered condition of the Church, there is also need of a more solemn sense of our responsibilities. There are scarcely any ecclesiastical matters except those which by our original declaration we debarred ourselves from legislating upon, which we may not discuss and regulate in our Synods, even to the extent of subdividing Dioceses, but it requires no great foresight to see that the whole tendency of recent decisions is to make us drift into the status of the Episcopal Churches of Scotland and America in our relation to the United Church of England and Ireland. The result is more to be apprehended because the Convocations of Canterbury and

York have at length been permitted to resume their legislative functions, and by a canon lately enacted, and probably by this time embodied in an Act of Parliament, the oath to be taken, and subscriptions to be made at ordination, are altered, and inasmuch as the new statute and canon will not be extended to Canada we shall have the anomalous spectacle of the same Church exacting different obligations from candidates for the ministry in different countries, unless our Provincial Synod thinks fit to adopt the alterations made by the English Convocations. (Stephenson: *The First Lambeth Conference: 1867* pp. 105–6)

The proposal from Canada was in two documents. One dated 16th September, 1865, from the bishops and addressed to the Archbishop of Canterbury begins: "We, the Bishops, Clergy, and Laity, of the Province of Canada, in triennial Synod assembled, desire to represent to your Grace. . . ." The second paragraph is as follows:

In order, therefore, to comfort the souls of the faithful, and re-assure the minds of wavering members of the Church, and to obviate, as far as may be, the suspicion whereby so many are scandalised, that the Church is a creation of Parliament, we humbly entreat your Grace, since the assembling of a General Council of the whole Catholic Church is at present impracticable, to convene a National Synod of the Bishops of the Anglican Church at home and abroad, who, attended by one or more of their presbyters or laymen, learned in ecclesiastical law, as their advisers, may meet together, and under the guidance of the Holy Ghost, take counsel and adopt such measures, as may be best fitted to provide for the present distress, in such Synod, presided over by your Grace. (Quoted by Archbishop Davidson in *Origin and History of the Lambeth Conferences of 1867 and 1878*, pp. 34–35)

The second document, dated 18th September, 1865, was from the Canadian Lower House and was addressed to the Convocations of Canterbury and York. The reason for a second document seems to be that the Lower House, while fully accepting the letter from the bishops, wanted particularly to make it clear that National Synod' should not refer only to the British Churches, which might then have been a legitimate interpretation. So one sentence reads as follows:

In desiring most earnestly to retain this connection, we believe that it would be most effectually preserved and perpetuated, if means could be adopted by which the members of our Anglican Communion, in all quarters of the world, should have a share in the deliberations for her welfare, and be permitted to have a representation in one General Council of her members gathered from every land. (Stephenson, op. cit., p. 156)

There seems to have been little subsequent discussion on the point. The course proposed by the Lower House was followed; probably that was always the intention. One can hardly suppose that it was ever seriously intended that the American Church should be left out.

The proposal for what became known as a 'pan-Anglican' conference was not uncongenial to Archbishop Longley. However he consulted with bishops in England, Bishop Fulford the metropolitan of Canada, Bishop H.J. Whitehouse of Illinois, and several Colonial bishops. At a meeting in February 1867, a motion by the Bishop of Oxford (Wilberforce) was agreed unanimously. It read:

We, the Archbishops and Bishops of English, Irish, Colonial and American sees, here assembled, pray your Grace, to invite a meeting of all the bishops of the various Churches holding full communion with the United Church of England and Ireland. (Stephenson, op. cit., p. 182)

Archbishop Longley sent out the invitations to the Bishops on 22nd February 1867 for a 'Meeting,' the first Lambeth Conference, at Lambeth on 24th to 27th September 1867.

For a study of recent developments in the Anglican Communion the agenda of that first Lambeth Conference does not need detailed consideration: the important thing is that the Conference happened. Archbishop Longley who gave the matter careful and judicious thought was well aware that it was, in his words, "entirely without precedent." In England particularly there was no shortage of opposition to the prospect of such a thing occurring. Anglican leaders in other parts of the world may have seen the lack of precedent, but they saw that as subservient to the need that had come to exist. Bishop Lewis of Canada is reported as having said to Longley in 1866: "Your Grace, do we not all belong to the same family? Why should we not meet?" (Stephenson, op. cit., p. 160)

Of the agenda all that need be said is this — and it must not be forgotten that the whole Conference, services, sermons and all, was assigned only four days — the items were only three in number:

1. Intercommunion between the Churches of the Anglican Communion
2. The Colonial Churches
3. Co-operation in Missionary action

This agenda was circulated as a 'confidential' document. It was revised, and ceased to be confidential. Parts of it were never discussed properly because there was not time. Item 2, about the Colonial Churches, was mainly about Gray, Colenso and the Privy Council, with Bishop Gray in full vigour. Archbishop Longley in his letter of invitation had asked bishops to suggest subjects for discussion. A good many did, but all were ignored. During the Conference twelve memorials for consideration of particular subjects were made known, but nothing more was heard of them either. Some subjects were assigned to a committee that met after the Conference.

Perhaps it was a hurly-burly of a Conference, yet it was dignified, impressive, and of a significance that created a precedent.

Longley's successor as Archbishop, Archibald Campbell Tait, had been no advocate of the Conference of 1867, but he was not unmoved by it, and, with a blending of caution and determination, held a second Conference in 1878. Under successive Archbishops, and with increasing episcopal attendance from around the world, the Conference has continued to meet about every ten years. Its effect was to consolidate the Anglican Communion at a time when its world-wide and apostolic character had become apparent. Consolidation was timely. It became a characteristic feature of the life of the Anglican scene, which Bishop George Bell, in his life of Archbishop Randall Davidson (page 299), described as giving "a special opportunity for knitting the various provinces and dioceses of the Anglican Church together in mutual counsel."

b. Lambeth Conferences in General

Some details of the Conferences are:

1. Number of bishops present:

1867   76

1948	329
1958	310
1968	459
1978	407

2. The Provinces represented were:

In 1867 — the four from the British Isles, the United States, and a cluster of dioceses under the contemporary designation of 'Colonial and Missionary'

In 1948 — Australia, Canada, China, England, India, Ireland, Japan, New Zealand, Scotland, South Africa, United States of America, Wales, West Indies, and some extra-Provincial dioceses.

In 1978 there were in addition — Brazil, Burma, Central Africa, China (Hong Kong only), Indian Ocean, Jerusalem and the Middle East, Kenya, Melanesia, Papua New Guinea, South America, Tanzania, Uganda etc., West Africa. (The Indian Province was incorporated in the united Churches in India, Pakistan and Bangladesh, and was no longer part of the Anglican Communion, but the united Churches in North India, South India and Pakistan did, and do, have membership in the Anglican Consultative Council.)

The Conference of 1948 exemplified some of the greatest virtues of the practice. After the break caused by the war, and the isolation and suffering that many dioceses had experienced, the coming together from all parts of the earth for the 'mutual counsel,' and the companionship with fellow Anglicans in Christ's name, was a valued and apostolic experience. In the years of separation problems had arisen, for example, about marriage and divorce, or about the status of Japanese bishops, for which a wider interchange than local discussion was sought. Similarly the hopes and problems relating to Church unity, particularly in a world which saw unity as a primary consideration for nations and Churches, were a catholic preoccupation. The world itself was changed and changing and it was vital that the Conference recognized that, and thought out the world-condition in a framework of Christian doctrine. And in people like Bishop Wand of London (the chairman of Committee I) there was a notable standard of theology available.

The Committees of the 1948 Conference were:

I. The Christian Doctrine of Man; and the Christian Way of Life
II. The Church and the Modern World
III. The Unity of the Church
IV. The Anglican Communion
V. The Church's Discipline of Marriage; of Baptism and Confirmation.

Lambeth Conferences were of great significance both for the Anglican bishops who came, and for members of other Christian Churches who wanted to know more clearly what Anglicans thought and stood for, and who within the western world and the developing world encountered variety in style and theology that indicated personal independence rather than a universal kind of witness. To Anglicans, more accustomed to diversity, disinclined to a present central authority, and looking to the gospels and traditions, the Conferences were much less of a problem. To many the experience of the Conferences was the proof of their value, and it had become difficult to conceive where the Anglican Communion would be without them. Both sides had a point.

In fulfilling their role the Conferences have worked to a pattern which owes a good deal to 'how things were done last time.' Often the scholarship has been great and impressive, and the work of a few scholars and men of experience has had great influence on the reports from the Committees which appear in the full Reports. But the Committees themselves are not the voice of the Conference. They, like members of the Conference in general, must put out resolutions for the full Conference to vote on. The number of resolutions has been astonishing; and there is an addiction for stating the obvious. Perhaps this is because some bishops feel that things that are obvious nevertheless cannot be said too often, and perhaps because some bishops, when they return to their dioceses, are able to point to a resolution as being largely their own work. But the result can be more unfortunate than that. Buried in the Committee Report on the Anglican Communion in the 1948 Lambeth Conference Report (Part II, pp. 84–86) is an impressive study of dispersed authority as an Anglican understanding of the way authority is exercised. The Conference passed no resolution on this, and so, even though a matter of weight, it has not the authority of the Conference of 1948. Perhaps this exclusion might be avoided by reference to the statement in the Council's Encyclical Letter, but it is not there either.

In the four Conferences from 1948 there have been 355 resolutions, as follows:

In 1948	118
In 1958	131
In 1968	69
In 1978	37

Many resolutions have been stillborn, or have died very shortly after birth. In recent years there has plainly been an effort by the administration to reduce the number, and the considerable success has added to the findings of the Conference.

To ask to whom the Conference reports, and for whom the Report is written, is reasonable, but it may also have proved useful at times that there is no certain answer to these questions. However, increasingly, in many spheres, the subject of responsibility and accountability is being raised. It was formerly possible to say that the Conference issued an Encyclical Letter to the 'Faithful in Jesus Christ.' This was widely read out in churches of the Anglican Communion, and it depended largely on the local priest and congregation whether anything further was done. As has so often been said, the Conference and its findings are advisory not authoritative. Such Reports and Encyclicals have undoubtedly expressed the mood and the hopes of the Conference, and have had some effect on the way the Church thinks. The last Encyclical Letter was in 1958. In 1968 there was instead a 'Message to the Clergy and Laity of the Anglican Communion.' In 1978 there was neither. Probably this was not deliberate, for the Conference of 1978 undoubtedly and correctly believed it had an audience in the Anglican Communion and beyond. But in a much more closely-knit world, the past, present and future do not have identical requirements.

Basically the organizational side of Lambeth Conferences has much that is unchanged since the beginning, although from 1948, as we shall see, there has been considerable change in its context. Continuing factors are that Lambeth Conferences have no Constitution, though habits and traditions have developed. They are summoned by the Archbishop of Canterbury who sends letters of invitation to Anglican bishops. Only bishops are invited, but whether this is restricted to diocesan bishops or whether it includes some or all suffragan or assistant bishops is variable. A consideration here is probably the growing number of dioceses in the Anglican Communion and the consequent increase in size of a Conference even if only diocesan bishops are invited. This may also be a factor in determining whether, even in an age of increased ease of travel, only bishops, and not a representation of the whole people of God which would include clergy and laity, are invited. In this the Lambeth Conference has a different membership from the Provincial Synods which are, among other things, the legislative bodies of the world-wide Anglican Communion, and which – some since before the first Lambeth Conference – have not been restricted to bishops. By 1978 the Conference included as non-voting participants a smaller number of clergy and laity from five continents who were the Standing Committee of the Anglican Consultative Council. It was no-one's fault in particular that this was not a very happy experience, but the development was good, and we shall see where it leads.

The agenda for the Conference derives from the Archbishop of Canterbury, but in fact he confers with others a good deal. As early as the second Conference in 1878 there was a suggestion that there should be a committee "such as should represent, more or less completely, the several Churches of the Anglican Communion; and to this committee it might be entrusted to draw up, after receiving communications from the bishops, a scheme of subjects to be discussed." This is the beginning of the Lambeth Consultative Body, frequently reconstituted since, until the 1968 Conference recommended (*Report*, p. 145) that its responsibilities be continued by the newly proposed Anglican Consultative Council. The 1968 Conference also recommended that the Archbishop of Canterbury should be asked to decide, on the advice of the Anglican Consultative Council, upon the calling of future Conferences, and on their time, place and agenda. This advice, how it was arrived at, and the decision of Archbishop Coggan, the Archbishop of Canterbury, is reported in the 1976 Report of the third meeting of the Anglican Consultative Council (pages 62–64).

The Conferences were held at Lambeth Palace until the Conference of 1968 which was held at Church House, London. The 1978 Conference was held at the University of Kent in Canterbury; for the first time the Conference was residential, and bishops from all over the world got to know one another better than they ever had before. No longer did bishops tend to lodge with like-minded friends. That Conference, while emphasizing the desirability for Lambeth Conferences to continue (Resolution 13), said: "While recognizing the great value which many set on the link with Canterbury, we believe that a Conference could well be held in some other Province." What will come of that we shall see. There are at least two motivations against it. A great many bishops, and also their wives, do like a trip to England. In earlier days when a majority of the bishops of dioceses overseas were expatriates, a journey to England was also a journey home to their social and ecclesiastical origins. As late as the 1920 Conference Bishop George Bell could think of the bishops as "coming home from the ends of the earth" (Bell: *Randall Davidson*, p. 1003). Secondly, on the whole, English dioceses are not eager about raising funds for their bishop to travel to a Conference not held in England.

Another continuing feature is that Lambeth Conferences are held — European wars permitting — about every ten years. Most bishops do not have an opportunity of attending more than two Conferences, if that. A bishop from overseas, an expatriate, who had been in episcopal orders for a very long time, when asked in 1978 how many Conferences he had been to, and replied with a twinkle "four, so far," was an exception. He is in fact now dead. But one can argue that the reply said something about the value of continuity. Once, not so very long ago, the world's affairs moved more slowly, and transport took time. In a world Church today, the greater speed of affairs, and the need to respond to major situations, make a demand in which continuity is important. One meeting in ten years may not be enough on its own.

The subjects discussed by Lambeth Conferences over the years are in themselves an illuminative and serious study. The Reports of the Committees, as we have seen, are often more important than the plethora of resolutions which, despite their number, are capable of overlooking some of the significant Committee material.

When one contemplates a century and more of Conferences, it is possible to sigh for the gospel. However, the record of the Lambeth Conferences is not to be condemned in a hurry. There are learned reports and essays (which often tend to date a bit); some subjects that may indicate little more than a fashion or debate of the time; some that having been raised at one Conference are by ten years later sorted out elsewhere. Some are an important feeling after policy, or correct and universal theology. Some smooth over, but cannot conceal, differences of churchmanship. Perhaps a criticism of the Conferences is that such differences, although diminishing, are yet insufficiently replaced by understanding and full co-operation. It is encouraging, though, to see how soon after something of an organizational sort-out in 1867, the Conference was discussing pastoral and parochial matters. The Conference of 1888 discussed 'The Church's practical work in relation to (a) intemperance; (b) purity; (c) care of emigrants; (d) socialism' — as well as having on the agenda polygamy and divorce. In 1897 there was 'The Critical Study of Holy Scripture.' The Prayer Book, Liturgical Revision, and many more subjects with a strong spiritual ingredient occur through the years.

Some subjects, and not always those one would expect, make recurrent appearances from quite early days. For example, the need for forming more Anglican Provinces was under discussion in 1867, even though the final sprint did not begin until the 1950s in Archbishop Fisher's time. The role of laity in the Church was under discussion at the same time, although statements about it go back much further, beyond John Keble's Assize sermon or the theological studies of Reformation divines.

While the recommendation for the Advisory Council on Missionary Strategy was not made until 1948, the subject of mission is seldom absent from a Lambeth Conference agenda. There is, indeed, here valuable material on the history of the Anglican concept of 'mission' from days when the function of missionary societies and the work of the Church in areas 'overseas' predominated to subsequent (and sometimes recent) understanding of autonomy and the essential missionary function of all baptized Christian people. In the 20th century re-union has moved, rightly, into a dominant position, and the Conference, being emphatic for the principle, has exerted considerable influence in the whole field of the ecumenical movement. Within the Anglican Communion, the Lambeth Conference became not only a source of advice but almost a court of appeal. In situations which were so different from one part of the world to another, and where sincere minds were often at variance, the Conference usually concentrated on giving encouragement and stating principles. To that extent it has been an agent of unity.

One of the principles is that the final object of all endeavours towards unity is that there should be one universal Church. The closer bonding that has developed in the Anglican Communion exists for this end, and is not in itself an end and final objective. If, in progressing towards unity a Church of the Anglican Communion were to see its way forward as uniting with great Churches in its own nation or area, it was encouraged to proceed if it felt that to be right, even though their unions with other Churches involved ceasing to be a member Church of the Anglican Communion. The possibility of events taking this course was expressed as early as 1930 in the Lambeth Conference's Encyclical Letter as the pressure for a union of Churches, including the Anglican, gathered strength in South India:

> After the union in South India, Anglicans who will be included in the united Church will not give up the use of the Prayer Book or discard any of the doctrines held in the Anglican Churches. Yet the united Church in South India will not itself be an Anglican Church: it will be a distinct Province of the Universal Church (*1930 Report*, p. 27)

In the history of Lambeth Conferences it is not surprising that no subject has received attention so consistently as the form, nature and organization of the Anglican Communion. The recognition of the Churches of the Anglican Communion as a world-wide fellowship or family within the one Church of Christ was a factor which made the first Lambeth Conference, or something like it, inevitable. Some of the thought on this matter in 1867 can seem primitive now. The little agenda as we have noted it for 1867 (page 64) includes 'Intercommunion between Churches of the Anglican Communion.' The principle was perceived and was forceful. Stages in the implications and the putting into effect of the principle occur in the major topic of nearly every Conference since. To follow them all through would make a fascinating history in itself. But our task is to pick up the story in the Conferences of 1948 and thereafter.

One of the great differences between the years after the Second World War and the 1860s has been the changing position of the Church of England in the Anglican family picture. In 1867 its dominance not only in England but in pan-Anglican activity as it was then appearing was virtually unquestioned. The dominance was assumed. A slightly different view may have been taken by some in the Protestant Episcopal Church in the USA which after the Revolutionary War (War of Independence) was an independent organization in America. By its own choice, however, it was in communion with the See of Canterbury. Its first bishop-to-be, Samuel Seabury, seeking consecration, came to England. But the requirements concerning sovereignty then existing for consecrations in the established English Church compelled Seabury to turn elsewhere. He was consecrated in the Episcopal Church in Scotland, in Aberdeen in 1784, the first 'overseas bishop' in the Anglican Communion. Shortly after, in 1787, with necessary changes having been made in the additions to the rite in England, two more American bishops, William White and Samuel Provoost, were consecrated in Lambeth Chapel (Carpenter: *Cantuar*, p. 286). The American Episcopalians then had three bishops on their own soil, and properly ordered consecrations could, and did, take place there. With the generosity of unquestioned independence the phrase 'the Mother Church' was still often used for the Church of England.

There is little exaggeration in saying that the first Lambeth Conference was a consultation with the Church of England. The pressure to hold it did not come from England, but was addressed to England, and it was reasonable that the decision to hold it should have been taken (in the face of some serious opposition in England) by the Archbishop of Canterbury, and that it was held in England at Lambeth Palace.

The experience of the early Conferences was considerable in bringing the Anglican Churches outside Great Britain into far greater knowledge of one another, and also the deeper knowledge of the theology of the universal Church led to a new confidence. The American Church, not British, not established, increasingly competent theologically, played a major part in this development. Without it the story might have been different when in this century non-British Churches in China and Japan became full members of the Anglican Communion, as subsequently did other Churches which indeed might have been, or become, adversaries of Britain politically. The important thing had become the nature of the apostolic Church, not the history of nations. More than half the dioceses of the Anglican Communion now are not in the Commonwealth. Such development meant there was no theological difficulty as colonies, of whatever attachment, became independent, or as Churches in countries with no association with British history, like

Brazil or Rwanda, became members of the Anglican Communion, or when South Africa left the Commonwealth and became a Republic.

The role of the Church of England in these and similar changes, which bring us into the most recent decades, had been a mixture of good and bad. The English contribution to scholarship and discussion remained very considerable, and outstanding people had given their lives and skills in building up the Church in other countries. While such extension of the Anglican Communion was admired and welcomed, comparatively few in England attached to it similar importance as to events on their own shores — even though the power and numbers of the old established Church were no longer what they used to be. The racial context in which a measure of disquiet was expressed in 1930 was that the Encyclical Letter (*Report*, page 23), after delighting that "among the bishops here assembled there are representatives not only of the western races but of the races of Japan, of China, of India and of Africa" (they totalled about half a dozen bishops out of more than 300) continued thus: "We must confess that as Christians we have only imperfectly realized this family life. There still survives among Christians the peculiar form of pride known as race superiority. Anglo-Saxons, perhaps, are specially liable to this infection." On the other hand, the great missionary societies in England, whose part in building up the Anglican Communion is of first importance, were giving expression to less national or racial views.

c. Lambeth Conferences, particularly 1948 to 1968, and the First Executive Officer

The Conference of 1948 met in a different world from those before the war of 1939-1945. Few bishops who came then had been at that in 1930. They valued the opportunity to assemble together, to be free of the isolation or sense of remoteness that had been the lot of many of them and their people, but they came also with thoughts engendered by the experience of those years. The gospel was imperative in scores of situations in ordinary people's lives. The mood apparent at the Conference was restless, and was more concerned with the practical than most that had gone before it.

It is not surprising that there was emphasis on collaboration, and less on isolationism or superiority, in 1948 and the following Conferences than in those of former time. And it was not only from the Conferences, but from the Church throughout the world that the pressures were coming. The divisions within the Church itself were even less tolerable, and there was a feeling that little that was effective had been achieved so far.

In 1948 the World Council of Churches was brought into being, with Anglicans playing a prominent part in the action. However, the theology involved in some of the endeavours towards unity, and some of the collaborations with other Christians that were proposed or undertaken made it clear that variety of churchmanship in the Anglican Communion (and elsewhere) could still be deeper than the pressures that had been generated to achieve greater unity at almost any cost.

The greater desire to press the practical side of Christianity and to answer people's questions to the Church about the environment in which they lived brought forward discussion of the Church and war, of human rights, of refugees and migratory labour, of industry and resources, and very soon of nuclear war. But this same desire carried the requirement that answers derive from a right context, not from zealous determination alone. The opening sections of the Lambeth Report of 1948 is in three parts — 'The Christian Doctrine of Man,' 'The Church and the Modern World,' and 'The Christian Way of Life.' The sections are still worth reading, and bear many signs of the hand of Bishop Wand. Parts may be dated, but the particular significance is the recognition that while theology is in a sense perennial, it must be related to the world of the time, and the lives that mortal men are actually living.

Similarly the Report in 1958 on 'The Holy Bible: its authority and message' eased the worries and problems of many by being both timely and timeless. Through Archbishop Ramsey it had a pattern of theology that was both trustworthy and required, and an element that approached poetry from Archbishop Carrington was, for many, a bonus that was welcomed. How direct an influence these Reports had beyond the membership of the Conference itself is difficult to say. Certainly by indirect routes they established confidence in many church people as the Church moved from years of war into years of revolt, revolution and renewal.

Experience in many situations during the war years changed outlooks. In the Third World as much as any there were new thoughts about universality and equality. The Anglican Communion was changing in its thinking about its nature as a 'family' from a mother Church and daughter Churches to that of a family of equals. This process was accompanied by the recognition and belief that the Church in any nation or race is properly a Church of the people there, an indigenous Church, not merely with its own membership but having within that membership its own officers and leadership. This study began by drawing attention to the enormous increase in the number of black African bishops from Africa. Indigenization has brought fresh attention to the membership of the Church being by baptism: it is baptism which makes the whole people of God with their universal ministry, a ministry within which some are assigned by God to particular ministries. The effect is to focus attention on the laity as essentially the same as those who hold other orders in the Church. The concept of the Church as the whole people of God is of course consonant with theology through the ages, and therefore with Anglican theology. Through the centuries, and at Lambeth Conferences with their wholly episcopal membership, it has tended to slip in and out of the picture (and still does). But since the war there has been a more lasting effect on much Anglican theology.

Two more of the prominent factors in the decades following the war must be recorded. The first, though widespread in human thinking, has an important ecclesiastical dimension for the Anglican Communion. The war had underlined the importance of communication. The development of the Anglican Communion spotlighted the need for communication and up-to-date information. In a world-wide Church it was essential that Provinces and dioceses knew about one another and could communicate; that problems, hopes, synodical debates and decisions were not divorced from consultation. A family without communication is hardly a family at all. The necessity of this development was stated repeatedly, and is still a long way short of resolution.

The second was the strongly growing demand for political independence in the many countries where it did not exist. Much of the map of the world was about to change.

With foresight and courage Archbishop Fisher recognized and tackled this situation. One may contend that in some respects he acted in an authoritarian manner, and that some of his ideas of the role of an Archbishop of Canterbury and of the Church of England had an imperial touch that was already old-fashioned. However, he made the important step forward, and for ever thereafter any move towards the position prior to his creation of new and autonomous Provinces must be accounted a throw-back. He authorized and supervised the creation in the Anglican Communion of new Provinces from dioceses and in countries where such a measure of standing and autonomy was not then generally envisaged. The struggle for political independence was still in process and its outcome not known. The ecclesiastical situation, the realities of which the Archbishop had rightly discerned in the years surrounding the 1948 Lambeth Conference, moved into an area which asserted the universalism of the Church, and the rightness of enabling a new expression of that universalism as soon as possible. The Anglican Communion entered vigorously into the international, inter-racial and inter-cultural existence which is the relevant expression of the universal Church. The dates of the Provinces that were formed in the years following the Lambeth Conferences of 1948 are given above on page 42.

The Conference of 1958 initiated another response to the changes in the Church which had become apparent after the war, and part in this must have been played by Archbishop Fisher who held that office until his retirement in 1961. How much of the future he foresaw is uncertain. He had much to do with the organizing of the two Conferences in his time, but the chairmen of the committees were all western: most were from the Church of England, and of the other seven three were expatriates. Nevertheless, he was among those who saw the need to bind the whole Communion more closely together.

In the Lambeth Consultative Body (LCB), which had an existence going back to the beginning of the century, there was an international committee, designed to meet between Lambeth Conferences, with this implied as one of its purposes, but it had not been able to do a great deal, not least because it was very seldom able to meet as planned. For one thing travel was inconvenient and expensive. There were several revisions of the Constitution for the LCB, a fact which testifies to the need. In 1930 (Resolution 50) the Lambeth Conference made recommendations again:

> The Consultative Body should be prepared to advise on questions of faith, order, policy or administration, referred to it by any

bishop or group of bishops, calling in expert advisers at its discretion.

It was to help the Archbishop of Canterbury in any matters he referred to it as well as assisting him in the preparation and follow-up of Lambeth Conferences. There were to be 18 members appointed by the Archbishop of Canterbury "with due regard to regional requirements." The idea seems all right; the practicality unreal.

In 1958 the Constitution was revised again (Resolution 61) with further changes that were of some significance. For one thing something was done about a supply of money for it. For another, its world spread — in the persons of the Primates — was specified; sixteen named Provinces of the Communion were to participate. Most significant, and with consequences that were to be far-reaching, there was to be a full-time secretary. This was the beginning of the function which soon became known as the Executive Officer of the Anglican Communion.

Similarly it was recommended in 1958 that there should be a full-time secretary for the Advisory Council on Missionary Strategy, a subject which again involved all parts of the Anglican Communion, not least in the situations where they were. (1958 *Report*, page 2/69 and Resolution 60). In that connection, as in other parts of the Report, and in the pressures of the previous years, the need is expressed for effective communication and collaboration in a Church which recognized its universality. This appointment, too, became the work of the Executive Officer.

The person appointed in due course (January 1st, 1960) to that task was Bishop Stephen Bayne, until then Bishop of Olympia, USA. The appointment soon proved to be outstandingly good.

The first Executive Officer of the Anglican Communion

There was in Stephen Bayne a streak of the prophet. A prophet in 'The Concise Oxford Dictionary' is defined as an "inspired teacher, revealer or interpreter of God's will." He was competent at ecclesiastical business which to some extent the two full-time secretaryships implied, but he was only incidentally a business man. He saw himself as the servant of all that part of the Church which is called the Anglican Communion — "he is a servant of all the Churches equally" (Bayne: *An Anglican Turning Point* p. 103). In a report to the Archbishop of Canterbury in 1960 he wrote: "For what is at stake, in this whole prodigious Anglican dream, is not that we shall somehow win more people to join our Anglican club or build a more efficient denominational power structure. . . . The point is unity; the point is that the Church is the one body in the world which is bigger than any human differences. . . . The Anglican Communion is not the whole Church, nor more than one of the scattered brotherhoods within the Church. But it is all we have — all I have at any rate — to begin with. It is my only way of joining redeemed humanity." (op. cit. p. 37)

Before he accepted the appointment both he and Archbishop Fisher felt their way as to what it might imply. One senses that Archbishop Fisher's most certain conviction was that he had asked the right man. Bishop Bayne's purpose was that he should discern what God wanted him to do. It may not be too much to say that a consequence of deliberations was that the Anglican Communion developed in a wholesome way, when it might have missed the chance altogether.

Some of the correspondence between them, before the appointment was clinched, is recorded in *An Anglican Turning Point*. A quotation is worth while. On 5th March, 1959, Stephen Bayne wrote:

> Most of all, I think the new officer must be one who will believe without weariness and without doubt in the vocation of our Communion and in the dream all of us share in some degree of what our common life and witness can be, under God. . . . My only strong feeling would be that there ought to be a certain degree of looseness, enough to make it clear that this new post is not an *English* invention, nor merely an extension of your own office — I say this knowing that you share it and understand the issues involved. Indeed the whole point of the office, as I see it, is to give articulation and expression to the corporate life of our whole Communion, and to give it a new and deeper level than our present patterns afford.

A few days later Archbishop Fisher replied and in the course of his letter said:

> You mention your own strong feeling that there ought to be a certain degree of looseness in the new post making it clear that this is not an English invention, nor merely an extension of my office.

With that I wholly agree. I might have been guilty of describing it as a sort of auxiliary office to me: I really never meant that... But, of course, in this office you are entirely your own master, responsible to the Anglican Advisory Council on Missionary Strategy for any tasks that you take on at their request, and responsible to the Consultative Body of the Lambeth Conference for any assignments you take on at their request (which means in effect at my request): so there we are. (op. cit. pp. 10–11)

The years after the Second World War and up to the appointment of Bishop Bayne were years in which the Anglican Communion was feeling after a more clear expression of its vocation as part of the one, holy, catholic and apostolic Church, and realizing that the responsibilities attached to that vocation had a unique element. Associated with this was the recognition of the place of the laity, men and women, in that divine society. It was this vocation, and the attempt to give expression to it, that was dominant in Bishop Bayne's thinking and made his appointment so right and timely. In his first year as Executive Officer his journeys took him to the Church in all the five continents. Before he ended his appointment he had given several accounts of what, as he saw it, the Anglican Communion was all about, and what was the role of an Executive Officer. Here is one account, from his address to the Anglican Congress of 1963 in Toronto, Canada:

The Anglican Communion is not an organization by which older and stronger Churches can extend their influence over younger and weaker Churches. We are not interested in branch offices around the world. We care rather for a household within which many Churches, representing many cultures and peoples, can take their self-reliant and buoyant place in full brotherhood, each giving and teaching, each receiving and learning. Therefore our organization must both reflect this and nourish it.

The Executive Officer is not a master of the Churches, he is their servant. It is the Churches who support him, who direct him in working out their common will. I do not speak of myself personally in this; I shall not hold this office for ever; I speak of any such officer. He is not an 'assistant to Lambeth Palace' or to the Archbishop of Canterbury. He is an assistant to every archbishop equally, and to every Church. He is obedient to no other person or body than ourselves, collectively, in our separate Churches. His work is simply and solely that of making the mutual inter-dependence of the Anglican Communion a little more real. (*Anglican Congress 1963, Report,* p. 186)

d. Anglican Congresses

As has been seen, Bishop Bayne was far from being a lone figure: rather, he was particularly adept at discerning what was happening. Some analysis of what was happening in the Church found expression in — perhaps provoked — two Congresses in those years. One was in 1954 at Minneapolis, Minnesota, USA, and the other, which has just been quoted, in 1963 at Toronto, Canada. These Congresses included large numbers of priests and lay people, as well as bishops. One of their aims was to bring to a much wider audience thoughts that were not unfamiliar at Lambeth Conferences, and to enable all sorts of people from all parts of the world to experience what in the universal Church, and not least in the Anglican part of it, they were full participants in. The Congresses succeeded in that great numbers of people came, and that many got a new and joyful understanding of their Church. The greatest effect was in the countries where the Congresses — the family gatherings — were held. Not surprisingly, the numbers who came from further afield were much smaller.

To the majority the most impressive experience was the personal meeting of peoples. The developments that were taking place were experienced. While the fundamental message of the two Congresses was similar, and some memorable speeches were made, it is of interest in looking back that in 1954 the speeches (except for 'overseas missions') were by churchmen of the western world. By 1963 a much wider field provided the speakers.

Something of what was being said in Minneapolis in 1954 may be indicated by reference to a few quotations from some of the speeches. Bishop Walter H. Gray, in his Introduction to the Report, reminded Anglicans:

Today this Church is established on every continent and among people of every race. . . . The pattern of expansion has been that the new sections of the Church, once fully formed, have been national in their organization and autonomous in their government. There is no joint central executive or legislative body in the

Anglican Communion. No one archbishop or bishop is supreme, and no national Church has authority or jurisdiction over any other. A special position of honor is accorded to the Archbishop of Canterbury as head of the primatial See of the mother Church of England, and the test of membership in the Anglican Communion has traditionally been whether or not a diocese is in communion with the See of Canterbury. It is this background that gives this Church on the world scene the name *Anglican*, though the actual titles of the different Churches vary a great deal. The word *Anglican*, therefore, in this context, no longer means simply *English*, but has come to be a term for the particular embodiment of the historic faith, order, and worship of the Catholic Church that is the heritage of this Communion. (*Report*, pp. 1–2: see also "Bishop Walter Gray and the Anglican Congress of 1954" by Borden W. Painter, in *Historical Magazine of the Protestant Episcopal Church*, Vol. XLIX, June, 1980)

It became clear to many that intervals of ten years or more between Lambeth Conferences gave the Churches insufficient opportunity to take common counsel in the face of the rapidly changing problems of the modern age. Moreover, since in our national Churches the priests and members of the laity share with the bishops the responsibility of decision in matters affecting our welfare, it was inevitable that there should come about a recognition that the clerical and lay representatives should share with the bishops the responsibilities of international gatherings. (ibid. p. 2)

The Anglican Congress of 1954 marks a new era in the history of the Anglican Communion in that it is the first representative gathering of the Church held outside the British Isles. (ibid. p. 3)

The most important phase of the Congress has been the privilege of worshiping together and finding at the altar of God the best basis for bringing together men of all races and from all continents. (ibid. p. 3)

Bishop Wand of London spoke on 'The position of the Anglican Communion in history and doctrine':

If I were asked to state in a single sentence the position of the Anglican Communion I should say that it strives to give expression to the full teaching of the Bible as reflected in the age-long history of the Christian Church. This implies both faithfulness to the original foundation of the Church and a constant adaptation to changing circumstances. It implies also a firm grasp of the principle of continuity which allows no essential break with the past or any departure from the lines laid down in our fundamental documents. (Report, p. 25)

In a passage that now seems a little strained and contrived, he defended 'parties' in the Church, but made a not unconvincing defence of 'comprehensiveness': "The idea that there was ever one sort of undifferentiated Christianity is a mere chimera of the ecclesiastical journalist." (*Report*, p. 44)

Archbishop Philip Carrington of Quebec spoke on 'The Structure of the Anglican Communion.' Like Bishop Gray, he emphasized that the Anglican Communion has no central executive office or body with powers to legislate for all. He stressed the nature of the role of the Archbishop of Canterbury as a unifying factor:

> There is no question about the loyalty and affection with which we regard the Archbishop, whether we think of the historic succession from St. Augustine, or of the present occupant of his throne. But, actually, he does not possess jurisdiction over the whole Communion. His position of pre-eminence would appear to rest on long-continued historic tradition, which has steadily increased in dignity with the expansion of the Anglican Communion. (*Report*, p 45)

By way of considering the Book of Common Prayer, and variant revisions of it, he says:

> It becomes clear then that the Anglican Communion refers . . . to a historical standard which is larger than itself. It falls back upon the Catholic tradition as a whole, especially in its most primitive phase in the period of the Apostles and their successors, always referring in the last resort to the Holy Scriptures as received and used in the Catholic Church. (ibid. p. 47)

The Congress of 1963 was in Bishop Bayne's time as Executive Officer and he played an important part in preparing for it. It was seldom innovative by intent. Rather his thoughts, and the developments underlying 1954 led to a greater practicality in

Anglican affairs. Some of this found expression in a paper by the Revd. Dr. Howard A. Johnson of New York, who made brief visits to many dioceses of the Anglican world:

> The main point I have to report is: The Christian Church — in spite of ineptitude here and there, in spite of bungling and of beggarly performance all too often — has made a world of difference in this world of ours. It has been like a shaft of light. (*Anglican Congress Report 1963*, p. 224)

The needs for better preaching, teaching and training were emphasized. The laity must be heard more:

> The skills, energies, and insights of the laity must be given scope as never before. It is not enough for the ladies of the Church to polish brass while the ship itself is sinking. The Church, after all, is ninety-nine per cent laity — a fact which clerical arrogance is always forgetting. (ibid. p. 226)

Three subjects may be picked out as receiving increased stress in 1963. They are

1. Reunion between the Churches, and the Anglican part in the endeavour;
2. Mission; and
3. Spirituality

Of mission, suffice it to recall for the present that the movement called 'Mutual Responsibility and Interdependence in the Body of Christ' sprang into being at a consultation organised by Stephen Bayne just before the Congress in connection with a meeting of the Advisory Council on Missionary Strategy (see page 176f).

Spirituality is to be fully aware of the world in which we live out our days, and of the things that are Caesar's, and to be aware also that life and destiny in this world are conditioned through and through by the things that are God's. It must be remembered that Archbishop Michael Ramsey was chairman of the Congress. In an age when new things caused excitement in all the Churches, and there was a pronounced disposition to break away from conventions, he did not shun all new ideas. But because for him it was not merely newness that had value, he had throughout the 1960s and 1970s a steadying effect. People listened to him about what in theology was permanent, or when he pointed an acceptable course. He, in a world that might discard every veil, spoke of mysteries that are beyond human understanding, and so of the sacramental nature of the Church and the divine revelation it has to safeguard. At the heart of his theology and his message to the Anglican Communion was the bible and the standards impressed on us by Christ. The most remembered and quoted of his words to the 1963 Congress was based on a passage from the Epistle to the Romans (14:7–8):

> For none of us liveth to himself, and no man dieth to himself, for whether we live, we live unto the Lord; and whether we die, we die unto the Lord; whether we live therefore, or die, we are the Lord's.

The chairman of the Program Committee of that Congress was the Bishop of Cariboo, Canada, Bishop Ralph Dean. In 1964 he succeeded Bishop Bayne as Executive Officer of the Anglican Communion, and held office until 1969. Working closely with Archbishop Ramsey — in so far as that was possible, for Archbishop Ramsey was *sui generis* in many ways — Bishop Dean continued the work of Stephen Bayne. From him he inherited 'the Anglican dream' and continued his understanding of the family and apostolic character of the Anglican Communion. Like Bishop Bayne he travelled widely and knew himself to belong equally to all the Provinces, their clergy and laity as well as their bishops.

There are clear signs that by 1968 the Lambeth Conference, of which Bishop Dean was the Secretary, was recognized as being an important voice, but by no means the sole voice of the Anglican family. The sale of Lambeth Conference Reports had passed its peak, and those of 1968 were less than half those of 1958. The developments that found expression in the ministry of Bishop Bayne were consolidated in the recommendation of the Conference of 1968 for a consultative council of the whole Anglican world. This was the logical development of Anglican experience during and since the war, and the expression of it in the appointment of Executive Officers. The form proposed for the Council (*1968 Lambeth Conference Report*, Resolution 69) was the work of many people at and before the Lambeth Conference of 1968. Several people have claimed, with modesty, to have had a hand in it, and many of them did. One name that should not be forgotten is that of Bishop Dean's colleague, Canon W.E. Jackson, of Canada — an observant, much-travelled and thoughtful man.

e. The Anglican Consultative Council

The recommendation for this consultative body was made by the Committee on 'Renewal in Unity' at the Lambeth Conference of 1968. The proposals were 'accepted and endorsed' by the Conference in Resolution 69, and so emanated from the Conference as a whole. The Council was not a passing bright idea, but was provoked by awareness of those changes in the Anglican Communion which we have seen were occurring in the previous two or three decades.

> The growing together of Christians has brought the Churches of the Anglican Communion to a new stage in their relations with one another and with other Churches and organizations. We appreciate the work hitherto done by the Lambeth Consultative Body, by the Advisory Council on Missionary Strategy, and, more recently, by the office of the Anglican Executive Officer and his advisory committee; but we believe that a more integrated pattern is now necessary, in which, as 'members severally one of another,' Anglicans may fulfil their common inter-Anglican and ecumenical responsibilities in promoting the unity, renewal, and mission of Christ's Church.
>
> We therefore propose the formation of an *Anglican Consultative Council*, which could continue the responsibilities hitherto entrusted to the Lambeth Consultative Body and the Advisory Council on Missionary Strategy, and the replacement of the office of the Anglican Executive Officer by a Secretary General appointed by, and responsible to, the Council. (*1968 Lambeth Conference Report*, p. 145)

In several respects the Anglican Consultative Council (ACC) was, and is, unique. It remains the only inter-Anglican body with a Constitution. Also it was authorized by the Communion as a whole. Resolution 69 referred the proposals to all the member Churches of the Anglican Communion for approval, stipulating that a majority of two-thirds in favour was required by 31st October 1969 if the

ACC was to come into existence. By that date I was the new Executive Officer (succeeding Ralph Dean). The replies from the Churches came in, and were unanimously in favour. The Council met for the first time in February 1971 at Limuru, Kenya.

An important feature of the ACC is its membership. This is not restricted to bishops, but includes clergy and lay people. Every Anglican Church has members, which it chooses itself, the numbers varying between one and three according to the size of the Church. The total number is comparatively small, partly to facilitate a frequency of meetings such as is thought appropriate for serious treatment of ecclesiastical affairs in the world today. The ACC meets every two or three years, and its Standing Committee annually. As far as possible the Council is to meet "in various parts of the world." (op. cit. p. 48/9)

Having been founded by the Churches, which normally means their Provincial Synods as the legislative bodies, and its membership being nominated by them, and its funds determined and supplied by them, the Council is responsible and answerable to them. In this answerability, too, it is unique.

The membership has its own feature, too, in that the united Churches of South India, North India and Pakistan each has its own full member. At the first meeting of the Council in 1971, it was felt that the achievement of union by these Churches, in each of which the Anglican Church had played a large part, was not simply an occasion for conveying congratulations and waving good-bye, but for sharing in their progression on the difficult path to unity, and for learning from their example. The time was not one for breaking connections; and also it was not one when anything that looked like an assumption of Anglican superiority should prescribe the way forward. So the ACC resolved to invite the three united Churches each to have one full member, chosen by them, of the Anglican Council. Each accepted, and their membership continues, to the advantage of the Council, and, one hopes, of the united Churches. This cannot be the end of the story when the goal of us all is unity and the universality of the one Church of Christ. All one can say is that it may be reckoned a positive beginning.

With one notable exception the Council appoints its own officers. The exception is the President who is always the Archbishop of Canterbury. A suggestion at the Lambeth Conference in 1968 that it might be otherwise happily made no progress. Although the Constitution does not require it, the three members successively elected as chairman so far have all been lay members: Sir Louis Mbanefo of Nigeria, Dr. Marion Kelleran of the Episcopal Church, USA, and Mr. John Denton of Australia. The role of these officers is so far inadequately defined. In the Anglican Communion it is not sufficient to say of the Archbishop of Canterbury only that he "when present, shall preside at the inaugural session of each meeting of the Council" (op. cit. p. 48/6); or to leave it to supposition that the chairman's only responsibility is to chair some meetings when they occur. However, though a few matters such as these need to be more specific, the Constitution and rules as proposed in 1968 are wearing remarkably well, not least because no more has been stipulated than seemed necessary.

In 1971, at the first meeting, the post of Executive Officer came to an end. The person holding that office, myself, was appointed Secretary General of the ACC, and re-appointments by the Council continued my office until the end of 1982, when the present Secretary General, the Revd. Canon Samuel Van Culin of the USA, was appointed. The ACC is alone as an inter-Anglican body with a secretariat (small as it is) continuously in existence, and with an income — deriving from, and devised by, all the Churches of the Communion.

The functions of the ACC cover an extensive area. Before listing them it is worth noting that while they can be amended it is not easily done, and requires widespread agreement in the Anglican Communion. Before amendments can be made, the Council must submit them to the member Churches of the Anglican Communion and ratification requires approval by two-thirds of them.

The functions of the Council are:

1. To share information about developments in one or more Provinces with the other parts of the Communion and to serve as needed as an instrument of common action.

2. To advise on inter-Anglican, Provincial and diocesan relationships, including the division of Provinces, the formation of new Provinces and of regional councils, and the problems of extra-Provincial dioceses.

3. To develop as far as possible agreed Anglican policies in the world mission of the Church and to encourage national and regional Churches to engage together in developing and implementing such policies by sharing their resources of manpower, money, and experience to the best advantage of all.

4. To keep before national and regional Churches the importance of the fullest possible Anglican collaboration with other Christian Churches.

5. To encourage and guide Anglican participation in the Ecumenical Movement and the ecumenical organizations; to co-operate with the World Council of Churches and the world confessional bodies on behalf of the Anglican Communion; and to make arrangements for the conduct of pan-Anglican conversations with the Roman Catholic Church, the Orthodox Churches, and other Churches.

6. To advise on matters arising out of national or regional church union negotiations or conversations and on subsequent relations with united Churches.

7. To advise on problems of inter-Anglican communication and to help in the dissemination of Anglican and ecumenical information.

8. To keep in review the needs that may arise for further study and, where necessary, to promote inquiry and research.

While there is no doubt that this Council of the Churches of the Anglican Communion gives expression to that universality which has been seen to characterize it, the years of the Council's existence have shown that it is not without shortcomings — some of which arise from an over-optimism about human nature — and that there are other areas where it has got ahead of the pack.

Among the shortcomings are these. It is too small, even though its present size facilitates a desirable family atmosphere at meetings instead of the formality of a large meeting. However, a Council of seventy or eighty people for a Communion of millions is questionable; and for great Churches to have the maximum membership, which is three, seems inadequate, although it is fundamental that every Anglican Province — even the small ones — should participate. If the Council is to work in the way that was clearly in the minds of the Lambeth Conference of 1968, it is essential that the Provinces feed matter into the Council's meetings, and that the members they have appointed convey back the advice and direction that the Council has decided on. But it is no easy matter for three people to report effectively to, say, the General Convention of the Church in the USA, or to the General Synods of the Church in England or Nigeria. Indeed, such bodies tend to be very inward-looking anyway, and references to the whole Anglican Communion and its views are infrequent. Moreover, what may be influential on the minds of a Lambeth Conference bent on change may not have an adequate counterpart in customary outlooks and assumptions. Britishness, romanticism, an eye to past national history, all have an understandable but nevertheless deflecting influence.

Particular attention may be drawn to two of the functions of the Council and the intention that it should enable the Anglican Communion to achieve 'a more integrated pattern.' At first it may appear that there is no provision for advising on action that might be taken in doctrinal matters or canon law. The provision is probably to be found in the first function given to the Council which is "to serve as needed as an instrument of common action" (*Functions*, No. 1). So it has come about that through the Council there has been set up for the Anglican Communion an 'Inter-Anglican Theological and Doctrinal Commission.' Recommendation in print was first made at the meeting of the Council in Trinidad in 1976 (*ACC-3 Report*, p. 21). Exploration of the ground was authorized by Resolution 8:

> The Council refers to member Churches the matter of agreement and discussion in doctrine and theology throughout the Anglican Communion.

The opinions of the Churches were then sought in three questions, the third being "Would your Church be in favour of co-ordination of doctrinal and theological study in member Churches by way of an inter-Anglican Commission?" Replies through the ACC meeting in 1979 were all affirmative, and the Council then recommended that the Commission be set up (*ACC-4 Report*, Resolution 14). Care was taken to spread the membership wide, and meetings lasting ten days each, with correspondence in between, were to take place every two years. The ACC Standing Committee was to determine the membership, the first subjects, and practical details. This it did in June 1980, determining that "The initial subject for the Commission to study and report on shall be 'Church and Kingdom in Creation and Redemption,' being a study of the relationship between the Church of God as experienced and the Kingdom of God as anticipated with special reference to the diverse and changing cultural contexts in which the Gospel is proclaimed, received and lived." ("Minutes of the 1980 Standing Committee," pp. 9-11)

The membership, like that for Anglican representation in inter-Church Commissions, is determined by the President and Secretary General of the ACC, in consultation with Primates. The present membership, with members drawn from all the continents, and with Archbishop Keith Rayner of Australia as chairman, is given in full in *Anglican Information*, No. 26, December 1980.

The other matter for particular attention at this stage concerns 'problems of inter-Anglican communication' (*Functions*, No. 7). The need for communication and the dissemination of information was clamant in the minds of those who came to the Lambeth Conference in 1948. The problem (which is by no means peculiar to Anglicanism) has been eased a little but is far from being resolved. Most of the principal world denominations, as well as the World Council of Churches, send out information regularly. It could be argued that there is too much. Little of it reaches the parishes, or even synods or comparable bodies. The efforts of the Anglican Consultative Council, similarly, show a limited development. In the days of Bishop Bayne and Bishop Dean *Compasrose* was a letter to tell bishops something of what was going on. Early in the 1970s this was superseded by *Anglican Information* which disseminated factual material from all the Provinces, and material of ecumenical origin, to bishops and many others throughout the Anglican Communion and beyond three times a year. This continues, and there is a case for sending it to parishes as well as dioceses; but with over 64,000 congregations the cost in production, circulation, translations and staffing, is out of reach. Anyway, as most of the information concerns Anglican matters that are over the immediate geographical horizon it is doubtful even now in how many dioceses it is read, let alone communicated. I recall a synod engaged in the important matter of a decision about ordaining women to the priesthood. Great satisfaction was expressed that I was able to say what the position was in other Provinces of the Anglican Communion. What to me was unsatisfactory was that every diocese represented there had received that information in *Anglican Information* long before. If I was baffled, the years of similar experience — not least I may say in England — have taught me not to be baffled. It is more important sympathetically to understand what as people we are all like — in a world and Church which buzz with change. Probably there is more progress than one realizes, and perseverance, like the ACC appointment of an Officer for Communication, is what in time will be most helpful to us all.

The Anglican Consultative Council exists, as we have seen, to meet the increased pressure for the Anglican Communion to develop its role as one universal body within the Church. The goal is excellent, but we have already glimpsed some of the reasons why it is not reached overnight. The matters that are considered and discussed at meetings of the ACC have their source in the direct involvement the secretariat has with issues all around the world, and from conferring about these in advance with the Primates of the Provinces. Also there are subjects which have their origin in our ecumenical affairs with other Churches. The agendas, with preparatory articles from significant and informed sources, are sent to the Council's members around the world well in advance of the actual meeting, and with the request that they are discussed as widely as possible. A list of the main subjects on the agendas is given in Appendix III.

Looking back over the Council and its antecedents, one has the impression that the element of prophecy — even of 'dream,' as he called it — which derived from Stephen Bayne was present in the ACC in its earlier years. More recently the element of vision has given place to a more overt concentration on efficiency as providing the way forward. How far this alteration is to advantage for the Council's undertaking is difficult to say. One is reminded at times of a phrase of Sydney Smith's in a different context, when he spoke of an "ungovernable passion for business." While the phrase may be taken as no more than a comment — Smith liked the man — it is also indicative of the danger to any ecclesiastical institution of declining in spirituality as it increases in either bureaucracy or nationalism.

f. Primates' Meetings

Small meetings of Anglican Primates, under the chairmanship of the Archbishop of Canterbury took place from time to time from 1908 in a group called the Lambeth Consultative Body. Its task was to assist the Archbishop before, after and between meetings of the Lambeth Conference. As we have seen, the plan did not work very well until the first Executive Officer became its secretary. A few years later, in 1971, it was superseded by the Anglican Consultative Council.

When the Lambeth Conference met in 1978, part of the organization set up for the occasion was a 'Primates' Committee.' This comprised the principal Primate from each Province, and was available for any major decisions that might have to be taken about the Conference, or for subjects on which the Archbishop of Canterbury wished to seek its views. The Conference itself recommended that there be subsequent meetings of the Primates, and that recommendation was followed. The purpose of the meetings was not made wholly clear, but basically it was advisory to the Archbishop of Canterbury. The membership is the principal Primate of each Anglican Province, and the first Primates' Meeting, called and chaired by the Archbishop of Canterbury, took place in November 1979.

The Anglican Communion now had three regular conferences — the Lambeth Conference, the Anglican Consultative Council, and the Primates' Meeting. For the sake of Anglicans and others, it was desirable to determine their relation to one another and to the task which, in many ways, they shared.

The Lambeth Conference therefore passed the following resolution:

> The Conference asks the Archbishop of Canterbury, as President of the Lambeth Conference and President of the Anglican Consultative Council, with all the Primates of the Anglican Communion, within one year to initiate consideration of the way to relate together the international conferences, councils, and meetings within the Anglican Communion so that the Anglican Communion may best serve God within the context of the one, holy, catholic, and apostolic Church. (*Lambeth Conference 1978 Report*, Resolution 12)

The Archbishop of Canterbury conferred with the Primates in the Primates' Committee which was meeting during the Lambeth Conference, and with their approval initiated the consideration by asking Bishop John Howe to write a memorandum on the subject as a first step. In April 1979 the memorandum from Bishop Howe was received by the Archbishop of Canterbury, and was sent to all the Anglican Primates, none of whose replies disapproved of it.

The memorandum concentrated on the conferences which might be thought regularly to deliberate on the Anglican Communion as a whole and with a wide range of its concerns. These were considered to be the Anglican Consultative Council, the Lambeth Conference, and the Primates' Meeting.

The possible purpose and contribution of Primates' Meetings was there described as follows:

> Assuming these meetings are established, each Primate would then participate in his capacities as chairman of both his General Synod and his House of Bishops, but especially as the representative person of the whole membership of his Province.
>
> From discussion with Primates themselves, the wish for meetings does not appear to derive from a desire to revive the Lambeth Consultative Body. Rather, in an environment of change and pressures, the recommendation for meetings of the Primates has arisen from a wish for an opportunity to hear and to learn from the experience of others, and for discussing ideas and responsibilities. The stimulus is not domination but reflexion — a belief that for the positions Primates hold it is especially important that there should be Christian companionship and discussion that are not hurried by the inevitable crowded agenda of more formal business meetings.
>
> The purpose of Primates' Meetings might then be:
>
> i. To confer on matters on which the Archbishop of Canterbury may wish to consult the Primates, including matters concerning the Lambeth Conference.
>
> ii. Bearing in mind the terms of reference of the Anglican Consultative Council:
>
> > a. to refer suitable matters to the Anglican Consultative Council;
> > b. to confer on the implementation of policy and proposals from the Anglican Consultative Council.
>
> iii. To share information and experience.

In my Review Address to the meeting of the ACC in 1979, an abbreviated version of the findings of the memorandum set out the relation and role of these three conferences as follows:

1. A *Lambeth Conference* must continue to be residential, in whatever country it is held. The West must recognize that the influence of the Third World will increase, and in time probably be dominant. The agenda should continue to encourage discussion on a wide basis, including especially matters of current concern to all or particular parts of the world. It will continue to advise through its resolutions. But at depth, especially as it is an occasional meeting, it serves as an extremely important indicator of the direction in which the Anglican family is moving.

2. A *Primates' Meeting* is mainly to enhance cohesion, understanding and collaboration in the family and to share information among the Churches, not least about the implementation of ACC recommendations made by the ACC under its terms of reference. The discussions can also be such as consider procedures which the Anglican Communion might wish to follow. For example, the Primates' Committee in 1978 agreed to a proposal that on some subjects, like, say, the nature of a Province, or the acceptable limits of marriage practice, there might be broad outlines for the Anglican Communion. Perhaps within this sort of free agreement among the Churches there are to be seen elements of that authority which some have found it a problem to locate.

3. The steady slog lies with the *Anglican Consultative Council*. It meets quite frequently and its secretariat operates all the time. It exists to serve the whole Anglican Communion, and its field is marked out by its terms of reference. They are very wide, and include a basic responsibility in the whole ecumenical area as well. Of its nature, a major activity of the ACC is to strengthen the relationships between the Churches. The selection by the Churches of their members of this Council is being increasingly realized as of primary importance, and so is the opportunity of the members to report back to their Churches. (*ACC-4 Report*, p. 74)

The agenda for the first meeting of the Primates' Meeting in November 1979 under Archbishop Coggan could not be determined until it was decided by the Primates what the Meeting was for. The

Meeting decided that the acceptable basis was the proposals of the memorandum. But the story has not stopped there.

In this study of development in recent years in the Anglican Communion, it is necessary to ask what part Primates' Meetings play, and here we move into what are, as yet, fields of uncertainty, though not without potential. The part to be played by Primates' Meetings is still undefined. The minutes of the 1979 meeting record that "in the discussion it was clearly recognized that decisions which have legal authority are made by the Synods of the Provinces which make up the Anglican Communion. The role of a Primates' Meeting could not be, and was not desired as, a higher synod in that sense. Rather it was a clearing house for ideas and experience through free expression, the fruits of which Primates might convey to their Churches" (1979 Minutes, p. 4). Despite the last phrase, it is not clear to whom the Meetings report, and to whom they are responsible. One aspect of the problem was illustrated when Archbishop Johnston of New Zealand said that a proposal there had been referred to the ACC who had replied at some length. He had since been asked to seek the opinion of the Primates' Meeting. He accepted that the Primates could not give the proposals the time that the ACC had done, and that in any case the most the Primates could do was to refer the matter back to the ACC (Primates' Meeting 1979, Minutes, p. 17).

At the second meeting (April 1981), the Revd. Professor Stephen Sykes, in some reflections he was asked to give on the Primates' Meeting, emphasized the need for greater definition in a number of areas of Anglican thought and expression. The point is important, but an implied question is whether a Primates' Meeting is the suitable, capable body to supply such definition. If not, who is? Where a Primates' Meeting, with its world-wide character and extensive knowledge of people, might be of help is in proposing scholars and others they believed would be of value in the quest for such definitions. Primates themselves are not necessarily the theologians for such work, and few of them, if any, were elected Primates for that purpose. An interesting observation made at that meeting in the course of a debate about authority was that "there was some discussion about whether authority should reside with a college of bishops, or with Synods as representing the whole people of God, and it was recognized that bishops, clergy and laity had different but related roles." (Primates' Meeting 1981, Minutes, p. 4)

Professor Sykes, in his 'Reflections' and on other occasions, made with emphasis the following point:

> May I again bring before the Primates my serious concern about the state of Anglican theological resources? We are, in my estimation, in danger of becoming the largest Christian denomination in Christendom without adequate provision of time and personnel for mature and careful thought. This constitutes an actual contradiction in our often repeated appeal to reason and conscience. It may be that the first priority is for a comprehensive review of resources for primary, secondary and tertiary theological education throughout the Anglican Communion. (Primates' Meeting 1981, Minutes, Appendix B, pp. 1–2)

As during the development of the ecumenical movement Churches have become more involved with one another, and with the world in which they live, the issue of beliefs and practices concerning authority has increasingly come under discussion. This has become apparent in the Anglican Communion as elsewhere. For most Churches the growing recognition of the diversity and importance of cultural differences of approach and understanding has been a factor here, and in the Anglican Church, perhaps more than most, there is the desire for an understood situation in which variety exists within acceptable limits.

The subject of authority was looked at during the Lambeth Conference of 1978 in a fashion that was tentative but not without yearning. Resolution 11 attached a rider that the Conference "requests the Primates to initiate a study of the nature of authority within the Anglican Communion." The request was taken up at the first Primates' Meeting in 1979 (Minutes, p. 10, and Appendix E). A discussion took place that was exploratory and fairly far-ranging. The aim became more to open up the subject than to draw conclusions. A direct consequence was that specific papers should be prepared on the subject for the next Primates' Meeting. These were assigned to Professor Stephen Sykes and Bishop Neville deSouza of Jamaica, both of whom were present at the Primates' Meeting of 1981. Also taken into account was a paper by the Revd. Philip Thomas on 'Some Principles of Anglican Authority'; and a list of 'Practical Implications of the Anglican View of Authority' was composed during the meeting by Sykes and deSouza. The Meeting commended "all four documents to the Churches of our Communion for study and comment" (Minutes, p. 6). They were duly printed as a booklet 'Authority in the Anglican Communion' which was sent by the ACC to the Anglican Churches. So far (by 1983) comments have come slowly. Two have been received, from Ireland and Wales; and two or three of the larger western Churches have promised replies in due course when appropriate committees have conferred and are ready to respond. One has to ask whether it is significant that there is no indication yet of any response from outside the western world.

The task of this study is not to pass a judgment on the theology contained in the papers, but to ask if there is evidence there of development in the Anglican Communion. Their existence, besides their seriousness and depth, indicates that there is. There is some investigation of authority as a Christian theological concept and topic before proceeding to the more particular experience of authority in the Anglican Communion. The investigation raises questions which, on the one hand, scholars of various points of view will be glad are introduced into the discussion, and which, on the other, give a guidance (but not a tyranny) that many good church people would welcome. The case for this constituting a development is strengthened, not weakened, by the fact that, while there is a remarkable amount of agreement, there is not too much. For example, the western, and often English, approach of Professor Sykes is to some degree countered by the Jamaican outlook of Bishop deSouza; their understandings of the place of laity within the ministry of the whole people of God is not quite the same; and one wonders how the Third World applies western ideas of 'criticism.' A value in these things is that we are not occupied with problems that pertain only to the Anglican Communion.

Before leaving this recording of the place that the consideration of 'Authority' appears to be taking in Anglican debate, a further note may be added about authority as it exists specifically in the Anglican Communion. Frequently assertions have been made that Anglicanism lacks authority in adequate measure. This is questionable. An analysis of the position of Christian Churches in general reveals that in most there is more diversity concerning authority than those said to be in authority in fact suppose. Certainly there is not in Anglicanism a universal code or constitution as those terms are normally understood within an organization; nor is there a central jurisdiction. But Anglican appeal to Christ and the gospel, and to faith and order in the apostolic and early Church is well known, although in this, as in any recourse to faith and scripture the element of human assessment cannot ever be excluded. This is ground that Anglicans and others have gone over many times.

In the course of preparing this paper I have read most things written by Lambeth Conferences, and by many other gatherings of divines as well. Many times the Anglican bases have been discussed and stated, not least by Lambeth Conferences in sections concerning the history and unity of the Anglican Communion, and while reports are sometimes dated, the measure of agreement, even with each decade adding or clarifying as it thinks best, is not to be set aside.

A consideration of the fundamental theology of authority is a lengthy business, and will take much time. Alongside that study a more immediate step could be taken. Lambeth Conferences, ACC documents, and other Anglican sources have written quite extensively on the subject of authority in the Anglican Communion. To gather and digest these has not been done and would be valuable. If and where there are disagreements they should not be carelessly eliminated; nor should the study be confined to the official parts of reports. Often the official resolutions of Lambeth Conferences seem short on inspiration. As we have learned from Professor Sykes, one of the most significant analyses of authority in the Anglican Communion is to be found in the published report of the 1948 Lambeth Conference. It was never authorized by the Conference — but it is none the worse for that.

g. The Lambeth Conference 1978

This brief following of international Anglican Conferences has shown that there has been a number of changes, or, maybe, developments, in the Communion. The Lambeth Conferences since World War II have led us to the appointment of the Executive Officer and thence to the Anglican Consultative Council. We have also seen the appearance on the scene of Primates' Meetings. Obviously the Anglican Communion does not stand still. To make some further analysis of the changes, a useful ground is provided by the most recent Lambeth Conference — that of 1978.

We have noticed (*see page 84*) that in at least one respect Lambeth Conferences are on the decline. In 1968 the sale of reports was less than half that of 1958, although the number of bishops present had increased by more than a third. The sale of the 1978 report showed that the drop was continuing. However, the popularity of the Conference with bishops seems as great as ever. Very few diocesan bishops do not come, and assistant bishops, who often are not on the membership list, long to come if they could. How is the change to be accounted for?

One factor is simply changes in the times in which we live. Travel is much easier and swifter than it used to be. Conferences are many, and, especially if you were not there, reports usually make dull reading and are not read. Communication, even with its many limitations, is more nimble than it was. Until fairly recently a Lambeth report was one of the best ways of learning about the Anglican Communion: now Anglicans suspect that they know it already. This is not always so, but a consequence is that most Provinces and synods are more inward-looking and concentrating on their own affairs than one would expect.

These are not the days of great men and memorable utterances: that too has affected Lambeth Conference reports. There is a greater quantity of sermonizing and exhortation. That need not be bad in its underlying content, but it does not generate eager consumers.

Probably these are not factors of profound theological importance, but they have their effect on a Conference that meets regularly — if only every ten years — and which may be seen as advisory at best.

The great increase in the number of new autonomous Provinces in the Anglican Communion, and with it of law-making bodies which include clergy and laity, inevitably brought changes in the role of Lambeth Conferences. So did the expression of these things in the creation by the Provinces themselves of the Anglican Consultative Council. But one would doubt if it is a direct awareness of these developments that has led to church members in general asserting that a Conference of bishops (with a very unequal representation) is an inadequate and therefore less significant symbol of the Anglican Church today. There is, for example, a widespread ignorance still about details of membership of the Anglican Consultative Council. But, regardless of detail, there exists an awareness throughout the

Anglican world that Provinces are bodies with a participation in the life and mind of the family which formerly they did not have; and a role of influence that Lambeth Conferences formerly had is no longer there. Too much could be ascribed to the outcome of theological reasoning: too little to 'feel.'

So a Lambeth Conference tends to be seen as 'another conference' — even if a rather special one. Like some other conferences, it is subject to fashion. We have noticed how it can produce contradictory resolutions about the decision-making process, reproducing the popular emphasis on laity in 1968 and on hierarchy in 1978. Esteem for 'small groups' has been manifest, as at many conferences, although the groups were not easily brought together again.

The point is that Lambeth Conferences have become less significant than they were. One of the factors is probably the decline of English dominance. Understandably at this stage the change may be difficult for some of the English bishops to adapt themselves to. It is not easy to realize that the norm may rest elsewhere. But in the Anglican Communion of today it is not necessarily a bad thing.

These paragraphs have focussed a good deal on the more recent of the Lambeth Conferences, and this may be a suitable point to include a few further observations that may have significance both for the present and for the future. We have noted that for the first time the Conference of 1978 was residential (*see pages 68,69*). The opinion was strong and widespread that any future Conferences must never be otherwise. Among the virtues were the understanding and affection that rapidly developed between people from all over the world — each with his own thoughts and problems — living together. Worshipping and praying day by day as one body was made possible as never before. Because it was an expression of Anglican universalism as it is, there was appreciation of the use of rites, and sometimes languages, that were unfamiliar to many, but all of which derived from current practice in the Anglican Communion — a procedure originating with the ACC. It was features like these in the Conference of 1978 that accounted for one Archbishop, from Africa, observing that "for me the Anglican Communion has come alive for the first time, and it feels like home"; and an English Archbishop saying "I felt I was at the rebirth of the Anglican Communion — a kind of recapitulation with a long evolution ahead."

Anglican diversity, indigenous and cultural, caused problems. One was, and is, languages. This has long been known at many meetings, like those of the World Council of Churches. 1978 was the first time languages other than English have been available, for hearing or speaking, at a Lambeth Conference. And that, surely, can be only a beginning. Moreover, if English is your language it can be difficult to remember all the time that many of one's brethren there are speaking and hearing in their second or third (or even sixth) language.

Several of the problems Anglicanism is going through arise from this world-wide nature of the Communion, and the diversity of Creation. In preparation for the last two or three Conferences 'Preparatory Articles' have been written and distributed in advance. Those for the 1978 Conference had a half-hearted reception, particularly in the west. The main problem did not concern the contributors, many of whom were eminent people in the Anglican and other Churches. The problem was that the 'Articles' derived from people of many countries and cultures, with unfamiliar expression or points of view. That is the way the Church is. They were not particularly British. As the editor I like to think that in another ten years' time they may be making their mark.

The last consideration here goes back to developments that were taking place before 1978. This is the matter of votes at a Lambeth Conference. It is true that generally votes are taken only when there is, or may be, an important difference of opinions. Each bishop has one vote. And that sounds fair enough. But in fact it means that the more dioceses a Province has, the more votes it has. The number of dioceses does not correspond to the number of church members, let alone active church members. Nor could it. Not only do Provinces wax and wane in their membership — although dioceses hardly ever cease to exist — but the approach to the subject of dioceses differs from one part of the Communion to another. Even were it desirable there is no quick way towards a uniformity in this matter; and no serious person in a Province of comparatively few dioceses is going to say, "Let us make more dioceses so that we have more diocesan bishops and thus more votes." I know of no clear solution to this problem, yet if the Conference's decisions are to be respected the present system will no longer do. For historical reasons, perhaps, it is understandable how in the past such a procedure should have come about. Most notably the preponderance of voting power lay with the Church of England and the Episcopal Church in the USA. But it cannot continue and anticipate respect. Here are some relevant figures for the last four Conferences: thirty years in which, as we have seen, there has been profound change, and in which much has happened to bring into being the world-wide Anglican family which contains so much of the pattern of the future:

Date of Conference	Number of bishops present	C of E percentage	ECUSA percentage	C of E plus ECUSA percentage
1948	329	32%	20%	52%
1958	310	16%	29%	45%
1968	459	24%	27%	51%
1978	407	11.5%	26.5%	38%

(Some variation, especially in the second and third columns, occurs because the number of assistant bishops invited to the Conference was not constant. England has a high proportion of assistant (which here includes suffragan) bishops.)

It will be observed that in general the English/American dominance is decreasing. And, as was noted at the beginning of this study, the indigenous representation from the developing countries is increasing. It was something of a disappointment in 1978 that more was not heard from the non-western bishops. It seems that one reason for this was a lack of confidence among them. For many this was their first Lambeth Conference; some were not confident that they would be understood correctly; some felt restrained by language difficulties. Thus, in the main, the western voice and style of thought — though the west may not always have wanted it — was almost as dominant as it always had been. It would be rash to assume that this pattern will continue much longer.

An important element in the 1978 situation was that political violence, or the threat of it, was causing tension between the Church and the State in a number of countries, particularly in the Third World. Bishops are more vulnerable than most. Some, probably more than the west realized, felt it unwise to say much, let alone to speak their minds, especially in plenary sessions. The most obvious predicament of this kind in 1978, and it must be allowed to suffice, was that of bishops from Uganda. Idi Amin was then President, Archbishop Janani Luwum had been assassinated the previous year, and the President's men were undoubtedly around the Conference and hearing the plenary debates. Those circumstances do not encourage uninhibited participation. One may anticipate similar pressures in various parts of the world in the years to come. From the Church's point of view the great satisfaction about the 1978 Conference is that they were there. That is more significant than that they had to be circumspect in speaking, but that certainly must be understood.

(The Ordination of Women to the Priesthood was a major subject at the 1978 Conference. The subject is treated on pages 152–166)

h. The Role of the Archbishop of Canterbury

We have seen in the previous sections that in the last 25 to 30 years there have been considerable changes in the Anglican world and its international conferences. These changes have inevitably affected the role of an Archbishop of Canterbury. Their effect on the Church of England is closely related, but that will be considered later (*see page 167f*). Here, where we have been looking at international conferences, attention is on the Archbishop's role, as the president of them all.

Although in line with what had been happening before, an irreversible change took place when Archbishop Fisher created new and autonomous Provinces of the Anglican Communion from dioceses which until then had come under his jurisdiction. The final stage was being entered upon of transforming the Anglican Communion from being a largely English outreach to being an international family of autonomous and equal Provinces. The Archbishop was more distinctly than before the 'first among equals' of the bishops, and the focus of unity in the family. We have seen this development come into being, and several consequences have followed. They, probably, are not complete.

The Archbishop has two major roles. He is, by appointment, the Primate of all England. And also he is the focus figure of the Anglican Communion, a body which grows in numbers and significance. A personal estimate is that his two roles are at present of about equal importance, and it is the role of focus person of the Anglican Communion which is growing, and will continue to increase. It is not an easy situation, especially as there is a limited appreciation of it in England. Also, as we have seen, the Anglican Communion has half its dioceses (though fewer than half its members) outside the British Commonwealth. For example, the Anglican Communion extends behind the Iron Curtain. Also the Anglican Province of the Southern Cone in Latin America includes all the countries there. Like any other Province of the Anglican Communion except England, while this Province is not under the Archbishop's jurisdiction or authority, he is for it a focus figure with a fatherly connection with the family. Two dioceses of the Province of the Southern Cone are in Argentina. (Incidentally, the Anglican community in the Falkland Islands is in the unique Anglican situation of being a parish that is no longer in a diocese at all. It avoids being adrift by a parochial attachment to the Archbishop who is, as it were, its Vicar.) The Anglican Provinces — their governments, context and people — will be less and less British-orientated and may not be sympathetic to western styles and standards. This is particularly true of the Third World, where the Church grows. The Archbishop's two functions, as they are at present — Primate of a national, established Church, and focus figure of an international Communion — do not make a comfortable blend. That international role which gives expression to the nature of the Anglican Communion will increase as the years go by.

It is both significant and relevant to note when, at their request, the Lusitanian Church of Portugal and the Spanish Reformed Episcopal Church were fully integrated into the Anglican Communion, the Commission which recommended this (October, 1979), after discussion with the bishops of those Churches, proposed that "Metropolitical Authority shall rest with the Archbishop of Canterbury in his capacity as the focus of unity of the Anglican Communion throughout the world, and as President of both the Lambeth Conference and of the Anglican Consultative Council" (*Report*: "The Iberian Churches," p. 12).

One has to allow, too, that, however mistaken it may be, many minds are not at all clear that the political element in the appointment does not mean that an Archbishop of Canterbury is expected to be motivated by his government's policies: there is then a supposition or a worry that political alignment may distort alignment with the gospel.

In the Anglican Communion, with the exception of England, bishops and primates are chosen by the Province concerned. The person of the Archbishop of Canterbury concerns them all. There is no great clamour at present for a voice in his appointment, and the Communion does have a small representation on the Commission that makes proposals for the office to the Crown through the membership on the Commission of the Secretary General of the Anglican Consultative Council. How long that will suffice is debatable.

The question has been raised at times, in an enquiring way, whether an Archbishop of Canterbury has to derive from membership in the Church of England. Given the form of the Anglican Communion now the theoretical answer is surely that he does, at present at any rate. The present practice is one with which the Churches of the Anglican Communion feel at home. For generations the practice has worked, and there is no significant pressure to change it. A respect and affection has surrounded those appointed to the office, and one suspects that any other system would be viewed with less confidence. Also, from the point of view of the Church of England, as long as the present form of establishment persists, a non-British citizen would be in a quite anomalous position in relation to the Sovereign and Parliament, and probably the Act of Settlement of 1707 presents barriers. The position of a *British* citizen who is not from the United Kingdom may pose fewer difficulties, at any rate in theory. A practical point is that in England the Archbishop of Canterbury is wholly or partially responsible for a large number of appointments and he needs a considerable acquaintance with the available personnel.

Again, in giving some consideration to this matter, we have become aware of the problems that face an Archbishop now as the Anglican-Communion-part of his double role increases. A quotation from Section 3 of the *Lambeth Conference 1978 Report* (page 104) is to the point:

We are confident that by the turn of the century, the role of the Archbishop of Canterbury as the acknowledged focus of unity of the autonomous Churches of the Anglican Communion will make the international aspect of the appointment even more demanding both in time and leadership than it is at present. We recognize that this cannot but have implications for the Church of England and for the province and diocese of Canterbury. (*Lambeth Conference 1978 Report*, p. 104)

England has difficulty in understanding the Archbishop of Canterbury's relation to the Anglican Communion. There is a tendency to regard him as a constitutional head with authority in all the Anglican Provinces rather than as the focus figure within a free family where authority rests with each Province and its own Archbishop and Synod. Nor is the Anglican pattern convenient for the media. An illustration is provided by the crisis that came upon the Anglican Church in Iran. Care for the Church and clergy there rested first with the Province of Jerusalem and the Middle East, of which Iran is a diocese, and its Archbishop (there called the President Bishop) Hassan Dehqani-Tafti, who happens also to be the diocesan bishop of Iran. Having been forced out of the diocese, any action in Iran was almost impossible for him. But he was able to enlist the help of the Archbishop of Canterbury as a person of stature and influence who was not an Iranian. The Archbishop's personal representative, Mr. Terry Waite, went to Iran to attempt to obtain liberation for church leaders in Iran — both the expatriate British and the Iranian nationals — as he frequently emphasized. In England, where the matter was given great coverage, one seldom heard of anything other than of the expatriate British. Understandably to those whose knowledge of the Anglican Communion was limited, the Archbishop of Canterbury's role was misunderstood as an international British affair.

Reference has just been made to the 'status' of the Archbishop of Canterbury. This is undoubtedly and rightly considerable. It arises partly from the position the Archbishop holds in England, and the 'feel' of the history behind it, and the wide recognition of this eminence. In more ecclesiastical circles, it arises partly from his central position as *primus inter pares* in the world-wide Anglican Communion. In so far as Anglicanism is identified with a person, it is with the Archbishop of Canterbury, and on numerous matters, within and without the Communion, his counsel is sought. Nowadays he travels a good deal, and rightly he is greeted with acclaim and enthusiasm — and sometimes a touch of human romanticism too.

It is virtually impossible for the Archbishop of Canterbury to travel with what might be called a low profile, or to visit churches where there is very little idea who he is, and where there is not a big congregation for the occasion. In consequence the role of some other people is important for the Anglican Communion, particularly that of the Secretary General of the Anglican Consultative Council. There is little reason why he should be particularly conspicuous, but he is owned equally by all the Provinces and they know it. Problems, fears and intentions of clergy and laity as well as of bishops are likely to be discussed informally with him, as well as those matters which relate to the ACC by Constitution, and he is assumed to have understanding of a variety of cultures. He is likely to know a good deal of what is going on when the ceremonial flags are not out. Through this kind and breadth of information, he is in a position to know something of the future course that things may take.

The following extract about the future Lambeth Conference in 1988 is from *Anglican Information* No. 35, December 1983, and is referred to above on page 59:

Lambeth Conference Announced

After consultations at Limuru, Kenya, with the Primates of the Anglican Communion and the Standing Committee of the Anglican Consultative Council, the Archbishop of Canterbury, Dr. Robert Runcie, has confirmed that a Lambeth Conference of Bishops will be held at the University of Kent, Canterbury (UK) in 1988. This will be the 12th Lambeth Conference. They have drawn together the chief pastors of the Communion most decades since 1867.

The aim of the Conference will be to promote fresh initiatives and renewal in four areas in the life of the church: mission and ministry; dogmatic and pastoral matters; ecumenical relations; and the transformation of the social order.

The Archbishop also confirmed that preparation for the Conference will begin immediately. Part of this will include a series of regional conferences, like the Pacific Basin Conference on Ministry, held in Honolulu in June. It is hoped that this will enable bishops to come to Canterbury well prepared and having contributed to planning an agenda which expresses local concerns. "I hope that the Lambeth Conference will not be seen as just another isolated conference which produces a report," the Archbishop commented. "This is why we have to begin now with our preparations. I hope that each bishop will be in close communication with his diocese about it and come reflecting its concerns — that each bishop will bring his diocese with him."

The Standing Commitee of the Anglican Consultative Council welcomed the announcement and agreed that its secretariat should take charge of planning and arrangements.

V

Unity and Ecumenism

a. About Unity

A way in which the Church manifests its organic nature is by the element of change. A way in which this change manifests itself is by variation in emphasis and concentration. For a century or more emphasis has increased on the importance of recovering unity in the Church, and on the necessity of eliminating the divisions which have, for whatever reasons, become established in the Body of Christ. This has become so obvious that it is difficult now to see how for so long the recovery of unity was not accorded the widespread priority it now has. The determination to recover the unity in Christ's Church, for which he himself prayed, has rightly become a major and virtually universal activity in the days in which we live. Sincerity and activity in this ecumenical response to Christ and the gospel provides a principal measure in the development of any part of the divided Church.

It is generally possible to see what forces brought about division: it is proving much more difficult to recover unity. Indeed, as the pursuit continues it is becoming apparent, in a way that had not been foreseen, that there is still no clear pattern of what the unity which the gospel calls for should be like in the present world. For example, should striving be towards unrestricted fellowship or towards an organic and visible unity which supersedes all differences?

This study does not require a history of the ecumenical movement, and various accounts have been written which do that. Attention here has to be on what part the Anglican Communion has been, and is, taking in the quest.

From the days when the movement was growing there has been Anglican support. Anglican belief in the nature of the Church and of the gospel made participation not only unavoidable but welcome.

"A continuing interest in the visible unity of Christ's holy Catholic Church throughout the world — this has been from the beginning one of the marks of the Anglican Communion" (Neill: *Anglicanism,* p. 366). The course that things took, as revealed by Lambeth Conference reports is interesting. The Preamble to the very first Conference, by general agreement, contains this:

> . . . secondly we desire to express the deep sorrow with which we view the divided condition of the flock of Christ throughout the world, ardently longing for the fulfilment of the prayer of our Lord: "That all may be one, as Thou, Father, art in me, and I in Thee, that they also may be one in us: that the world may believe that Thou hast sent me"; and, lastly, we do here solemnly record our conviction that unity will be most effectively promoted by maintaining the faith in its purity and integrity, as taught in the Holy Scriptures, held by the primitive Church, summed up in the Creeds, and affirmed by the undisputed General Councils, and by the drawing each of us closer to our common Lord.

For its date the passage is remarkable, but one senses that idealism outstrips the realities of the aspiration.

The subject of unity recurs in the second Conference of 1878, but the focus is on unity within the Anglican Communion. Later on in the 19th century this was followed by consideration of relationships, and then of possible procedure towards unity, with some other denominations. In the 1908 Conference came (though as the last item on the agenda) 'Reunion and Intercommunion.'

Wars affect the Church. And the relationship of Christians who confess the one Lord becomes a more acute problem as stresses are shared and the needs of the world increase the common ground. There is more recognition that a way to increased unity must be found. Reunion was a concern of many Churches and individuals, even if the complexities of the problems were being understood only erratically. Christian minds were becoming turbulent. It was in this context that in a quest that was now for world reunion the Lambeth Conference of 1920 produced the famous document 'An Appeal to all Christian People.' The direct effect was probably disappointing, but Anglican commitment was fairly plain, and future discussions, though viewed with apprehension by some Anglicans of various schools of thought, were definitely aimed at reunion and unity. By

1948, and the verge of our period, the Lambeth Conference had a long committee report on 'The Unity of the Church,' and a Conference resolution (No. 51) which reads:

> The Conference records its thankfulness to Almighty God for the revival of interest in the cause of Christian unity which has been increasingly manifested in many parts of the world. It also pays a tribute of gratitude to all in our own and in other Communions who have displayed courage, enterprise and vision in the service of this cause.

However, it was not until the Conferences of 1968 and 1978 that Observers from other Churches were actually named in a Conference report.

It would be misleading to imply that all Anglicans have been enthusiastic for ecumenical endeavours in general, or that among those who were there was an overall ecumenical policy held by Anglicans as a Communion (cf. The Rev. Canon Christopher Hill: *Preparatory Papers for ACC-5*, 1981, p. 201, para. 2). Some, while not resisting the principle, were apprehensive about the form some proposals were taking. They feared, and not without reason, that the essential nature of the one Church was jeopardized by muddled ideas, however enthusiastic, or by a wrong identification of fellowship with unity, or by the predominantly protestant course that seemed to characterize some ecumenics. A consequence was diverse Anglican reaction to many of the schemes that the quest for union was producing. One course that events have been known to take was this: If one believes, as most do, that the unity of the Church is in accordance with God's will, then a proposal for an Anglican Church to enter into serious discussions aimed at greater unity with a Church of another denomination cannot reasonably be refused. There is a feeling, not least among Anglicans generally in the region concerned, which implies how good it will be when other people are like us. (Members of the other Church doubtless feel similarly.) Very often eventually some sort of positive recommendation comes out of the discussion, but invariably it involves changes, usually by both Churches. And then dreams evaporate, and the project dwindles in committees and the ecclesiastical media. Probably something good survives, and serious (not hostile) thinking is done. But nothing has happened quickly.

Through the 20th century, if not before, most of the major Christian Churches had given much time and effort to work for reunion. Sometimes the aim was to justify the position a Church had taken up and to manifest its wider acceptability, sometimes the aim was a greater degree of communion or inter-communion, sometimes the aim was to increase understanding and collaboration. Discussion often centred on ministry and episcopacy, and this brought the Anglican Communion to the middle of much effort and dialogue. By the 1960s Anglicanism already had a long ecumenical history. But on the episcopal side particularly, not much had actually been achieved. And within Anglicanism itself the accepted ecumenical duty was combined with worry: the more catholic Anglicans fearing what the more protestant ones might agree to, and *vice versa*.

On the episcopal front the creation after years of discussion of the episcopally structured Church of South India was arrived at, as we know, with a good deal of anguish, and a union was achieved which to many seemed more regional than universal. But with the two largest and best known of the historical episcopal Churches — the Roman Catholic and the Eastern Orthodox — there was no significant progress although some symbolic gestures were made. Rome was so large, monolithic and right in its own eyes, that for few of its principal figures could ecumenics be much more than a friendly call to other Churches to come home. The Orthodox Church felt sympathy for an episcopal Church which was not fettered by the papacy or the protestant reformation; but to what extent its ministry and doctrines were those of the ancient Church was a matter requiring much testing and discussion, and which, because of the restrictions on the collaboraton among the Orthodox Churches, made any general agreement either way an almost theoretical decision of the future.

In the Churches of the Christian world the quest for unity went on: there was no question of it dying out. The Anglican Communion pressed on. But there seems cause for supposing that by, say, 1960 ecumenics was engaged in more from a sense of duty than of expectation. If there was an expectation it was that in a cause which was so plainly in accordance with divine intention God would do something. Sooner perhaps than was generally expected, He did.

For many people, perhaps for most, a major change has come about with the entry first of the Orthodox Church and then of the

Roman Catholic Church into the ecumenical movement. This has given the quest for unity as a response to Christ's intention for the Church a universality that it desperately needed. The desire for reunion is not protestant or catholic, but Christian. Though it is very apparent that unity is not in consequence just round the corner: the hope is that there is now one corner fewer to go round.

b. Ecumenism, with particular reference to Anglicanism

The pressure for unity developed with the realization that unity was not only a good thing but necessary. This became increasingly apparent as denominations moved beyond their traditional areas, and encountered one another increasingly in the vast areas of mission and extension. Both the extent of identity of purpose and the differences of faith and emphasis came into focus with a new importance and dis-satisfaction. Even the acuteness of some of the conflicts increased the hopes that these might be transcended in a decline in differences and divisions. In the main loyalty to the tradition received, and the belief that one's own tradition was right, were impressive, however much divisions were regretted. The issues of 'What kind of unity?' and of how to achieve it were more and more relevant and unavoidable.

Several factors appeared on the scene, and most of them are still with us today. They need not, though, be regarded as necessarily excluding one another, although some seem to be in decline. One line of thought concentrates on local or regional union. In the country or area as many denominations as possible are encouraged to participate in formulating and carrying out a plan for a united Church. With this approach goes an emphasis on 'multi-lateralism' — several local (or bigger) Churches working together for a form of union that they can all accept. Some of the concentration here may be on achieving forms of words or wider practices — not necessarily superficial — that are generally acceptable. A great achievement in this area has been the creation of the united Churches of India and Pakistan. A problem that has been emerging here is that the united, national Churches themselves experience an isolation from the Churches of the rest of the world. Even though their world bodies have normally assented, often with enthusiasm and admiration, to the terms of union, the new united Church cannot be fully identified with any of them. For example, in India and Pakistan, the Anglican 'Church of India, Pakistan, Burma and Ceylon' was fully participant from the beginning of the planning, and became part of the united Churches as they were created. They ceased to be an integral part of the Anglican Communion, as they did of the other parts of the divided Church from which they had sprung. Stephen Neill, writing of the Church of South India, explains — "It was agreed from an early date that the resulting Church would not be in any sense an Anglican Church; it would be an independent regional Church" (Neill: *Anglicanism*, p. 380)

A feature of the unions in India and Pakistan is that the resulting united Churches include the historic episcopal ministry in their form of Order. This contribution came from the Anglicans alone, to whom it is essential. To span the gap which had existed since the Reformation between episcopal and non-episcopal Churches was a unique and great achievement. Thus multi-lateral and limited regional discussions aiming at union are by no means impossible, but undoubtedly they are difficult, and in recent years they have generally broken down or lost impetus — so it has been in the USA with COCU (*Consultation on Church Union*), with the Anglicans and Methodists in England, in Australia and elsewhere. One can contend that the role that was often ascribed to Anglicanism by Anglicans — largely on the basis of it being both episcopal and reformed — that it is a 'bridge' Church carries less conviction than it did. There is a wider supposition now that the high road to reunion is seldom established by building bridges: progress by convergence has become a more acceptable highway.

Anglicanism continues in commitment to the multi-lateral approach as well as to the bi-lateral. If this Anglican concern with both the classic processes should seem a well-intentioned attempt to run with the hare and hunt with the hounds, that is not really the case. The situation is that, other than God Himself, no one knows how reunion will come, or even how long the road is. The reasonable approach seems to be that in so serious a matter if doors are open a little you try to open them further; if doors are open further, you try to go through them, looking for guidance from the Holy Spirit. The Anglican Church may be confused or disagree on matters concerning reunion: what is not in question is its commitment to the quest.

Why then down the Covenant?

Thus the whole field of activity given by the Anglican Churches to the Anglican Consultative Council was prescribed in only eight functions: but of these eight, three concerned the ecumenical commitment.

The bi-lateral procedure by which unity is sought may be assigned two main forms. Two Churches work together for unity (or more unity) between themselves. This may be either between those Churches in one locality or nation, or between two Churches on a world-wide basis. The former of these two approaches has two particular difficulties. One is that Churches, as a whole or in parts, have very different patterns of construction. What with one pattern may be possible may be not only difficult but almost incomprehensible in another; moreover, that diversity may not be apparent for some time, and when it is, the future and the outcome have to be considered deeply in a changed context. A second difficulty can arise where limitations in consultation and communication give rise to one part of a Communion making headway of a kind that another part of the same Communion does not know much about and which, when it does, it has difficulty in supporting. What happens then is uncertain, and may come near to putting the whole process into reverse. An example is the growth in the Episcopal Church, USA, with great diligence of collaboration with the Lutherans, about which some parts of the Anglican Communion are not well informed (in a sense perhaps through their own fault), and may yet express dismay. In England the Covenant scheme with some of the non-episcopal Churches, failed to win the Synod's support, but if it had there is uncertainty what would have happened in the Anglican Communion. Anglican Covenant schemes in South Africa and Wales were different, and there is no certainty that other parts of the Anglican Communion where the Church lives alongside the same non-episcopal Churches as England would have decided they could go along with England's scheme. One can say that the danger arises as much from faulty communication as from a particular approach to unity: the point to be made is that it exists.

A form of the bi-lateral approach which has increasing prominence, and a penetrating, long-term hopefulness, is that between the Churches or traditions in their universal, or world-wide, manifestation. It is to be recognized, though, that these are manifestations with basic variety. On the one hand there are world-

wide associations, or fellowships, or similar confessional attach-
ments, often relating to a particular Reformation leader or theology,
for example, the World Alliance of Reformed Churches, or the
Lutheran World Federation. On the other hand, there are the single
families of Churches where the unity is seen as provided and compelled by one, holy, catholic and apostolic Church — for example,
the Anglican Communion and the Orthodox and Roman Catholic
Churches. Bi-lateral conversations of this kind can and do involve
any of the world-wide Churches or Confessions, but the determination with which the Second Vatican Council brought the Roman
Catholic Church into the arena of ecumenical activity has given a
new realism to discussions of unity with that Church. While its
essential universality makes bi-lateral work with other world bodies
the natural procedure, and that is the dominant style of the work of
the Vatican's Secretariat for Promoting Christian Unity, it does not
follow that their attention is restricted to the Orthodox and Anglican
Churches. Other Confessions and Communions are partners in
discussions with them, as for example the Lutherans, the Disciples of
Christ, and the Methodists.

The Anglican Communion is at present a participant in four bi-
lateral discussions on the world basis. The Anglican membership
represents the whole Anglican Communion, and the members of the
four Commissions are appointed by the President of the ACC (the
Archbishop of Canterbury) and its Secretary General and with consultation with Primates. The four Commissions are with the
Lutheran Church, the Orthodox Churches (Anglican/Orthodox
Joint Doctrinal Discussions), the Roman Catholic Church
(Anglican-Roman Catholic International Commission, usually
known as ARCIC), and with the World Alliance of Reformed
Churches. Reports from Commissions are received by the Archbishop of Canterbury on behalf of the whole Communion, and are
sent by the Secretary General of the ACC to all the Anglican member
Churches so that the ACC can learn their views. This is particularly
important in a world Communion when a Commission proposes
lines of action or policies. The procedure may take some time as
reports are likely to be referred by the member Churches to their
synods, and not all synods meet very often — and some are occasionally forgetful.

The Anglican Communion, though certainly with a smaller individual membership than the Romans or the Orthodox, and probably smaller than the Lutheran, Methodist or Reformed Churches, is geographically very widespread. Thus the decision by all the member Churches of the Anglican Communion on major matters of reunion is important. Also it is to be realized that not all parts of the Anglican Communion are directly involved in the immediate affairs of every Commission, although they are involved in the principles.

The work assigned to the four present Commissions is not in all cases the same. In some cases the two Churches have thought best at this stage to focus in a particular area and for a limited number of meetings: such are the Commissions with the Lutherans and the Reformed Alliance. In the case of the discussions with the Orthodox the purpose is more of exploration and understanding in great or typical areas of faith. With the Roman Catholics the ultimate objective, approached step after step, is visible unity.

An account of these four Commissions will be found as follows: Lutheran — pp. 129f; Reformed — pp. 133f; Orthodox — pp. 134f; Roman Catholic — pp. 141f.

The World Council of Churches

Integral to the whole ecumenical movement and the course which development has taken is the World Council of Churches. Its history and influence are much wider than the concerns of the Anglican Communion, but an evaluation of the part played in ecumenical endeavours by the Anglican Communion requires a primary concern with this Council. As the Anglican Provinces have come into being they have of their own wish joined the Council. As is well known when, as a culminating step in a long process, told in many histories, the WCC was constituted in 1948 at Amsterdam, the declaration of the Constitution was made by the then Archbishop of Canterbury, Archbishop Fisher. In the years leading up to, and following, 1948, the names of Anglicans who were especially prominent in the life of the Council have frequently been emphasized — Charles Brent, William Temple, George Bell, Geoffrey Fisher, Oliver Tomkins and others. Nowadays regret is sometimes expressed, at Geneva and elsewhere, that, with the exception of

Perhaps the Methodist have fallen over!

Archbishop E.W. Scott of Canada, such Anglican eminence and influence on the Council seems to be a thing of the past. But before regret is too soundly endorsed some of the changes that have taken place may need to be noticed. In 1948, and the following years, leadership in the Church was widely expected to be white, and of a European cast of theology. That is no longer so. In 1948 there were delegates of 150 Churches at Amsterdam, and with a strong western predominance. There are now over 300 member Churches. Moreover, concern with poverty, injustice, oppression, liberation is an aspect of the Christian gospel which is more at the forefront of much belief, moral preoccupation, and politics too, among the countries of the Third World than it has been in the Anglicanism which tends to look to Britain. The World Council reflects the thoughts of its own membership. One can contend that the World Council has its faults, limitations and biases, but one may question how far the leadership of a former day is appropriate now. What is for consideration by all Christians in a changing world is that the principles of the Christian faith, and its moral base, do not change.

An advantage which the World Council has is that it is not a Church. This gives it a facility for looking around at the whole scene, for exploring issues that Churches seem to have left alone, for not being hampered by the particular style or gait that a Church may develop over the centuries. Both Churches and Councils are objects of loyalty, but the two loyalties are not of identical kind. A Council may more easily gather stones together, but also more easily, and without strain on loyalty, consider whether the time has come to cast away stones. The flexibility proper to a Council may propose to the Churches, as nothing else can, that in a known situation their performance is not all it should be. The Churches sought and seek unity: in their meeting together as the WCC they discovered the need to consider whether such an objective could be contemplated by Christians apart from contemplating also the unity of mankind.

The objective of this paper is not to argue the rights and wrongs of the matter, but to propose that it was right that such a question should be asked. But one must doubt whether such a question could have more than a limited usefulness if it were asked by a denomination or two. In fact, in coming from the Council, which one must remember is a Council of *Churches*, it has the wider impact, and is probably affecting a review of Christian thinking and social behaviour which is still in process.

It is unlikely that every Church and its members is going to like all that the Council says and does. Among so large and diverse a body that would be incredible. The role of the Anglican Communion, one would suggest, is to participate as constructively as possible, to hear and help formulate the questions, to realize the relevance of its own universality, to face, and if need be question, the social and political issues facing Christian people of the one creation, to review seriously, and it may be to approve, the diversities in its own ranks — and also to propose where and when a time has come in the affairs of the Churches to cast away a few stones.

As has been said, a history of the WCC would not be appropriate to this study. A convenient account of some of the work for reunion (both before and after the actual formation of the World Council), particularly as it concerns the Anglican Communion, is given by Bishop Stephen Neill in *Anglicanism* (pp. 366-383). And a very valuable account of all union discussions on both international and national bases is given in *Confessions in Dialogue* ('Confessions' is here used as meaning 'denominations'). This book was compiled jointly by the Faith and Order Commission of the WCC and the World Confessional Families (see pages 124,125). The third and updated edition covering 1959-1974 was published in 1975.

At or near the centre of every quest for an increase in unity, and in inter-communion, is the issue of ministry, and of the episcopal ministry. It can be said with some justification that ministry is not a subject which dominates the gospel and epistles. Indeed, loyalty to the gospel is to be found everywhere among those who together seek for unity, yet ministry and episcopacy are omnipresent problems in the divisions. It is clear from the records of Anglican quests for unity which, as Neill says, reach out "literally in all directions in the Christian world," that episcopacy is always an essential at the heart of Anglican thought. There are signs that sometimes they wish it was not so. The Lambeth Quadrilateral of 1888 in stating the four essentials from an Anglican point of view for a re-united Christian Church names one as "The Historic Episcopate, locally adapted in the methods of its administration. . . ." Eighty years later, at the Lambeth Conference of 1968, a modified, but unconvincing, adjustment was made to the words, thus: "Common acknowledgement of a ministry through which the grace of God is given to his people" (*1968 Report*, p. 123). It was unconvincing to many, Anglicans and others, because it appeared to be a form of words which obscured real disagreements, however much one might regret the disagreements.

Within the Anglican Communion itself there is, as we have seen, a good deal of diversity. However, throughout the Communion the structure and Order is episcopal, and the Anglican Churches are committed to it, and would not have it otherwise. This might be thought remarkable, but only by a superficial estimate. The episcopal and apostolic ministry is seen not as in any way separate from the gospel, but characteristic of the Church which has its foundation in the gospel and the apostolic foundation of it. It is seen as an element in the God-given tradition (παράδοσις) of his one Church, and its proper universality in time and space. It is seen as a uniting factor without which reunion can never be complete. The pomp and earthy power and corruption that some bishops have achieved is deplored and denounced; the virtual necessity at the Reformation of discarding some forms of episcopacy as it was then encountered is widely understood and the need for reform widely agreed. What has lasted in approval is not bad bishops, but the principle of a universal ministry which is a bond of unity and fellowship, and which is rooted in the apostles and the gospel.

Influenced by their own settings this has been said by the Romans, the Orthodox, the Anglicans, and others, some protestant as well as catholic. Within broad limits we have seen how each Church in discussions for unity has ministry in the centre of its vision. Each tends to lay stress on its own style, or on a style which it hopes will be acceptable to its own members as well as the other Church involved. The importance — even though it is sometimes emphasized to the exclusion of almost all else — of belief about ministry is obvious. But because no one Church is ever at ease about one other Church raising the subject as an issue of universal importance, we have here the sort of issue the Churches might raise together for widespread general consideration. This is the sort of major undertaking which the WCC might encourage and facilitate. And it has done so. One doubts if any other organization could. Plainly in this kind of activity the Anglican Communion has a part humbly to play: it may not stand aside. The World Council raised the issue in a booklet (Faith and Order Paper, No. 111) published in 1982 called *Baptism, Eucharist and Ministry.*

An extensive account of the WCC is relevant to this study only in so far as it serves to indicate where particular developments in the Anglican Communion might lie. With this booklet Anglicanism can contribute importantly to the quest for a consensus among Christians on baptism and eucharist; however, the responsibility of Anglicanism may be appropriately indicated in this study by a measure of concentration on ministry.

The booklet is the outcome of years of preparation, with help at the beginning from Orthodox and Lutheran members of the Council, and then through the Council by successive drafts to the member Churches for comment and revision. An earlier draft had the fascinating title *One Baptism, One Eucharist, and a Mutually Recognized Ministry.* On the whole responses came more from individuals specially committed to such study for unity than from Churches as a whole. Responses came from some Anglican quarters, and encouragement from the Anglican Consultative Council in 1979 (*ACC-4 Report,* page 13). A problem, not very well coped with by Anglicans, is the abundance of documents of one sort and another on which views and comments are invited: they shower down like rain into a fleece of wool, with a similar propensity for disappearance. Some, however, like this one, are of especial importance.

This booklet, under the guidance of the Commission on Faith and Order of the WCC, took its final form at a conference in Lima in 1982. There were participating members from a diversity of traditions. Copies were then sent to the Churches asking for their official response.

The Anglican Churches (Provinces) belong severally to the WCC. That they should reply is of great importance. It is not a quick procedure for us or for anybody else. Synods and world consultations are likely to be required, and care and prayer are needed whether replies express approval, disapproval or doubt. Development in the Anglican Communion is inseparable from taking seriously *Baptism, Eucharist and Ministry.* Here, to conclude this section is one quotation from the part of the document on Ministry (pp. 28–29).

The primary manifestation of apostolic succession is to be found in the apostolic tradition of the Church as a whole. The succession is by expression of the permanence and, therefore, of the continuity of Christ's own mission in which the Church participates. Within the Church the ordained ministry has a particular task of preserving and actualizing the apostolic faith. The orderly transmission of the ordained ministry is therefore a powerful expression of the continuity of the Church throughout history; it also underlines the calling of the ordained minister as guardian of the faith. Where churches see little importance in orderly transmission, they should ask themselves whether they have not to change their conception of continuity in the apostolic tradition. On the other hand, where the ordained ministry does not adequately serve the proclamation of the apostolic faith, churches must ask themselves whether their ministerial structures are not in need of reform. *Don Cuf'lt is a [oov Guardian no doubt!*

To assess the present Anglican condition it is necessary to expand a little on what has been said so far, and to record some of the impressions one has gathered. (In doing this, use will be made of a Review given by me to ACC-5 in 1981: *Report*, pp. 18–21)

Beyond any particular accomplishments of Churches in the ecumenical field, the great achievement of many Churches is that they no longer think in terms of running on parallel courses with the hope that ecumenical industriousness will result in a bridge being thrown across the intervening separation. Instead, Churches are converging; and effort to this end is deliberate. Convergence involves the discovery of common ground, the discounting of factors that are idiosyncratic, or that do not matter fundamentally after all. Also it involves disregarding differences that are, when all is said and done, tolerable. The hopefulness of convergence is that it ends in meeting — and that at the point of meeting is the common Christ, more clearly seen. This situation requires the question: "What, in consequence and as a practical step, can we now do together?"

Good relations are necessary for convergence to achieve its end in unity. Good relations among the Churches prevail to an extent that was almost inconceivable in the lifetime of some of us.

However, there is evidence for thinking that there may be a decline in zeal for ecumenical achievement — at least in the institutionalized form that has been known in the past:

> Some would disregard the rules or traditions that would seem to keep us apart, as tiresome and out-dated. There is a good deal to be said for that, especially when it is seen that the Christ of everyone is the same person, and the need of the world is for Christ. Christ, for Christians, has a pre-eminence without rival or competitor within the diversity of faiths and denominations.
>
> But the discounting of orderliness has been tried before and is never very successful. It achieves a re-arrangement of the pattern of the cracks rather than a restoration of wholeness.

But on the one hand it can be said that a bigger view of requirements of institutional procedure has made possible new visions of ecumenism in the Roman Catholic Church; while on the other hand a Pentecostal view would regard ecumenism as having no distinct roots, but springing out of the gospel, so that it is the proclaiming of the universal gospel which alone matters. Institutions and boundaries and special movements are as often as not impediments to what the Church is really about. Hence forms of Pentecostalism are to be found in most Churches, including the Roman Catholic.

As far as Anglicanism is concerned, the view and practices of the Third World are various. Some are on good terms with Christians of other Churches, but seem in practice to do little about it. To some the divisions are a regrettable addition or importation, and the extent of already existing collaboration — including with the Roman Catholics — can come as a surprise. Other Anglicans take what now seems a rather out-of-date view of ecumenics, and meanwhile wait for someone else to give a lead. But before reaching that particular assessment, consideration must be given to the particular culture, history and motivation.

The ecumenical movement produces a great many studies which crowd the shelves of libraries and furnish diplomas and doctorates. That, too, is a phenomenon worthy of consideration in any assessment of development.

A problem which does not always seem to get the attention it deserves is the reasons that account for different denominations still existing, especially after so much study and care. One factor not to be under-rated is the matter of where you were born. Why, we may ask, do we belong to different denominations? Both 'denomination' and 'church' indicate community. An unattached serious Christian individual — even if that person is a hermit or anchoress — is virtually a contradiction in terms. There is a general human need for community, and denomination is one form of community as well as being of the nature of institutions amid which, and with which, we live. For the majority of people which Church you belong to depends on where you were born. For example, if you were born in Italy or Latin America you are probably a Roman Catholic; if you were born in certain parts of Germany you are probably a Lutheran, and so on. When you are at a conference on unity, which side of the table you are on is decided in fair measure by where you were born and who your parents were. Your profound commitment to your faith is at least as much by accident as by decision. Nevertheless what one believes one cannot ignore. But the significance of it all is sometimes less conclusive a view than we sometimes think. Perhaps it means that one must recognize even more sympathetically that other people are as committed as one's self; and that "Brothers, come home" is not an ecumenical statement.

The 'Christian World Communions'

Happily it has been recognized for a long time now that the path to unity is paved not with bayonets, politicians and anathemas, but by such virtues as listening to one another and finding out what is meant. Talking with people is generally more productive than talking about people. This line of thought, which is characteristic of the best ecumenics of our day, underlies the coming together every year of the Secretaries of most of the larger Churches or Communions of the Christian world. The gatherings are informal and without a Constitution. They have been taking place annually for about 25 years, and will continue. They are held in places with special connections with one or more of the participating Communions: Athens, Geneva, Lake Junaluska USA, London, Rome, Sofia and the like. They used to be known as meetings of the Secretaries of the World

Confessional Families, but as we have seen 'Confessional' is a difficult and inappropriate word for some — not least the Anglicans — although for most the purpose of these informal meetings was more important than the name. However, at the proposal of the Lutherans, the name is now adjusted to 'Christian World Communions' and no one's theology seems troubled. In fact this matter of a comfortable name is more complicated than might be guessed. One of the first things one learns from such a gathering, perhaps as nowhere else, is how much difference there is in the way Churches in their world-wide dimension are organized and operate. The one-ness of catholicism, for example, is different theologically and in practice from the one-ness of alliance.

The purpose of the meetings is for the Secretaries to know one another better and to know one another's Communions better. There is no specific plan for union, although information about any discussions in which particular Churches are engaged are of common interest. For one thing approaches to matters of union are very different among the Communions, and for another the Secretaries (and the one or two consultants they may have with them) have no authority beyond that which derives from membership of their Church and the job they have been asked to do. They are not appointed representatives in a special cause. The common factor is the wish to serve Christ better.

An encouraging aspect is how many meet. The membership, though quite informal and generally without official representation, includes Secretaries from Communions which are not in the World Council of Churches. In the past 25 years the number of Secretaries present each year has grown from seven until now the following bodies are represented in most years: The Anglican Consultative Council; the World Baptist Alliance; the Patriarchates of Constantinople and of Moscow; the Disciples and World Convention of Churches of Christ; the Friends' World Committee for Consultation; the Lutheran World Federation; the Mennonite World Conference; the World Methodist Council; the International Old Catholic Bishops' Conference; the World Alliance of Reformed Churches and the International Congregational Council; the Reformed Ecumenical Synod; the Roman Catholic Church's Secretariat for Promoting Christian Unity; the Salvation Army; and the General Conference of the Seventh Day Adventist Church. The World Council of Churches always accepts an invitation; and occasionally one or two other invitations are accepted.

Always such meetings have been useful for communication and for elucidation. But one feels that in recent years a development has been taking place, a development which probably owes much to these Christians being 'gathered together,' and a consequent increase in affection and esteem. Usually the Secretaries give some account of current matters in their own Churches. This used to be fairly brief, and many of us assumed a duty to keep some polish on the image of one's own denomination. The approach is changing. Failures and worries figure more in the accounts, and advice is sought. Common beliefs begin to be discerned where they were not really suspected before, not least about how the Scriptures are the ultimate resource to everyone. The sort of issues raised in *Baptism, Eucharist and Ministry* do not come as a surprise. Principles and procedures are enquired about, not to score points but to understand motivations. Recently a practice has been introduced whereby the Secretary of one of the Communions gives a description, or 'profile' of his Communion, with a consequence that one sees rather better from his angle — and maybe so does he.

Here, as I see it, is a development on a very wide scale, and as in other cases of hope, convergence is at the heart of the matter. My belief is that Anglicanism is being called to play a useful part in this process which compels us to realize in a practical way, and in terms of common faith, that we may not stay where we are.

These meetings, though quite widely reported to the Churches by the Secretaries, do not have as wide an audience as they might — though too wide or formal an audience might destroy them. What the future should be is a problem, but it is important that the Anglican Communion should not miss out on what is happening.

Here, after considerations about the course relationships between the Anglican Communion and other churches are taking, is a suitable place to bring together some topics which until now we have allowed to go by without further discussion, to which they are entitled. They are topics that concern (a) an idea that the Anglican Communion might 'disappear,' and (b) Anglican discussion of a 'Wider Episcopal Fellowship.' In the 1960s especially, and as

Anglicans perceived that involvement in the ecumenical movement was likely to effect changes in the Anglican Communion, a fear was expressed that Anglicanism might 'disappear.' More than one line of thought lay behind this notion. In one instance it derived from a supposition that Anglicanism lacked, and should not lack, a special and separate identity. But, as we have seen, the basis of Anglicanism is the recognition of the continuity of the one universal Church with Christ and the gospels and the apostles. The identity of the Church and that of Anglicanism are inseparable. If, for the sake of argument, it were considered a possibility that the universal Church should cease to exist, then there would be no point at all in Anglicanism continuing. One seldom hears that kind of fear of Anglican disappearance expressed now: it might be fair to say that the point of concern is more that as progress is made towards unity Anglicanism might be slower than it should be in becoming involved.

A more impressive cause of the disquiet arose from such events as the coming into existence of the united Churches in India and Pakistan, and the corollary that the Anglican Church of India, Pakistan, Burma and Ceylon — at least as far as all the dioceses of India and Pakistan were concerned — ceased to be part of the Anglican Communion. That remarkable achievement of union had at the same time brought into existence a measure of dis-union. It was not a purpose of the uniting Churches all to become Anglicans, but — as we have seen — "it was agreed from an early date that the resulting Church would not be in any sense an Anglican Church; it would be an independent regional Church. . . and its relationship with the Anglican Communion would have to be gradually worked out" (Neill: *Anglicanism*, p. 380). The resulting problem has not yet been solved, and short of the reunion of the whole Church itself it may not be.

A reaction of many Anglicans was to perceive that further national or regional unions which were achieved, as one hoped would be the case, with full participation by the Anglican Church of the region, would lead to further diminishing of the Anglican Communion. Some chose to speculate on the position that would arise if a local English union scheme took the Church of England out of the Anglican Communion. That has not happened, but it is not impossible. In fact, unions of the South and North India episcopal type

No Servant Ikutance lies at failure.

have not recurred, which may or may not be considered a pity, but in consequence that aspect of Anglican concerns about the disappearance of the Communion has dwindled.

The Wider Episcopal Fellowship

However, one reaction to the developing ecumenical situation was to consider whether there might not be the possibility of a Communion, or at any rate a fellowship, which was bigger than the Anglican Communion and which could take it and other Communions or Churches into its embrace. What was seen as the common possession was episcopacy, which is, moreover, of its very nature, a key factor in unity. In 1948 the Lambeth Conference was speaking with serious hope of 'a Larger Episcopal Unity' (Resolution 74), and before long the Anglican Communion was using the phrase 'Wider Episcopal Fellowship.' This resolution was followed up by one in 1958 that recommended "that within the next five years the Archbishop of Canterbury (Archbishop Michael Ramsey) should invite to a conference representative bishops from each Province of the Anglican Communion, together with representative bishops from each Church possessing the historic episcopate with which Churches and Provinces of the Anglican Communion are in full communion or in a relation of intercommunion" (*1958 Lambeth Conference Report*, Resolution 16). Such a meeting was held at Canterbury in 1964. Reactions varied, as did the bishops. In a consideration of the Wider Episcopal Fellowship by some responsible Anglicans three years later, the view was given that "hitherto the prevalent idea among many Anglicans had been that this Fellowship might, in due time, replace the Anglican Communion and the Lambeth Conference by enabling both to be part of a wider whole. More recently, however, some serious objections have been raised against this assumption. On the one hand it is becoming clear that to interpret the W.E.F. as a fellowship of churches puts too great emphasis on a particular view of episcopacy. . . ." (Advisory Committee to the Executive Officer meeting in 1967).

The Lambeth Conference of 1968 passed a resolution (Resolution 65(a)) similar to that of ten years before, but through the Anglican Consultative Council, Archbishop Ramsey expressed the view that preparations for such a major conference should include Regional Conferences to prove and prepare the way. He was also convinced that churches attach different significance to the episcopacy in their systems.

In 1978 a resolution (No. 13(1)) similar to previous ones had support, but nothing has come of it, nor have regional preparatory conferences taken place on any significant scale. In places, notably the Episcopal Church of the USA, hopes and activity relating to the idea of a Wider Episcopal Fellowship have a good deal of life in them. In most places the problem, at least for the present, seems to float in and out with the tide, hoping that perhaps there may come a more momentous stirring of the waters.

c. The Anglican/Lutheran Commission

There is a good case for putting the four Commissions in alphabetical order, but there is convenience in taking the Commissions with the Lutheran World Federation and the World Alliance of Reformed Churches in close proximity, and therefore the latter will be taken directly after the Lutheran Federation.

The direction of movement in the relationship of Anglican and Lutheran Churches is usefully expressed in some paragraphs in the 'Introduction' to the report of the 'Conversations' of 1970–1972 (*Anglican-Lutheran International Conversations*):

1. In spite of occasional contacts and a common awareness of great areas of affinity in doctrine, worship, and church life, Anglican and Lutheran Churches have in the past lived largely in separation and in relative isolation from one another. One painful manifestation of their separate existence has been the absence of *communio in sacris* between Lutheran and Anglican Churches (apart from that enabled by regulations concerning different grades of intercommunion between the Church of England and various Scandinavian Lutheran Churches).

2. A new situation has been created by more frequent encounters in recent times, both between Churches and individual members of the two Communions; the recognition of new, converging tendencies in their biblical and theological thinking; the realiza-

tion of their common task of mission and service in the modern world; more frequent but still responsible acts of intercommunion; and the encounter of Lutheran and Anglican Churches in union negotiations.

3. This situation demands not only better mutual knowledge and understanding and closer co-operation. It calls at the same time for a reconsideration of the official relationships between Anglican and Lutheran Churches leading to more appropriate expressions of our common faith, witness and service.

and

44. Modern scholarship (exegesis, patristics) has in many ways served as a means of convergence between different denominations. This also applies to and has consequences for our evaluations of early tradition. But even if there remain a number of different emphases in this field, they are certainly not of fundamental importance, but rather expressions of different histories, ways of thinking and life, which should be a source of mutual enrichment and correction.

Already there is the intention to identify ground common to both Churches:

10. We have attempted to articulate lines of thought which are already accepted in much of the past and present thinking of our Churches. This implies that we tried to be as representative as possible of the traditions and present developments in our Churches. We hope that the articulation of current tendencies may itself advance and extend our ecumenical unity.

Also the fruits of ecumenical experience are brought to bear in the endeavour to avoid unnecessary clouding of issues, for example:

11. We are aware that in every ecumenical conversation the delegates from both sides develop an increasingly friendly relationship; understanding develops, deep spiritual fellowship grows, and with it a strong desire to express the maximum agreement possible. Those they represent are not going through the same experiences, and there is always a danger that both sides, or at least one, will prove to be so far ahead of their constituency that little good will come of the encounter.

12. This is particularly true in the matter of language. Phrases have come into currency and have worked their way into the life and thought about Lutheran and Anglican Churches. In some cases the words correspond to those used on the other side and mean much the same thing. Sometimes the words sound similar, but mean something different. Sometimes the very words are strange and foreign in the ears of another tradition in the life of the Church.

13. In conversations like ours each side becomes familiar with the language of the other. Sometimes particular phrases become expressive of particular points of agreement or disagreement, and thus a special language makes articulate to the participants the spiritual or intellectual processes in which they have been engaged. Their constituencies have not become familiar with this language.

The two Communions, with the recognition in their Churches of world-wide mission, were emphasizing that the base for their ecumenical activity together must also be world-wide. In exploratory preparation for the 1970 Conversations a committee was set up by the Archbishop of Canterbury and the General Secretary of the Lutheran World Federation. The committee produced a Memorandum in 1967 proposing the appointment of 'a representative Anglican-Lutheran Commission' by the Lambeth Conference and the Executive Committee of the LWF. The Memorandum proposed that the Commission should —

a. conduct a worldwide Anglican-Lutheran dialogue;
b. consider other contacts and areas for practical co-operation;
c. report regularly to their respective appropriate authorities. (op. cit. page 7, para. 7)

The Lambeth Conference concurred in 1968, and it was further agreed that "the conversations should begin by discussing the general mission of the Church in the world and only afterwards proceed to questions of doctrine and order, though major issues should be faced as soon as possible" (page 7, paragraphs 7 and 8). The Lambeth Conference, doubtless with an eye to proceeding step by step, and to avoiding lengthy conversations that might provide exercise for scholars more than they influenced the Churches, suggested the conversations "should be held on four occasions over a two-year period" (ibid. No. 8). The result was the Conversations of 1970–72. For each Church the membership came from three Continents.

The subjects which were investigated were: Sources of Authority, The Church, The Word and the Sacraments, Apostolic Ministry, and Worship. The Recommendations were focussed on matters that the Commission considered were already possible, and on steps that ought to be taken. Great mergers belonged to a later step, but logic had indicated that it might be less far away than had sometimes been supposed.

A consequence of that Commission was that in 1976 the Anglican Consultative Council and the Lutheran World Federation agreed to recommend regional dialogue in areas where the two Churches were particularly in contact: the USA, Europe and Tanzania (*ACC-5 Report*, page 36). The results were various, and while some progress was made and a good deal was learned, the general picture was that progress on a world basis, while highly desirable and inspirational, is more often talked about than effected.

In 1981 the time seemed to have come, if momentum were not to be lost, to resume the wider involvement (see *ACC-5 Report*, Resolution 2). Consultation by the agencies of the two Communions — the ACC and the LWF — resulted in the following purposes being agreed for the new Working Group:

a. assess the results of the dialogues specifically proposed by the previous Working Group in the three regions of Europe, Tanzania and the USA;

b. make recommendations with the intention of proposing how the two Communions might achieve full communion;

c. suggest, if possible, procedures that would assure closer co-operation between the two bodies. (ACC Standing Committee, May 1982, Minutes pp. 6–7)

It was also advocated that observers might be invited from the Roman Catholic Church and the World Council of Churches. One does not suppose that (b), or even (c), would be to the comfort of mind of every member of the Federation and the Anglican Communion. What is significant is that the greater concentration on seeking truth and unity by concord put increased pressure on establishing a process by which there would be an achievement of common action.

The Group met in England in November 1983 with promising results.

d. The Anglican/Reformed Commission

The account of the Commission with the Lutheran World Federation has indicated that while denominational loyalties are not under attack the recovery of unity does not lie in re-examination of old wounds, but of recognizing that much is already held in common and discovering how to go forward from there. That, too, characterizes much in the work that is developing with the Commission of the Anglican and Reformed Churches. Similarly the two Commissions have aspired to extend discussions that have frequently had a national emphasis to matters that have an international implication. Also a procedure towards unity that goes step by step has acquired prominence. The Anglican/Reformed Commission (whose first meeting was held in 1981) restricted itself to four annual meetings. It does not assume that the end is near, but in the Commission itself, and also more widely, the way forward may be ready for re-assessment by then. Moreover, there must be time for adequate communication with other Churches.

Anglican and Reformed Churches have engaged in discussions for a long time, but progress, except on a personal level, has been meagre. Known disagreements, most often about ministry and episcopacy, have become rocks towards which most dialogues head. As with the Commission with the Lutheran World Federation, increasingly examination is of the very considerable areas of agreement, and the question is how things look from there. Here are two quotations:

> We decided to draw a line under the past and look towards the future together, and started from a position which may well not be within the experience of our local churches.

The second is:

> From the beginning we were determined, in accordance with our mandate, and in the spirit of *Philippians 3:13*, "forgetting what

lies behind and straining forward to what lies ahead," to discover each other's faith as it is today and to appeal to history only for enlightenment, not as a way of perpetuating past controversy.

The first quotation is from a personal account of the first meeting of the Anglican/Reformed Commission (1981) by the Revd. George Braund, the Anglican secretary; the second is from the Preface to *The Final Report* (pages 1–2) of the Anglican/Roman Catholic International Commission, published in 1982.

It is encouraging that the Anglican/Reformed Commission does not feel committed to a precise agenda; indeed, it very much looks to the Holy Spirit for guidance as to what it should be about. At what is quite an early stage in its affairs an adequate description of its work and dialogue was provided by the account in the *ACC-5 (1981) Report* (page 38):

> The first full meeting of the Anglican-Reformed Commission took place at the beginning of this year and it examined some Latin American perspectives on Christological thinking, the Incarnation and the unity of the Church, and the relation between Christ, the Kingdom, and the Church. Discussion led to two unanimous convictions. First, the Church was constituted by the free grace of God in Christ; and for this reason Christian Churches had to accept each other, since God in Christ has given himself for all, and we are accepted in Christ, though unacceptable. Second, this same Church was a provisional expression of the Kingdom and did not fully actualize, in any of its manifestations, the promise of its own life.
>
> At its second meeting next year it is planned to discuss what attitude Anglican and Reformed Churches should have towards mutual recognition and the nature of organic unity; the content, context, and goal of the Church's mission; and the relation of 'orthopraxis' (e.g. action in regard to racism and the poor) to church unity. It is hoped the final report will be completed in 1984.

e. Anglican Discussions with the Orthodox (and Oriental Orthodox) Churches

Dialogues between the Anglican and Orthodox Churches have been, and are, characteristically discussions by theologians. What they will be in the future remains to be seen. But for the Orthodox, and for Anglican understanding of the Orthodox, this theological approach has been necessary. Understandably for Anglicans in general, and for those whose approach to rapprochement between Churches was in a western style of more discursive ecumenics, the seemingly precise and even obscure requirements which the Orthodox theologians appeared to compose, gave the impression that, even if much in Orthodoxy was admirable, discussion was like getting in a tent where there was little room to move. Some, however, in both Churches, saw a good deal further than this. And more in both Churches developed this understanding in the years after the second World War.

The Report of the fourth meeting of the Anglican Consultative Council in 1979 has a passage on Anglican-Orthodox relations which, while dated in some ways, makes points which illustrate some of the past and of the present attitudes:

> It must first be admitted that to many Anglicans there is a seeming remoteness and irrelevance to dialogue with the Orthodox Churches. This is not only due to their geographical distance from many Provinces of the Anglican Communion. Even where Anglicans and Orthodox live side by side (and Orthodoxy is more widely dispersed than is often imagined), there remains a cultural isolation which divides. There is also a serious difficulty of theological language and proportion.
>
> Yet we contend that the Orthodox tradition does have a direct relevance for other Christian Churches. We see today a search for authentic spirituality: the Orthodox tradition has much to offer from the richness of its spiritual and liturgical heritage. We see today a renewal of experience and understanding of the Holy Spirit: Orthodox theology has always stressed the Church and Sacraments as the sphere of the activity of the Spirit. (*ACC-4 Report*, p. 3)

Contact and discussion between the Churches has quite a long history, but the aims have not always been the same. This was partly because the two sides were ignorant of factors influencing the other's approach. Anglicans might talk too soon and too easily of the possibility of division in the Body of Christ, and about reunion; at a fairly early stage they would want to discuss paths to intercommunion, and to urge the acceptance of Anglican Orders. But for the Orthodox the starting-point (and perhaps the consummation) of these things was total unity in dogma.

As is always the case, understanding increased through meeting together. There developed a deeper understanding of one another's beliefs. There might not always be agreement, but it became possible to agree to differ. Common ground was identified and seen to be considerable. In writing of the present Commission which had its first full meeting in 1973, the co-Chairmen, Anglican and Orthodox, stated:

> A theological dialogue of this kind pre-supposes two things. No participant is asked to begin by surrendering anything which he holds to be of the essence of the faith once delivered to the saints. All participants in mutual respect agree to find their starting-point in the things which we hold in common. It could be said that the first three years have been a search for such common ground and a discovery that it does exist." (*Anglican-Orthodox Dialogue* (see below) p. 2)

The theologians have encountered many difficulties, and sometimes the differences have seemed almost too much to persevere with, and there has been reason to fear the dialogue might not go on — at any rate for a time. But that has not been the case. Both sides, on suitable occasions, have emphasized their gratitude for what has been achieved, their sure confidence in the work of the Spirit therein, and their wish and expectation that the Discussions will go forward.

An important stage in the Discussions was reached in *The Moscow Agreed Statement* which was agreed by the Anglican-Orthodox Joint Doctrinal Commission when it met in Moscow in 1976. The text of this Statement has been issued a number of times. In a book entitled *Anglican-Orthodox Dialogue*, published in 1977 (SPCK: editors, Archimandrite Kallistos Ware and the Revd. Colin Davey), a history is given of Anglican-Orthodox Dialogue from 1920 until the Moscow Conference in 1976; an account of the Moscow Conference itself; and the full text of the Statement.

The Statement is in 32 paragraphs under seven headings:

1. The Knowledge of God
2. The Inspiration and Authority of Holy Scripture

3. Scripture and Tradition
4. The Authority of Councils
5. The Filioque Clause
6. The Church as the Eucharistic Community
7. The Invocation of the Holy Spirit in the Eucharist.

The extent to which the two Churches are growing in mutual understanding is indicated by the fact that such subjects could be considered and discussed together. Of course there is not agreement throughout on the subjects themselves, nor does there pretend to be. The communiqué from the Moscow Conference emphasizes the unprecedented extent of representation of both the Churches of the Orthodox Communion and of the Anglican Communion, and says that the conversations "made it clear that there are still many differences to be reconciled and many divergent points of view to be overcome before further substantial progress can be made," and also that "the delegates on both sides would agree that during these conversations the opportunity of growing into better acquaintance and understanding with each other has been a blessing for which they give thanks to God" (ibid. page 38).

At this point one may ask why two Churches which for a long time have been thought by many to have so much in common should have so much difficulty and proceed, particularly on the Orthodox side, with so much caution. Illumination will come from reading the book just mentioned; but it may serve a useful purpose here to indicate some of the differences which become apparent there. One Church is Eastern and the other Western, with distinctions of history, cultural influence and academic practice, but at Moscow an expression of the common ground was given when Archbishop Stylianos of Australia said that "The Church remains faithful to the unchanging identity of Scripture and Tradition, while at the same time being open to the findings of scholarly work" (ibid. p. 50). Differences that originate in that divergence of East and West — for example, concerning the place in revelation of the Cappadocian Fathers on the one hand and of St. Augustine of Hippo on the other — seemed, interestingly, to contribute more to the Churches' problems in establishing their common ground than did any fundamental difference of view to be associated with the Reformation. One feels that the Anglican respect for theologians is less inclined to isolate theologians, and one senses that the disinclination to separate them from the pastoral experience of the Church as a whole, and from the world of today in which we live, proved less uncongenial to the Orthodox than was expected. One of the other differences, known previously but elucidated less, was difference of language and forms of expression. Many examples could be given, and of the progress in understanding made, but one must suffice, and that can be taken from the *Moscow Agreed Statement* itself, paragraph 3, which is in the section on 'The Knowledge of God':

> To describe the fullness of man's sanctification and the way in which he shares in the life of God, the Orthodox Church uses the Patristic term *theosis kata charin* (divinization by grace). Once again such language is not normally used by Anglicans, some of whom regard it as misleading and dangerous. At the same time Anglicans recognize that, when Orthodox speak in this manner, they do so only with the most careful safeguards. Anglicans do not reject the underlying doctrine which this language seeks to express; indeed, such teaching is to be found in their own liturgies and hymnody.

The history of Anglican-Orthodox relations up to 1976 is to be found in Ware and Davey. The first authorized Commission met in 1931, and some progress was made, but the second World War intervened and the relationship, which had become complicated, needed new life if understanding was to develop significantly. The desirability of resuming the dialogue was agreed when the Archbishop of Canterbury, Michael Ramsey, visited the Oecumenical Patriarch of Constantinople, Athenagoras I, in 1962, and the first steps were taken to setting up a Joint Commission. Preparatory conferences were held on both sides, separately, and the full Joint Commission held its first meeting in 1973. This Commission in due course at a conference in Moscow produced the Moscow Agreed Statement of 1976.

In 1976 an issue on Anglican minds was the need to involve a wider audience and wider participation. In discussions at Moscow of the Commission's future the Anglican chairman, Bishop Robert Runcie of St. Alban's (now Archbishop of Canterbury) said: "We have learnt how to speak to one another, but not yet how to speak to our Churches," and that the difference in atmosphere between the Oxford (1973) and the Moscow conferences was astonishing; but that at the same time the work of the Commission had remained virtually unknown to the great body of believers on either side. Discussions were being carried on largely in a vacuum. Similarly the Revd. John Riches (Anglican/Scotland) asked that the Church's role in a changing society should be explicitly mentioned in the future agenda (Ware and Davey: *Anglican-Orthodox Dialogue* pp. 78–79). Such recommendations were not uncongenial to the Orthodox who, with the Anglicans, agreed unanimously to the publication of the Moscow Statement. In the following year, 1977, the Archbishop of Canterbury (Archbishop Donald Coggan) and the Oecumenical Patriarch (Demetrios I) met in Constantinople and expressed the hope "that the agreements already reached by this Commission would be more widely shared among the faithful of our two Churches, for the promotion of the Ecumenical Movement and Christian Unity" (ibid. page 94).

It may not be presumptuous to think that the Orthodox have a respect for the Anglican involvement in the affairs and problems of the world of the present day and their direct impact on the lives and decisions of ordinary Christian people whose lives have to be lived in that context. The Orthodox may have hesitations, to say the least, about some aspects of Anglicanism, but they are aware and grateful that it has much in common with themselves. And they are aware that the spread of Orthodoxy, and the increasing involvement of recent generations with the world about them, give Anglican Christian experience a content that is important to them.

After the Moscow meeting of 1976, and the widespread approval of the Statement and of the work the Commission was doing, it was generally hoped that the discussion would continue constructively and unabated. But a crisis was already developing which is to be discerned in the references in the Statement to the acceptance by some Anglicans of the permissibility of women being ordained to the priesthood. At the meeting of the Commission at Cambridge in 1977 the storm broke. The Secretary General of the Anglican Consultative Council, at the request of the Commission, gave an account of how the matter stood in the Anglican Communion. This account was neither for nor against, but to the majority of the Orthodox present it became apparent, as it had not before, that in several parts of the Anglican Communion women had, constitutionally, already been ordained priests and were functioning as such; and that in other parts, although no ordinations had taken place, the serious view had been given that there was no theological objection to such ordinations. In those circumstances the Orthodox expressed serious doubt whether the Anglican-Orthodox discussions could continue. At that stage the matter of whether the ordination of women to the priesthood was permissible was barely discussable. However, while the Orthodox arranged discussion among themselves of the Anglican behaviour, consideration of the future of the Commission and its agenda went tentatively ahead.

As far as easing the problem was concerned, the Lambeth Conference of 1978 was not a happy occasion. The Orthodox, through their official observers, asked the Anglicans not to proceed further, and expressed the fear that the consequences of so doing might bring about a drastic reversal of the hopes of unity between Orthodoxy and Anglicanism. The message did not come across as clearly as it might to the majority of the Anglicans, who for their part felt that the Orthodox had not perceived the strong belief of many Anglicans that the responsibility lay among themselves to determine what courses Anglicans should adopt. While the Conference took careful note of what they felt were the views and practices of other Churches they did not reverse existing Anglican procedure but proposed careful restraints and balances on procedures for the years immediately ahead (Resolution 21).

(In this study the subject of the Ordination of Women is dealt with as a separate subject on page 152)

In the months that followed, relations between the Churches eased a little, and the process was greatly helped by journeys made by the Bishop of St. Albans, Robert Runcie, then the Anglican chairman of the Commission, to a large number of Orthodox Church leaders in the east to manifest brotherhood, strengthen the fellowship that was developing, and to discuss theological matters in the way that can be done advantageously only in small gatherings. At one time it had seemed that the Commission might not continue, or only with a very restricted and formalized agenda. Happily it is agreed that the Commission continues and with an agenda and procedure that follows on from what has gone before, although, of course, the practice of some Anglicans about the ordination of women adds to the problems: it is not eliminated.

Concerning the Oriental Orthodox Churches, the Anglican Communion is concerned in developing old relationships in what seems a practicable way. An account is given as follows in the *ACC-4 (1979) Report* (page 5):

> For many years there have been cordial relations with the Oriental Orthodox Churches, which are those ancient eastern Churches which for various reasons did not attend, or could not accept, the Council of Chalcedon in 451. They include the Coptic Orthodox Church, the Ethiopian Orthodox Church, the Syrian Orthodox Church, and the Armenian Apostolic Church. In recent years there have been personal meetings between leaders of the Anglican Communion, including the Archbishop of Canterbury, and the leaders of some of these ancient Churches (for example, the Coptic Church and the Armenian Church). There have also been valuable exchanges at other levels. While it is difficult at the present to envisage how there could be a formal dialogue between the Churches of the Anglican Communion and the autonomous Oriental Orthodox Churches because of their number and variety, we nevertheless strongly affirm the desirability of increasing visits and exchanges in order to further mutual understanding.

The next Council meeting, ACC-5 in 1981, was able to express satisfaction that Bishop Henry Hill of Canada, who had succeeded Bishop Runcie as the Anglican chairman of the Anglican-Orthodox Commission, "should visit the leaders of these ancient Christian communities to discuss ways of strengthening the links and fostering an appropriate means of theological dialogue between these Churches and the Churches of the Anglican Communion" (*ACC-5 Report*, p. 42). The offer of these visits was warmly received, as indeed, in due course, has been Bishop Hill himself. What developments in relationship are possible we shall see, but there is no doubt that Christian brotherhood will renew its strength.

f. The Anglican/Roman Catholic International Commission (ARCIC)

Talks with the Roman Catholic Church in recent years have attracted more attention than any other in which Anglicans have been engaged, and this not only among the Anglicans. One reason for this is that many Churches agreed, whether they had said it or not, that the reunion of the divided Christian world could not be brought about without the inclusion of the great Roman Catholic Church. In short, without them the goal of the ecumenical movement was unattainable.

In the past century or two, it has been widely understood that the Roman Catholic Church believed itself to possess a responsibility for defining dogmas, and uttering more or less the last word. The Anglican Church, and other Churches affected by the Reformation, did not, which in the Anglican case resulted in openness, or comprehensiveness and flexibility, which Rome could not easily appreciate (cf. Prof. E.R. Fairweather: essay "Where Should Dialogue Begin?" pp. 40–41, in *Anglican/Roman Catholic Dialogue* edited by Clark and Davey, 1974). A notable illustration in the stalemate centred on biblical interpretation. Rome appeared to lay down the law in a way that impressed few outside the Roman obedience. Those who were strongly opposed to Rome had reached this position principally because they saw dogmas, even arbitrary dogmas, overriding the Word, so that closer relationship with Rome was to be resisted. Others opposed the closing of doors by Rome to biblical scholarship, and their failure to participate in academic study of the Bible and the critical debate about the Bible which from the nineteenth century on had been a central issue in Christian witness and scholarship in the western world. The Roman monologue rendered dialogue impossible.

Already it is difficult to recall how rigid the fences were. To the outside world the change in the Roman Catholic stance, and its attitude to other Churches, seemed to come very suddenly. The Second Vatican Council (1962–65) is seen as the time when the windows were opened. In fact the pressures within the Roman Catholic Church had been increasing for years before that, but for the Christian world at large Vatican II and the Schema and Decrees it produced is reasonably reckoned the point of change.

An account of Anglican/Roman Catholic relations from 1864 until after Vatican II by Bishop (now Cardinal) J.M.G. Willebrands, delivered in January 1967, under the title *Why is Anglican/Roman Catholic Dialogue Possible Today?* is printed on pages 26 to 36 of the book edited by Clark and Davey referred to above. This is a valuable paper for understanding what happened before Vatican II, and the contrasting possibilities of the subsequent situation to which the present Anglican/Roman Catholic dialogue belongs.

Reference has been made in this study to the fact that a warmth of friendly understanding is generated by people meeting in person rather than by dilating at a distance. No small part of this present situation has come about through personal meetings of Archbishops of Canterbury with Popes: first Archbishop Fisher with Pope John XXIII in 1960, then Archbishop Ramsey with Pope Paul VI in 1966, Archbishop Coggan with Pope Paul VI in 1977, and Archbishop Runcie with Pope John Paul II in 1980 (in Ghana) and in 1982 in Canterbury.

The hostility of the Vatican Secretariat of State in 1959 to Archbishop Fisher's visit to the Pope soon became difficult to believe. An illuminating account of events is given by Archdeacon Pawley in a book by him and his wife, published in 1974 (up-dated and revised edition 1981) *Rome and Canterbury through Four Centuries* (pages 315–317). The sole reference to the Archbishop's visit in *Osservatore Romano*, which is recorded in the book, namely, "Dr. Geoffrey Fisher had an audience with His Holiness" was produced successfully to cause amusement and amazement at a reception given in the Vatican for Archbishop Coggan in 1977.

The *Decree on Ecumenism (Unitatis Redintegratio)* in referring to 'Churches and Ecclesial Communities Separated from the Roman Apostolic See' *(Decree III)* says (section 13):

> Among those in which some Catholic traditions and institutions continue to exist, the Anglican Communion occupies a special place.

In the discussions after the Council a good deal of attention and hope seems to have been attached to this sentence. Without doubt, there it stands, but one has the impression that there is less concentration on it at present. This may be as well. From the Anglican point of view what is significant and hopeful for the future (though hardly for the immediate future) rests on a wider foundation. The possibility has appeared of a constructive dialogue with Rome aimed at visible unity, and the Anglican Church has seized it and perseveres in it energetically.

What is required of this paper is not to recount the history of events so far but to study what development there may have been. That there is true development we have just indicated. The following points of a historical kind are sufficient here.

1. In March 1966 the Archbishop of Canterbury, Michael Ramsey, and Pope Paul VI met in Rome 'to exchange fraternal greetings' and, as Archbishop Ramsey fully intended, to make advances that might be possible in the 'new atmosphere of Christian Fellowship' and to initiate "sincere efforts to remove the cause of conflict and to re-establish unity" *(Common Declaration, 1966)*. In their *Common Declaration* they go on to say "they wish to leave in the hands of the God of mercy all that in the past has been opposed to this precept of charity" and there follows the quotation from *Philippians 3:* "Forgetting those things which are behind, and reaching forth unto those things which are before, I press towards the mark for the price of the high calling of God in Jesus Christ." The Declaration continues:

> They affirm their desire that all those Christians who belong to these two Communions may be animated by these same sentiments of respect, esteem and fraternal love, and in order to help these develop to the full, they intend to inaugurate between the Roman Catholic Church and the Anglican Communion a serious dialogue which, founded on the Gospels and on the ancient common traditions, may lead to that unity in truth, for which Christ prayed. The dialogue should include not only theological matters such as Scripture, Tradition and Liturgy, but also matters of practical difficulty felt on either side.

2. In consequence a Joint Preparatory Commission was set up and after three meetings produced in 1968 its Report, called the *Malta Report*. The work and papers of the Joint Preparatory Commission are recorded in a book *Anglican/Roman Catholic Dialogue* edited by Bishop Alan Clark and the Revd. Colin Davey, 1974.

3. The subsequent Commission, known as the Anglican-Roman Catholic International Commission (ARCIC I), met frequently from 1970 to 1981. As it went along it produced Statements and Elucidations (the well-known *Agreed Statements*) on Eucharist, on Ministry and Ordination, and on Authority. These, with an account of the Commission and its work, were published as *The Final Report: Anglican-Roman Catholic International Commission* in 1982.

4. The subsequent and continuing Commission, with revised membership (ARCIC II), held its first meeting in August 1983 (*see below*, pp. 150–1).

Part of the background that developed with the new relationship was the growing friendship and relaxation between the two Churches. To some extent this is normal in inter-Church dialogues among the participants, and does not depend on the meetings being held in the same place. The meetings of the Anglican/Roman Catholic Commission took place in several different places in Europe, but the association with Rome itself was a factor in the personal relationships that developed, and which led to discussions and explorations which ranged far beyond those directly required by the Commission. Also the Anglicans had a natural point of contact with Roman Catholics for talking about problems as well as hopes in the Vatican Secretariat for Promoting Christian Unity which had come into being shortly before Vatican II.

A point, though, which Anglicans tended to forget, especially those without direct acquaintance with the Commission, was that for the Vatican and the Secretariat, Anglicanism was not the only pebble of its kind on the beach. Rome, through the Secretariat, is deeply involved in unity matters and discussions with a considerable number of other Churches and Communions, as well as with the WCC.

On the Anglican side one of the consequences of Archbishop Ramsey's visit in 1966 was the establishment of the Anglican Centre in Rome. This is not directly involved in the work of the Commission, but is unique among the Churches as a base for discussion, collaboration, study (particularly through its library) and friendship both for Anglicans and Romans. Soon in its existence the Centre came under the umbrella of the Anglican Consultative Council, and was clearly the property of the whole Anglican Communion. It has become better known both among Anglicans and in Rome, and provides an important added dimension to the two Anglican churches there with which it exists in close collaboration.

Here, where mention is being made of the relationships that have developed, it is necessary to go back to the Commission itself. From time to time I have been able to sit in at meetings and have observed a turn of events which, while not foreign to other ecumenical dialogues, has an inevitability and emphasis here which are memorable. Discussion of a well-known subject gets under way, with both sides, albeit charitably and with learning, putting the familiar Anglican or Roman point of view. Then quite suddenly, and without effort or contrivance, all the participants are engaged together in a joint quest for the truth in Christ of the matter in hand. This is ecumenics as it is often wished for, and less often achieved. This is a basis of characteristics of ecumenical discussions, such as the discovery that there is more common ground than one had supposed, or the rejection of the assumption that a return to old differences is the beginning of the way to unity. Studying issues and solving problems are to a great degree things done together. The points are not new: they have been perceived in other Commissions and Declarations, but in the ARCIC dialogue they have come more readily than realism led us to suppose.

However, there are other factors which are taking longer. There was a wave of optimism as the changes manifested by Vatican II were observed. Among Anglicans some envisaged a considerable measure of reunion being achieved within a generation, and perhaps some Romans did so too. Others, even then, were much more cautious or even fearful. It is now clearer that although much is possible, procedure by stages, which the Commission aims at, is a fairly lengthy business. No discredit is done to either Church by the fact that a touch of near romanticism in the early days is giving place to realism as the relationship develops. Mountains make a magnificent view but travelling through them, even in good weather, makes for hard going. The trip takes time.

The consequences of Vatican II are considerable, but so much new vision cannot be expected to go without reaction. It is widely felt that a measure of conservatism is gaining ground in the Roman Church, at any rate for the time being. This means that the times are not easy within the Roman Church itself, either among scholars or in many dioceses or congregations. A problem which many Anglicans have discovered is that their understanding of the Vatican itself is limited. Wherever Anglicans come from they are likely to think like Anglo-Saxons. The Vatican, much larger, and with a longer history, is more diverse. There are problems, even disagreements, between one Congregation or Secretariat in the Vatican and another. What appears to be agreed or approved with one body, even with the Pope, may yet have ridges to cross or conclusions to justify. For an agreed document to be ready for print is not to say that it will be printed. Years after Father Ronald Knox, once an Anglican, had become a Roman Catholic, he observed in a personal letter: "He who travels in the barque of St. Peter had better not look too closely into the engine-room" (Penelope Fitzgerald: *The Knox Brothers* 1977, p. 258). He was very Anglo-Saxon.

Relationships between Roman Catholics and Anglicans in different parts of the world have and do vary considerably, but one of the effects of the new developing ecumenical collaboration is that differences are diminishing. Certainly Anglicans in general have a better understanding of Rome, and Roman collaboration and kindness are welcomed all over the world. Similarly the visits of Pope John Paul II to many countries have helped draw Christians together and reduce suspicion. Anglicans rejoiced at the visit to Canterbury and elsewhere in England, though some in other parts of the Anglican Communion were uncertain whether a measure of Roman confusion was identifying the Church of England with the Anglican Communion itself; but they were not too worried, and cheered heartily all the same.

The assessment and the degree of acceptability of ARCIC-I is a matter for the two Churches. As the character of the document had no exact precedent in either Church it could not be fed into an established groove. And as its implications affected the whole of the two world-wide Communions a vital first step was to gather views and reactions over a wide field. The reception of the Report has its own big importance.

In September 1981 the Anglican and Roman Catholic co-chairmen of ARCIC-I wrote to the Archbishop of Canterbury, as President of the Anglican Consultative Council, and to the Pope, saying:

> We venture to suggest that the two following questions be put to the appropriate authorities in both our churches.
>
> We ask whether the Agreed Statements on Eucharistic Doctrine, Ministry and Ordination and Authority in the Church (I

and II), together with the Elucidations are consonant in substance with the faith of Anglicans (the letter to the Pope here reads "faith of Roman Catholics")?

We also ask whether the Final Report offers a sufficient basis for taking the next concrete step towards the reconciliation of our churches grounded in agreement in faith?

On the Anglican side, the ACC, meeting later that month, commended "to the Churches of the Anglican Communion the two questions proposed by the co-Chairmen" *(ACC-5 Report,* Resolution 4b). In conveying this resolution to the Anglican Churches I explained that the reply from each Anglican Church must have the authority of its Provincial Synod. The closing date for replies was given as 1986, and the suggestion was made, which so far is accepted without discussion, that in the light of the replies the decision of the Anglican Communion might be determined at the Lambeth Conference in 1988. Of course each Church itself decides by what process it will arrive at the response its reply shall contain.

The Roman Catholic procedure is told in a paragraph of the 'Foreword' by Bishop Alan Clark, the Roman Catholic Chairman of ARCIC, to *Observations on the Final Report of the ARCIC* by the Sacred Congregation for the Doctrine of the Faith, 1982. Bishop Clark writes:

> In due time the Holy Father authorized the Secretariat for the Promotion of Christian Unity to set in motion the process of evaluation of the *Final Report* by inviting the views of Bishops' Conferences, particularly in countries in which the Anglican Church is also present, "to send a considered judgement on the work done, above all as to whether it is consonant in substance with the faith of the Catholic Church concerning the matters discussed" and seeking their views "on the agenda for the next stage of this dialogue" (Letter of Cardinal Willebrands, 17th March 1982).

Before looking at the agenda for ARCIC-II it is worth noting two interesting points. On the Roman side, the ARCIC-I *Final Report,* which was ready before the end of 1981, was not released for publication for several months. That the evaluation is to be made by Bishops' Conferences far and wide, which is likely to involve reference to clergy and laity, is a procedure which is pleasing from an Anglican standpoint. What had not been generally realized was that during those months the Vatican's very influential Sacred Congregation for the Doctrine of the Faith would compose its own *Observations* on the Report. It is felt by some who were engaged in the ARCIC dialogue and by many who followed its progress that this publication may be intended as a guide to the Bishops' Conferences. However, it has to be noted that the ARCIC Report is essentially doctrinal, and therefore has a particular concern for this Congregation. What the effect of *Observations* will be one cannot say. It is very cautious in the support it gives to the ARCIC Report, but some would say it is not very impressive theologically, and that it has not really grasped the principles which underlie the task of the Joint Commission. What effect it has will be seen in time. But Anglicans need to appreciate the role of the Congregation for the Doctrine of the Faith, and that appreciation of the role of the Vatican Secretariat for Promoting Christian Unity is not the whole story.

A point on the Anglican side which the ARCIC discussions have emphasized is that the construction of the Anglican Communion, with its admirable emphasis on the autonomy of its Churches or Provinces, and its method of arriving at decisions by consultations, is less effective than it might be in providing overall policies. One can contend that other world Communions may reasonably expect there to be an overall ecumenical policy. They do not find one. There is also the danger, from an Anglican point of view, that different Anglican Churches, engaged in their own, even parallel, inter-Church discussions may inadvertently go in differing ways that are not readily acceptable to one another. It does not, however, seem desirable, or indeed possible, to have an ecumenical policy laid down for all by a central authority, but the present capacity for divergence (with lack of good communication an underlying cause) will not do, and may well be considered ecumenically unreasonable. One may suggest that the direction for the Anglican Communion to pursue is that proposed elsewhere in this study, namely that the Anglican Churches need to, and could, agree to limits within which decisions — probably to some extent various within themselves — are taken, and which therefore are acceptable to all. Less formally, but equally practically, this procedure must be accompanied by communication and sharing of information within the family.

Finally, some matters concerning ARCIC-II, which, at the time of drafting this, is holding its first meeting.

There is a momentum in the Anglican-Roman Catholic unity dialogue which has given it a special prominence, as has already been indicated. Some of the matters it is discussing have yet to achieve a measure of agreement which already exists in dialogues with other Churches, such as matters concerning the Bible, canon law, the eucharist, and even ministry, but although ARCIC, like some other dialogues, has an eye on stage by stage progress towards visible unity, there is here a different sense of possibility, almost of destiny, which is of the substance of the momentum.

As ARCIC-I moved towards its conclusion it became the view of both Churches that the developments achieved through the ARCIC dialogue must not be allowed to grow cold. It was clear that any decisions about ARCIC-I were unlikely to be available for several years. Meanwhile ARCIC-II should take up and carry forward the work. Of course their agenda might well have to undergo revision when decisions or major observations became available about ARCIC-I. So factors underlying ARCIC-II are the work, and not least the unfinished work of ARCIC-I, together with a gathering together of issues which from the point of view of one Church or the other, or both, required to be taken next. These composed much of the substance of the Common Declaration of Pope John Paul II and the Archbishop of Canterbury at Canterbury in May 1982.

Obviously there are points in the agenda for ARCIC-II which will have a particular Anglican interest. Besides the emphasis on the importance of pastoral and practical steps, especially stressed by Archbishop Runcie, on justification, on both *Apostolicae Curae* and also the ordination of women, there is one other matter, before stating the programme for ARCIC-II, which should be mentioned. Impressive as the meetings of ARCIC-I were, one should also observe that the membership was entirely white and male and north-Atlantic. With ARCIC-II, in both Churches, this is changing.

The Programme for ARCIC II with explanatory notes has been presented as follows:

1. To examine, especially in the light of our respective judgements on the Final Report, the outstanding differences which still separate us, with a view to their eventual resolution.

   a. Matters possibly arising in due course from official reactions to ARCIC-I.

b. Other matters not dealt with by ARCIC-I:
   — Justification by faith (cf *ACC-5 Report*, p. 40, para. 4)
   — The joint examination of principles of Christian morality in order to discern what range of options is compatible with unity.

2. To study all that hinders the mutual recognition of the ministries of our Communions.

   This is perhaps the most urgent of the matters referred to the new Commission. Within a process of reconciliation between our Communions, and in the context of the work already done:
   a. What is required for recognition and reconciliation of ministries?
   b. How the particular problems arising from *Apostolicae Curae* and the ordination of women are to be resolved.

3. To recommend what practical steps will be necessary when, on the basis of our unity in faith, we are able to proceed to full communion.

   The Commission will need to examine:
   a. Patterns of Anglican/Roman Catholic relationships and full communion.
   b. Pastoral and practical steps necessary for the achievement of unity:
      — those that require proposals from the Commission
      — those that may first require preparation of material at regional level.

VI

Some Current Anglican Affairs

a. The Ordination of Women to the Priesthood

Within the Anglican Communion, and under the Constitutions of their Churches, women are being ordained to the priesthood. By the end of 1983 about five hundred had been ordained. The first constitutional ordination of women took place in Hong Kong in 1971. Subsequently there have been ordinations in Canada from 1976, in New Zealand and the USA from 1977, in Uganda in 1983, and probably in Kenya. But the discussion about whether it is acceptable, even whether it is possible, to ordain women to the priesthood continues both within and beyond the Anglican Communion. It is not for this study to argue the theology, and to declare who it considers right in the matter and who wrong, but it is suitable with so recent a practice to give a more lengthy account than usual of what has taken place in these last few years.

The subject of the ministry of women, with some reference to priesthood, has quite a long history in the Anglican world, particularly in the Church of England. The fresh stirring of the subject might be assigned to the Church of England's report in 1966 entitled *Women and Holy Orders*.

The question had been raised. Professor Alan Richardson, then Dean of York, in preparation for the Lambeth Conference of 1968, wrote an article on the subject — "Women and the Priesthood" in *Preparatory Essays* (page 295) for the Lambeth Conference. While maintaining that some of the most frequent views against such ordinations are inadequate, he also points out that those whose position is that there are no serious theological arguments *against* are in fact talking about logical not theological arguments. In speaking of theological considerations he goes on to say:

The question, however, remains whether such a decision taken by a single separate branch of the Church (for example, the Anglican Communion) could possess such authority; it would not be reverting to an ancient practice (as, for example, restoring the Cup to the laity), but would be making an innovation for which there was no ancient or ecumenical precedent. This is the crucial question which underlies the debate whether the Anglican Communion should proceed to the ordination of women to the priesthood now. It is a profoundly theological question, since it raises the issue of authority in the separated branches of the universal Church of Christ. It goes much deeper than discussions about whether such unilateral action would help or hinder progress towards organic unity amongst the Churches. *(1968 Preparatory Essays, pp. 296–7)*

When he has moved to sociological considerations, he says (p. 298): "The underlying difficulty is, of course, not sociological at all; it is basically the result of a failure to reach a proper understanding of the Church's priestly ministry." And again: "This is why the concentration of attention upon the question of the ordination of women to the priesthood is mistaken; it diverts the mind of the Church from the more important question of the nature and function of an ordained ministry in a secular society."

However, the Lambeth Conference of 1968 did concentrate its attention on — among other things — the question of the ordination of women to the priesthood, and found itself of the opinion that such ordinations were by no means invariably a bad thing, and so it played a major part in setting flowing a stream which will not arrive at its end for a long time yet. The Conference passed five resolutions on the subject (Nos. 34 to 38) of which the first two are:

Resolution 34
The Conference affirms its opinion that the theological arguments as at present for and against the ordination of women to the priesthood are inconclusive.

Resolution 35
The Conference requests every national and regional Church or Province to give careful study to the question of the ordination of

women to the priesthood and to report its findings to the Anglican
Consultative Council which will make them generally available
to the Anglican Communion. *(1968 Lambeth Conference Report)*

The resolutions were not particularly contentious. The results of
voting by the Conference could be recorded on a specific request
from the Conference, and some results were so recorded. But there
was no request for votes to be recorded on any of these resolutions.

The resolutions derive from the report of a committee of the Conference on Renewal in Ministry (of which Archbishop Coggan —
then of York — was chairman, and Archbishop Beecher of East
Africa vice-chairman) and its particular sub-committee (No. 21) on
Women and the Priesthood. The officers of this sub-committee were
Bishop W.W. Davies of Nova Scotia, Bishop E.J.K. Roberts of Ely,
and Bishop D.S. Rose of Southern Virginia. The report of the committee is on pages 106–108 of the Conference Report. Because of the
influence on the subject that this report had, it is suitable to quote
from it, even if at some length.

> We find no conclusive theological reasons for withholding
> ordination to the priesthood from women as such. We think it
> worthwhile to make the following points:
>
> The appeal to Scripture and tradition deserves to be taken with
> the utmost seriousness. To disregard what we have received from
> the apostles, and the inheritance of Catholic Christendom, would
> be most inappropriate for a Church for which the authority of
> Scripture and tradition stands high.
>
> Nevertheless the data of *Scripture* appear divided on this issue.
> St. Paul's insistence on female subordination, made to enforce
> good order in the anarchy of Corinth, is balanced by his declara-
> tion in Galatians 3:28 that in the one Christ there is no distinction
> of Jew against Gentile, slave against free man, male against
> female.
>
> It appears that the *tradition* flowing from the early Fathers and
> the medieval Church that a woman is incapable of receiving Holy
> Orders reflects biological assumptions about the nature of
> woman and her relation to man which are considered unaccep-
> table in the light of modern knowledge and biblical study and
> have been generally discarded today. If the ancient and medieval

assumptions about the social role and inferior status of women are no longer accepted, the appeal to tradition is virtually reduced to the observation that there happens to be no precedent for ordaining women to be priests. The New Testament does not encourage Christians to think that nothing should be done for the first time. *(1968 Lambeth Conference Report*, p. 106*)*

The Conference, in Resolution 37, had recommended that "before any national or regional Church or Province makes a final decision to ordain women to the priesthood, the advice of the Anglican Consultative Council be sought and carefully considered."

The Conference also asked, as we have seen, that every national and regional Church or Province "give careful study to the question of the ordination of women to the priesthood and to report its findings to the Anglican Consultative Council which will make them generally available to the Anglican Communion." (Resolution 35)

By the time the Anglican Consultative Council held its first meeting in 1971, under the presidency of Archbishop Michael Ramsey, it was known that eight Anglican Churches were acting on Resolution 35, but none had completed its study. However, the Bishop of Hong Kong (Bishop Gilbert Baker), acting through the Council of the Church of South East Asia, had asked the ACC for advice on what course to follow, as recommended by the Lambeth Conference Resolution 37, since his diocesan synod had approved in principle the ordination of women to the priesthood. (This was in response to the Lambeth Conference of 1968, and not the previous action of Bishop R.O. Hall, the former Bishop of Hong Kong, whose action in ordaining a woman during the exigencies of the Second World War had not been supported by the bishops; though one might contend that the ordination had some influence on the later events there.)

The Anglican Consultative Council, at Limuru, at its first meeting in February, 1971, passed the following resolution:

In reply to the request of the Council of the Church of South-East Asia, this Council advises the Bishop of Hong Kong, acting with the approval of his Synod, and any other bishop of the Anglican Communion acting with the approval of his Province, that, if he decides to ordain women to the priesthood, his action will be acceptable to this Council; and that this Council will use its good offices to encourage all Provinces of the Anglican Communion to continue in communion with these dioceses. *(Resolution 28(b): ACC-1 Report, p. 39)*

This was carried by 24 votes to 22, with several abstentions: a narrow majority. The key phrase, which was not arrived at lightly, was "if he decides to ordain women to the priesthood, his action will be acceptable to this Council." One can question whether the remainder of that sentence which says the Council will encourage other Provinces to continue in communion goes beyond the constitutional powers of the Council. The majority of those present, from Anglican Churches all over the world, thought it did not. In fact, neither then nor afterwards, as the ordination of women in the Communion became more widespread, has communion within the Anglican Communion been broken off, though at times it has been strained.

Later that year, on Advent Sunday 1971, and after much consultation and prayer, two women, Jane Hwang and Joyce Bennett, both of whom had served in the Diocese of Hong Kong for several years, were ordained to the priesthood.

In the years that followed, in accordance with Resolution 35 of the 1968 Lambeth Conference, studies from the Provinces and dioceses were coming in, and through the Anglican Consultative Council were made known and available to the Anglican Communion. Particularly these were made known to members of the ACC, which met again in 1973 in Dublin. The Report of that Council (*ACC-2*, p. 39f) observes:

> The present position with regard to the Ordination of Women indicates clearly that there has been considerable movement since Limuru 1971.

The Council had before it a summary of resolutions adopted by the Churches, which nevertheless indicated that studies were far from completed, and that final decisions might not be arrived at for some time. Of ten reports available, besides Hong Kong which had, of course, already acted, three Churches expressed approval in principle of the ordination of women, four said final action was pending, and two said that as far as they were concerned the time was not right. None recorded specific disapproval of the principle. Several

Churches, mostly in the Third World, indicated that they would like a consensus or lead to follow before deciding what they should say.

More detail of the positions taken up by Anglican Churches is given in Appendix IV. In November 1971 the ACC had started to produce and circulate *Anglican Information* which was a circulation three times a year to all Anglican dioceses and numerous other recipients (not all in the Anglican world) of information of many kinds which came to the ACC from all over the world. As news came from time to time summaries were included of "The Position So Far." Here are two of the statements from the ACC meeting in Dublin in 1973 (*ACC-2 Report*, p. 41):

The Council . . . adopts the following statements as the mind of the Council:

i. The Council agrees to recommend once more that, where any autonomous Province of the Anglican Communion decides to ordain women to the priesthood, this should not cause any break in communion in our Anglican family. (Carried: in favour 50, against 2, abstentions 3.)

ii. The Council recognizes that any firm decision on the ordination of women to the priesthood will have important ecumenical repercussions, which need to be taken into account; but this consideration should not be decision. The Churches of the Anglican Communion must make their own decision. (Carried. in favour 54, against 1, abstentions *Nil*.)

Concerning the statement (i) above, it is notable that this large majority came from a Council whose members were appointed by all the Anglican Churches. The two abstentions came from expatriate bishops of overseas Provinces, one of whom had retired and was participating in the Council as an 'alternate' member for a Province which had already decided it did not object to the principle of ordaining women to the priesthood.

The material which had been gathered from the Anglican Churches for *Anglican Information* up to December 1977 was printed in *Preparatory Information* (pages 69–75) for the Lambeth Conference of 1978. That, with a few adjustments, is now reproduced here in Appendix IV (pages 228–238), together with such information about decisions and reports as was received subsequently, and which is dated accordingly.

From the record given in Appendix IV of the decision in the Episcopal Church, USA (ECUSA), it is apparent that there was considerable tension on the issue in that Province of the Anglican Communion. This is true, as anyone knows who was at the General Convention of 1976. The issue had become inflamed by two services to ordain women to the priesthood, one at Philadelphia in 1974, and one shortly afterwards at Washington, D.C., before any constitutional assent had been given. This makes it more understandable that the Church there became so engrossed with the matter that views and feelings, either way, in other parts of the Anglican Communion seemed to become rather remote factors. Also it became increasingly probable during the debate that some members of the Church would break away if the decision of General Convention should be in favour of the ordination of women. It was in favour, by a narrow majority, and a number of members of the Episcopal Church did separate from it. This separation, however regrettable, was constitutional. If a point is arrived at where any Christian cannot any longer in conscience accept, or tolerate, the Constitution of the Church to which he belongs, he can no longer in conscience continue as a member of it.

An alternative route, which some have taken, in the USA and elsewhere, is to accept, if it is at all tolerable, whatever decision has become incorporated in the Constitution as the mind of the Church. They may feel, and reasonably so, that they should continue to press an alternative point of view which perhaps may bring further change, but they do not feel it would be right for them to cause a division in the Church. Many have commended the Canadian procedure whereby the views of other Provinces and of Churches that are not Anglican were taken into account in reaching a decision, and in which a conscience clause was included which aimed to make toleration possible where compulsion would be unacceptable.

The decisions recorded from *Preparatory Information* give Anglican views up to the end of 1977, and, in a few cases, beyond. To give an account of factors being considered by bishops at the Lambeth Conference of 1978, and of their resolutions on the subject, attention must also be directed to views being expressed in Churches other than the Anglican Communion.

Non-episcopal Churches, in the main, were not opposed to Anglican proposals that women should be ordained priests. As Professor Alan Richardson had said in 1968 (*Preparatory Essays*, page 296), this is the outcome not simply of belief in the 'priesthood of believers' — which, in fact, is a very widely held belief — but of whether there is or is not a distinctively priestly function. On the whole, the Anglican proposal was welcomed, or even considered somewhat overdue.

We have already noticed how deeply disturbing the proposal was to the Orthodox, and, in the main, still is. Anglicans were careful, even those who disagreed with the Orthodox, to acknowledge the worry and shock their procedure, and maybe their theology, was causing for many Orthodox, and to give assurance that the protest was heard and given careful consideration. For a time it seemed that the official Anglican/Orthodox Discussions might be broken off, but happily this has not happened. The temperature had moderated a little, but the implication is not that the problem has gone away.

The Roman Catholic opposition to the ordination of women to the priesthood is considerable. The rapprochement with the Anglican Communion which has slowly been developing in recent years, and the indications of convergence, have certainly not been forwarded by the Anglican action. The Roman Church has made it plain, and understandably, that ordination of women has created another major difference between the Churches, and one which will not be resolved easily. It was desirable that some consideration should be given to the effect of this on the improving relationship of the two Churches — for example, how realistic was the continuation of ARCIC? A Consultation — often referred to as the 'Versailles' Consultation, because that is where it met — was arranged by the Vatican Secretariat for Promoting Christian Unity and the Anglican Consultative Council, and its agreed purpose was to consider "to what extent and in what ways churches with women priests and churches without women priests can be reconciled in sacramental fellowship."

Each Church had five members appointed by the organizing bodies. It was made clear that the findings of the Consultation would be only that of its members. The Consultation met for several days in February/March, 1978. In brief, the members of the Consultation were of opinion that the discussions aiming at unity could continue despite the differences of view about ministry which was the reason for the Consultation. Here it must suffice to reproduce only one paragraph — the final one (No. 8) from the report:

> While we do not underrate the reality of this obstacle, we are convinced that our communions ought to maintain that deep trust in each other which has been built up over recent years. We have a grave responsibility to continue and intensify co-operation and dialogue in everything that promotes our growing together towards full unity in Christ. In this the churches will be sustained by their confidence and hope in the Holy Spirit, who alone can bring the effort to fulfilment. *(Anglican/Roman Catholic Consultation, No. 8)*

The Old Catholic Church has taken a position in many ways similar to that of the Roman Catholic. The Anglican and Old Catholic Churches are in full communion, and, despite some tension, this continues, but with one exception. The exception is the Polish National Catholic Church in the U.S.A. In 1978 their General Synod "voted to terminate sacramental inter-communion with the Episcopal Church and the Anglican Church of Canada because of their decisions to remove canonical barriers to the ordination of women to the priesthood. Relationships remain cordial and contacts continue. The Episcopal Church, however, remains in sacramental communion with the Old Catholic Churches in Europe." *(The Episcopal Church Annual 1982, p. 331)*

To some Anglicans these ecumenical reactions meant more than to others. What may be said is that far and wide they have been taken into account, humbly one believes, as conclusions and decisions were sought. Often underlying the debate in the minds of individuals and of synods was the difficult question of what it is permissible for a single Church, Denomination, Communion to do when the one, holy, catholic and apostolic Church is divided.

At the Lambeth Conference of 1978, the subject of the ordination of women was uppermost in the minds of most of the bishops there. There were different views and much heart-searching, and bishops came from dioceses which manifested a diversity of opinions and decisions. In the course of the Conference it became apparent how deep was the desire to preserve the unity of the Anglican Communion and of the episcopate. Here, albeit rather long, as the subject made necessary, are the relevant resolutions (Nos. 21 and 22) of the Conference:

21. Women in the Priesthood

1. The Conference notes that since the last Lambeth Conference in 1968, the diocese of Hong Kong, the Anglican Church of Canada, the Episcopal Church in the United States of America, and the Church of the Province of New Zealand have admitted women to the presbyterate, and that eight other member Churches of the Anglican Communion have now either agreed or approved in principle or stated that there are either no fundamental or no theological objections to the ordination of women to the historic threefold ministry of the Church.

   We also note that other of its member Churches have not yet made a decision on the matter. Others again have clearly stated that they do hold fundamental objections to the ordination of women to the historic threefold ministry of the Church.

2. The Conference acknowledges that both the debate about the ordination of women as well as the ordinations themselves have, in some Churches, caused distress and pain to many on both sides. To heal these and to maintain and strengthen fellowship is a primary pastoral responsibility of all, and especially of the bishops.

3. The Conference also recognizes
   a. the autonomy of each of its member Churches, acknowledging the legal right of each Church to make its own decision about the appropriateness of admitting women to Holy Orders;
   b. that such provincial action in this matter has consequences of the utmost significance for the Anglican Communion as a whole.

4. The Conference affirms its commitment to the preservation of unity within and between all member Churches of the Anglican Communion.

5. The Conference therefore
   a. encourages all member Churches of the Anglican Communion to continue in communion with one another, notwithstanding

the admission of women (whether at present or in the future) to the ordained ministry of some member Churches;

b. in circumstances in which the issue of the ordination of women has caused, or may cause, problems of conscience, urges that every action possible be taken to ensure that all baptized members of the Church continue to be in communion with their bishop and that every opportunity be given for all members to work together in the mission of the Church irrespective of their convictions regarding this issue;

c. requests the Anglican Consultative Council

    i. to use its good offices to promote dialogue between those member Churches which ordain women and those which do not, with a view to exploring ways in which the fullest use can be made of women's gifts within the total ministry of the Church in our Communion; and

    ii. to maintain, and wherever possible extend, the present dialogue with Churches outside the Anglican Family.

6. Consistent with the foregoing, this Conference

a. declares its acceptance of those member Churches which now ordain women, and urges that they respect the convictions of those Provinces and dioceses which do not;

b. declares its acceptance of those member Churches which do not ordain women, and urges that they respect the convictions of those Provinces and dioceses which do;

c. with regard to women who have been ordained in the Anglican Communion being authorized to exercise their ministry in Provinces which have not ordained women, we recommend that, should synodical authority be given to enable them to exercise it, it be exercised only

    i. where pastoral need warrants and

    ii. where such a ministry is agreeable to the bishops, clergy, and people where the ministry is to be exercised and where it is approved by the legally responsible body of the parish, area, or institution where such a ministry is to be exercised.

7. We recognize that our accepting this variety of doctrine and practice in the Anglican Communion may disappoint the Roman Catholic, Orthodox and Old Catholic Churches, but we wish to make it clear

a. that the holding together of diversity within a unity of faith and worship is part of the Anglican heritage;

b. that those who have taken part in ordinations of women to the priesthood believe that these ordinations have been into the historic ministry of the Church as the Anglican Communion has received it; and

c. that we hope the dialogue between these other Churches and the member Churches of our Communion will continue because we believe that we still have understanding of the truth of God and his will to learn from them as together we all move towards a fuller catholicity and a deeper fellowship in the Holy Spirit.

8. This Conference urges that further discussions about the ordination of women be held within a wider consideration of theological issues of ministry and priesthood. *For the motion 316, Against 37, Abstentions 17.*

22. Women in the Episcopate

While recognizing that a member Church of the Anglican Communion may wish to consecrate a woman to the episcopate, and accepting that such member Church must act in accordance with its own constitution, the Conference recommends that no decision to consecrate be taken without consultation with the episcopate through the primates and overwhelming support in any member Church and in the diocese concerned, lest the bishop's office should become a cause of disunity instead of a focus of unity.

In this matter of the ordination of women to the priesthood, where there is still so much debate, and where no convenient history yet exists, it has seemed necessary to go further into the history of the discussion and decisions than with other subjects. To complete this account, here are a few of the thoughts and observations that one has noted from watching, discussing and listening in the recent years.

1. In many parts of the world the views of the laity are only appearing slowly. Often, for quite a long time, lay people were not really interested, and are inclined to suppose this is a matter for the professionals which does not particularly concern them. As they begin to think otherwise, their views may appear to be based on

practical, and even local, experience, and are not very appreciative of the theological factors involved. But before hastening to an assessment of their views, it is well to contemplate what is the role of the laity: is it that they should all aspire to become theologians? And one needs to ask what is the significance that when they vote their majority tends to coincide with the majority vote of bishops?

2. The debate about the ordination of women roughly coincides in time with the movement for women's liberation, on which many feel passionately. How far the issues reasonably relate together is a matter of personal judgment: what is certain is that they are not at all the same thing.

3. This debate about whether women should be, or even can be, priests often develops and maintains a party or churchmanship character. Partly this is because the theology involved in supporting either point of view is complicated and the practice develops of following the line of contention of the theologians, and of the school of thought that one prefers on other matters. Thus, as in other matters of theological difference, if one knows what is a person's churchmanship one can make a guess that is likely to be right about his position in this debate. An objective assessment built on the evidence is not very frequent. However, it is not absent, and in this particular debate a personal attempt to assess the evidence objectively is more frequent than in older discussions and differences that have become more stereotyped. What is regrettable is when evidence is sought not for its own sake but because it is considered to support whatever is the position one has already taken up.

4. A contention which is worthy of sympathy is that in so important a matter as this, which concerns the ministry of the Church, it is unacceptable that one part of the broken Church should act on its own. The view of this kind one most often hears expressed concerns Rome, or possibly the Orthodox. The point is that agreed common action which becomes available through the achievement of reunion (or something very near it) precedes decision in such a matter as this because the whole Church is concerned. However, it is increasingly frequently pointed out that visible union, even with Rome, is exceedingly unlikely to come about in this century, and a general reunion in the Church can obviously

be expected to take longer. One is, in fact, facing an argument for indefinite postponement. Whatever one's views may be, the difficulty caused by this contention for women who believe that they have a vocation to the priesthood to which they are called by the Holy Spirit is clear. One can understand their hesitation about waiting for many years — indefinitely it may be — for a decision to be possible, and even so not knowing what the verdict then may be.

At the heart of this matter, whatever one's views on ordination may be, is the necessity of the hard recognition that while the Church is divided one has to acknowledge the fact and make decisions in that circumstance.

5. The strains and worries in the Anglican Communion which result from different decisions in different parts of the world are comprehensible. Some of these differences seem to be in part due to lack of communication and of sharing concerns and decisions more widely in the Communion. One doubts that anyone was in a position to determine when the issue about ordaining women should arise in the Anglican Communion, but one may suspect that had it arisen some ten years later, assuming that communication within the family had improved by then, the handling of the situation — even if the results had been much as they are — would have been done better. Not least, the participation of the Third World would have been less hesitant and unsure.

6. Over the years one gets the impression that some of the opposition to ordaining women which emanated from parishes has decreased with actual experience of women priests: a phenomenon foreign to the previous assumptions they had, and had inherited. From experience they have discovered it was not so bad as they thought. On this basis some have indeed become advocates.

7. Also one notes that, even where ordaining women is favoured, the arguments against it which carry weight are moving from the theological to the practical: difficulties focus on the family and physical things which are thought by many to play a dominant part in the woman's role. Views in this area depend on what is accepted as the woman's role. That in the west is a matter of debate; and the outlook of the Third World is different again.

8. There are women priests in the Anglican Communion. It is idle to suppose there will be any significant undoing of that situation.

b. Communication

We have seen how in recent years the Anglican Communion has matured as a family. We have noted that a system has developed, fundamentally admirable, whereby decisions are made within the family by the member Churches consulting together, and then within their own Provinces (in the light of the common conferring, and of their own conditions and culture, and of their own autonomy) making constitutional rules or canon law. This procedure assumes as essential the communication and the sharing of information. Professor John Macquarrie, while taking a less enthusiastic view of the Anglican structure of autonomous Churches, makes the point that each autonomous Church "ought to be in constant consultation with its sister Churches." This is said in the context of a consideration of Anglican procedure concerning the ordination of women *(Lambeth Conference 1978 Report,* Appendix I, p. 118).

In this study reference has repeatedly been made to the importance of communications. Almost any Church or ecclesiastical organization needs increasing efficiency in communication to perform as adequately as it should, and the rapidly developing performance of the secular world serves to emphasize that the capacities exist, at least in proportion to the funds available. The purpose here is to consider whether Anglican improvement in communication, an improvement which is virtually inevitable, is sufficient to be reckoned a development.

The Anglican Consultative Council has been aware of the need, and so too, it seems, was the Lambeth Conference of 1968. As yet the possibilities of the universal Anglican Consultative Council itself do not seem to have been realized, nor do the capacities of *Anglican Information* and other more *ad hoc* circulations. But they are welcomed, as was the appointment for the Communion of a Communications Officer. Old habits and assumptions and isolations are not changed overnight, but they are changing. Widespread consultation has been less customary than one might suppose. This is changing slowly but significantly.

In the parishes throughout the world there is variety in how far membership of the Anglican Communion is understood. To some, not least the newer Provinces, it matters a good deal. Some of the older ones tend to think still in old contexts like 'overseas missions' or some kind of, unconsciously assumed, racial superiority.

An agent of communication can be the Church press. A limitation it still suffers is that most papers have a churchmanship bias, or were founded with the purpose of undergirding and promoting a party approach. A difficulty which perhaps is insoluble is to produce a paper which can be of the widespread circulation that is appropriate to a world-wide Communion. Difficulties include the cost of rapid transport, the wide differences in national economies, language, varieties of culture and education. To cope with even some of these problems would need subsidy from somewhere. Information from other Churches makes for mutual appreciation and understanding. On the other side of the coin it serves to diminish the occasions when other Churches misunderstand Anglicanism. This kind of misunderstanding is not of a superficial character, and considerable and lasting disagreements between Churches have arisen from different implications being attached to the same word. And the rubrics of a period can imply to others permanent formularies. Understanding, in these troublesome cases, is usually best achieved by talking to one another — by intelligent communication.

To prescribe that there be more newspapers and journals does not, of course, do much to solve our problems. People can have too much. One which in some quarters could meet a need is a paper or journal, monthly perhaps, and of no particular or consistent angle of approach, which was composed of articles and competent discussions of the current affairs concerning the Church, or the Church and the world. The Romans have something like it in English in *The Tablet*. There is no doubt that such a publication would need a fairly large financial support, but that could be a more useful expenditure than some in which we engage.

c. The Anglican Communion and the Church of England

Of the twenty-seven Churches which make up the Anglican Communion one is the Church of England. While that statement may be correct as a fact, it nevertheless ignores the prestige and seniority which give the Church of England a special place. Nearly all the dioceses, of which there are now more than 400, by one route or another, can trace their Anglican origins to the Church of England. The exceptions occur mostly in pre-Reformation dioceses in Celtic areas of Britain. The situation began to change as autonomous Provinces, with their own Constitutions and Canons, began to appear; but those Constitutions usually had a deliberate and distinctly English quality. The faith was expressed by reference to English formularies, and to the Book of Common Prayer, as are the Orders of ministry. The bond of ecclesiastical unity is frequently by reference to the See of Canterbury or the Church of England, though increasingly to the Anglican Communion at large. Reference to England as 'the mother Church' was not uncommon in earlier days, from the founding of the Episcopal Church in the USA onwards, though now the degree of affection in the term has increased while any acknowledgement of ecclesiastical subservience has decreased.

As the Anglican Communion has developed its universality and internationalism, the relation to the Church of England has changed in a way that to most, including England (when it is realized), is a happy and acceptable thing. The Anglican Communion, for those who believe in the Anglican faith, is the desired development of much that has gone before: there is a more developed expression of catholic universalism, of the equality of human family relationship throughout God's creation, and of Christian affection. Moreover, as is intrinsic in the international Body of Christ, the Church and the State are separate things, though each may exist to serve the other as responsibility requires, and as obedience to the gospel permits.

Within the Anglican Communion the Church of England is the only member Church that is 'established', as the description is. This means in effect that the Church's affairs are to some extent controlled by the State, and the Church is the official Church of the country. In the past, in England as in many other areas of the west, it was the natural assumption that in a Christian land the people and the powers were of one faith: *cujus regio ejus religio* became a way of expressing it. In theory allegiance to the crown and to the papacy was all part of one Christian pattern. Tensions between crown and pope, however, could reach, and, as in England, pass breaking point. But the Church of England remained the official Church of the whole

State. The struggles in England in the centuries after the Reformation related directly to what should be the Christian faith of England — of the Church of England.

Time passed, and situations eased. Other expressions of Christian faith, or none, became allowable in England. Citizens could choose to be outside the established Church and of such rules of crown and parliament as controlled it.

In the days of English greatness, nevertheless, the Church of England had a status which should not be underrated. It was a dominant Christian force in the imperial realm. Combined with the increasing emphasis on the gospel and evangelism which we have seen was integral in the life of the Church overseas, and strengthened by the English missionary societies, the Church of England developed characteristics with a resemblance to those of the mother of a family. Certainly it was the centre for a Christian activity far wider than that of England alone. At that stage it was no surprise that the Church of England, with its attributes and long traditions and learning, should be looked to for leadership and advice. The internationalism which brought about the first of the Lambeth Conferences not unnaturally led to the Conference being in London with the Archbishop of Canterbury in the chair.

When considering that Conference it is interesting to keep in mind that in the immediately previous decades — since the passing of the Reform Bill in England in 1832 — the Church of England had been much engrossed with its own role in the nation. Bishop Blomfield of London (who resigned through ill-health in 1856) was a man of insight, energy and independence of mind. Of him Dean Carpenter has written that "he saw the contemporary plight of the Church in practical terms. Only a Church radically reformed in its structure could, he was convinced, perform its necessary task of restoring national morale. Equally important, he was prepared to co-operate with the Government in bringing this about" (Carpenter: *Cantuar*, p. 294).

However, at the same time the Anglican Communion was coming into being, and after some initial problems, associated with Bishops Gray and Colenso in South Africa, the growing Communion made it clear that an aspect of Anglicanism to which it did not aspire, even if it were possible to do so, was establishment, and the submission in ecclesiastical things to England's crown and parliament, however much it might think well of them on other counts. Certainly English establishment was not possible with countries that were not British. The gospel, the faith and order of the catholic Church, participation in the family — these were at the heart of things.

One might expect that the Church of England with its special position in a Christian nation would maintain a great numerical strength, but this is not so. Among those with no particularly active Christian commitment it has a fairly large nominal membership, as would any established Church. Some of the nominal members would support a bazaar. The active membership, as we have noted, is anywhere difficult to determine. A reasonable measure for England devised by the Church Commissioners for England (*The Historic Resources of the Church of England*, 1983, Schedule 3) is to add 50% of the total on electoral rolls to 50% of the total on the 'usual Sunday attendance' list. One then gets a total for Church of England membership of 3.25% of the population. Even in the west, where, in contrast to many other parts of the world, church membership has declined markedly in the last twenty years, this is a dismal figure. For many people coming to England from other parts of the Anglican Communion, to find such scanty, and often elderly, congregations is a chilly experience.

But as the established Church, the Church of England still has access to grandeur and wealth that give it a place of its own in society. The holders of its top offices, whether they wish it or not, have a special relationship to the crown and to the top ranks in government and the social order which derives from history and tradition rather than from the requirements of the gospel. A kind of neutrality may be expected of it, and of this situation Dr. Peter Hinchliff has observed ". . . the civil service model of neutrality is dangerous because it suggests that the churches, like civil servants, ought to be servants of the government" (Hinchliff: *Holiness and Politics*, 1982, p. 7).

In government the established Church has an influence, but not a decisive influence, on public morality. This may not be wholly bad in that the part of the population which has no real or specific belief and standards no longer feels compelled to act as if it had. But a dilemma that is not resolved is that of loyalty to the English establishment and loyalty to the universal Church. An odd and partly unexplained consequence is reversion to the Old Testament and praying for victory in battles. Marble memorials in churches make a prominent feature of weapons and military attire. Loyalty to a nation and loyalty to God have usually become divergent since Christ transcended Jewish belief in an elect nation. Loyalty to a nation tends to over-ride other loyalties, or consumes them into itself. Loyalty to God is not excluded. An effect of these and other factors has been to locate the strength of the establishment in the middle classes, who had become a dominant force in government and economics by the 18th century.

To the working classes the status attaching to ecclesiastical establishment is generally of less account. However, where the Church shows real concern for the sick and the poor, and an understanding of the people of the industrial world, there is more respect for the Church, whichever denomination it may be. Not infrequently it is the Church of England, through its parish clergy and those who work with them who manifest this kind of response to the gospel. But in the policies and politics of the nation, whether in the cabinet or the trades unions, the voice of the established Church has had no noticeable influence for a long time. It may be surmised that a problem confronting the Church of England is that its inheritance having become so much more secular over the decades it still cannot make up its mind to abandon secularism and stake all its inheritance on the gospel.

Reference to the wealth of the Church of England is not a reference just to its treasures and great buildings, which are part of its inheritance, but to money. The amount received from resources other than present giving within the Church is more than that for the whole of the rest of the Anglican Communion put together. The total which the Church of England gives annually to all the missionary societies for the work of the Church in other countries and specialized fields is trifling compared with what it receives itself from what are termed its 'Historic Resources'. (A very good report on these Historic Resources is given by the Church Commissioners for England — who manage them and much more — in the book referred to above.)

The situation can be given a still sharper edge by drawing attention to the following: in most parts of the Anglican Communion, indeed in most denominations in most countries, a congregation needs to provide a church and a place for the minister to live in, all the running expenses of the church, and the minister's stipend, or it does not have a minister or a church. The Church of England assumes most of these things will be provided — that always there will be a church close at hand. Church members for decades have been accustomed to paying only a fraction of the stipend. Recently, mainly under the pressures of inflation, this has risen to nearly half — which is not an impressive figure. The Church of England now relies a little more than it used for its existence on giving, but giving that can still be eclipsed by the claims of the organ fund or that finds suitable expression in the sacrifices endemic to a coffee morning.

One sad effect has been that with past endowments generally maintaining churches and clergy, the churches have continued in those locations where they were, even when the population has moved elsewhere. New towns have been growing apace. As the Church of England inherited virtually all the medieval churches the effect of all this has been far too many churches of which a great many are in the wrong places. Churchpeople from other parts of the Anglican Communion, the developed as much as the undeveloped world, are often amazed when they come to England at finding churches so close together. Even more injurious has been the failure of a practice of Christian giving to develop. Even in church matters what people together pay for they value and use. The Ecclesiastical Commissioners come near to this point when they say "Levels of giving are usually and necessarily in an inverse relation to (diocesan) income from historic and other sources" (op. cit. page 52). Even more impressive may be the reaction of a member of an English parish who for some reason has for a time been attached to an American one.

Although it may not be directly to our point, fairness demands that one say that while the size and use of the wealth of the Church of England requires great changes for achieving response to the gospel in other parts of the world as well as in England, it must be accepted that to change habits takes time. Customary practices cannot be altered fundamentally overnight. That is a kind of revolution which, however right, people do not wish on themselves. Moreover the Church of England has literally thousands of medieval buildings which under present arrangements it needs somehow to maintain, whether it really needs them or not.

Underlying this reference to the wealth of the Church of England and its historic resources is the contention that the resources could with great advantage be spread much more widely in the Anglican Communion for the salvation of souls — the purpose for which the

Church of Christ was created — than is in fact the case. The main consideration here is that these resources are by the law of the land restricted in their use to England. The Church Commissioners are 'for England,' by law. As far as their responsibility is concerned — and one is very much aware of this as one reads their report on the Historic Resources — the Anglican Communion seems not to exist. Yet the Church of England is part of the Communion and would have little significance without participation in its mission and universality. The point is not to criticize the Church Commissioners but to say that it is more than time that the law was changed, and in the interests of fulfilling the gospel the established Church should do something about that.

It may seem strange that, nevertheless, within the Anglican Communion, the Church of England is held in high, though varying, esteem by other members of the family. This is, of course, in part due to its unique history and to its part in bringing the Anglican Communion into being, though some find its self-confident assumption of its own superiority (an assumption of which it is often quite unaware), extremely tiresome. On the other hand, among the autonomous fellow members of the family the expression 'mother Church' is still encountered. The reputation of the Church of England's academic prowess still stands high, but in the older Provinces this is more frequently rivalled now, and in the Provinces of the developing world England's general ability to appreciate other cultures and their contribution to the faith is often questioned. But it still has a status in Church and State which is impressive. One detects this particularly in dioceses that until not so long ago were British colonies and dominions. Old outlooks do not vanish overnight, and conservatism reappears in times of disillusion, and there is a good deal of disillusion, whether expressed or not, in recently independent countries. But these things will not last. Appreciation of an old regime may be expressed, even nostalgically, but there will be no return to it. Freedom and independence, despite the worries and troubles they may bring, have a value in the hearts of people which those who have not been without these things will never understand.

Rather dissimilar is the outlook of the increasing number of dioceses that have no British connection, past or present. For them the status of the Church of England may have an undoubted attraction, but in the political pressures of the world, that too will not last, and could even be dangerous. The attraction is the faith and universality of the Anglican Church — and for them particularly the name 'Anglican' is rather a trouble.

And for some in the Anglican Communion, probably very aware of their own independence, and perhaps also aware of a long association with England, there is a romanticism which readily accords the Church of England its special place and parental role in the Anglican Communion. A guess is that romanticism, political weather permitting, has a quality that will enable it to last rather longer, but certainly not for ever.

d. Property

Big museums usually have a department displaying a great range of Christian craft work — gold and silver vessels and dishes, paintings, sculptures, vestments of outstanding richness, and much else. Often these are from the Middle Ages, the ages of faith as they are sometimes called. Often notices tell from what churches they came, and perhaps the name of the noble donor. They are very valuable and impressive displays, and very disquieting — disquieting not because a museum is not their originally intended place, but because they exist at all.

Similarly, if one goes into a great church or cathedral anywhere in the world, there are likely to be two reactions: one is of admiration at such impressive Christian splendour and skill, the other is of a kind of dismay that this is the best we can do about honouring the gospel of salvation and the kingdom of God. If we see this beauty and magnificence as the way to the foot of the cross, then we have not understood the way. All too easily a dichotomy is unconsciously achieved: an appreciation of the splendour, and an approving attention to the Son of God saying to Pilate "My kingdom is not of this world."

This dilemma is not difficult to state, but the problems to which it gives rise are not comfortably resolved. The examples chosen highlight the conflict. But are not great cathedrals built to the glory of God, and there is nothing else like them? And whatever one may think now, they can hardly be allowed just to fall down. So, one can argue, there is no alternative to finding the vast amounts of money to keep them up. It is difficult to be convinced all the time. The case for medieval bishops' houses and for palatial ecclesiastical residences is less good.

Partly what makes the problem is the need throughout the world to evangelize, to enable the spreading of the gospel. That is the greatest Christian purpose for the use of abilities, resources, time and money. No Christian building compares in its significance with the ancient temple of the Jews in Jerusalem, yet of this Christ was prepared that as a consequence of people committing themselves to the faith that he taught, "one stone should no longer stand upon another." It is as much of a paradox in a great new church of the developing world as in a great church of the old world that there should be at the centre a near-naked figure upon a cross.

Again, for the other side of the argument, the case can be put that if great churches cease to be the ideal then church buildings must be simple and not costly — and probably not very conspicuous. That may be a move in the right direction, though in most places it is not a route that would appeal to everybody. It is expected that churches will be outstanding, and changes about things like that do not come about in a hurry — not least among people who seldom use the buildings and therefore hear less often the gospel that might compel a revolution in their assumptions. One has to ask what in the purposes of God is the function of such buildings? In the parts of the world that need them, Christian buildings of some sort have a high claim on nearly all Christian resources. Perhaps buildings that are not particularly eye-catching would attract fewer people: that may be so, but it is by no means certain, nor in the Christian context is it to be assumed that success and crowds are to be identified. There are many parts of the world where one of the greatest Christian duties is to draw adherents of other faiths to Christ — that is undoubtedly true, and it may be contended that rather inconspicuous places of Christian gathering will not help in that mission; however, the attractiveness of the humility of Christ may be most discernible in simple things.

To consider property it has been easiest to take churches and cathedrals as illustrations, but, of course, they constitute only a part of the story. That can include a wide range of present or hoped for acquisitions, from land (of which the Church in some parts of the Third World, too, has quite a lot) to a variety of endowments, and even special wool for making special hassocks. But underlying the debate, not least for a universal Church, is the question as to what for all people is the way of salvation, and what is the gospel for?

Note must be taken that in the process of thinking about the things that are suitably done in Christ's name there may now be parallel standards which are required by secular authority. Particularly in developed countries these are not low. Hospitals, community welfare, equipment, colleges may in these circumstances make considerable demands: they may even be the good reason for some acquisitions of property.

The purpose of this section of our study is to emphasize that there is an issue and a problem here if we are to consider development in the Anglican Communion. My own experience asserts the existence of the problem, and also that it is very doubtful if we have yet got a good enough answer to it.

e. The Anglican Communion and Mission

This section of this study is not much more than an appendix. The point is not that mission is a subject which is suitably 'tacked on,' but the opposite. The Church and mission are in large part synonymous. By the nature of the subject here, mission has repeatedly come into the picture, and is of the substance of the study. The Church, church membership, and mission are inseparable.

There exist many good histories of mission. The major denominations of the world, and the World Council of Churches, missionary societies and fellowships have produced them. Often there are analyses made which have a depth which, like the histories, have a lasting significance and quality.

Mission is not something the Church *does*, it is part of being one, holy, catholic and apostolic. Mission is about being sent. So, too, in its Greek origin is apostle. At once we are involved in a 'mark' of the apostolic Church and of its ministry, and behind that, and towering over it, is Christ the Redeemer Himself and his words "As the Father sent (Greek: *apostellein*) me even so I send you" (John 20:21. Note: the second use here of 'to send' has the Greek word *pempein*; the meaning does not seem to be significantly different. Perhaps the implication is less particular and more general). The death which was for the whole world and its generations was died in loneliness on a certain day. The outreach to the whole world, and to all the individual lives of which it is composed, is the mission laid upon the Church.

In a great, but nevertheless limited, form emphasis on mission was concentrated on spreading the faith particularly to the pagans. A definition on these lines is at the beginning of an article on 'Missions' in *The Oxford Dictionary of the Christian Church*. This emphasis is a main factor in the work of great travelling Christians from Francis Xavier to David Livingstone, and is the foundation of most missionary societies. It dominates what the earlier Lambeth Conferences have to say about mission, where 'missions' are characteristically 'foreign' and relate to work by expatriate Anglicans for the extension of the faith among non-Christian, or pagan, peoples. Such Anglican missionaries achieved great things, in large measure through the support and inspiration they had from the missionary societies. And as the societies relied largely on the parishes, not least for money, the Conferences gave much thought to advising on how best that could be ordered. However, into these discussions, which contained much that was very serious, and a little that was romantic, there also appears from time to time, almost it seems by chance, that even greater theology of mission which concerns the very nature of the Church. And, in a hesitant way, thoughts of the one universal ecumenical Church creep in after a fashion:

> We aim . . . at extending not the Anglican Church with its special characteristics, but the Holy Catholic Church in its essentials, which each new Church, as it grows up, many exhibit under characteristics of its own. (*1920 Lambeth Conference Report:* SPCK 1948 edition).

Recent years have seen increasing expression of the relation of mission to God's mission in Christ, and to God's whole work of creation. Here it must suffice to make two quotations: the first from the 1971 *ACC-1 Report*, where the creative discussion of mission and evangelism was outstanding, and the second from the Faith and Order Conference in Bangkok in 1973. Here is the quotation — rather long — from the *ACC-1 Report* (pages 41–42). Under the heading 'Contemporary Questionings' the passage proceeds:

In every place and time Christ's mission takes different forms and is described in different terms. In our own time there are vast varieties of situations. There are places where the simplest verbal communication of the gospel brings a response of faith, conversion, and baptism. There are other places where Christians find it almost impossible to find words and deeds which are capable of conveying to their neighbours who and what Christ is. But some things can be said which, while not complete, are generally applicable to our situation today.

a. There is the conviction that God is at work in the world, far beyond the boundaries of the Church — in movements of liberation and humanization and in movements of radical renewal in the ancient religious systems. In many cases these movements can be traced to the impact of ideas which have their roots in the Bible. In some cases we see secular agencies accomplishing reforms for which the Churches laboured but which they were not able to achieve, and we are compelled to recognize God's healing and liberating work.

b. There is the deep sense among peoples everywhere of the meaning of being a human being; of the reality of our common humanity in spite of all that divides us; and of the indignity which men suffer through countless denials of their humanity in the structures of our political, economic and cultural life. This is expressed in a great variety of ways; perhaps most notably in the intense feeling of young people in many lands of revolt against all institutional forms which seem to prevent us from simply being human with one another.

c. There is, therefore, a recovery of biblical perspectives which had been forgotten; a vision of salvation as God's total, all-embracing gift of healing and liberation for his whole creation; of this salvation being concerned with men's bodies as well as their souls, with their corporate life as nations and societies as well as with their personal and private life; of the mission being God's mission rather than ours, and of its dimensions being greater than the creation and growth of churches.

The Bangkok Conference spoke of Church growth "as being at the same time (i) the numerical growth of the Church; (ii) the development of a new man in every person; and (iii) the rooting of Christians' faith in local realities and their commitment to society" (Quoted in *ACC-2 Report*, page 51).

The drawing of attention to mission as integral to the Christian life of each baptized person in the place where he or she is has, as one of several consequences, the putting under review of the work of missionary agencies. They are not just concerned with other people 'out there'; and phrases such as 'overseas missions' or 'foreign missions' are questionable indeed.

The closer relating of God's mission and God's creation has led to an appreciation by many that the activity of God goes beyond the frontiers of the Church. Inevitably this leads to consideration of the form that dialogue should take with people of other faiths and ideologies, from Confucianism to Communism. But there is also Christian emphasis that salvation is through Jesus Christ and none other. Here, among the Christians themselves, there is sincere disagreement and uncertainty. The value is that the issue has been raised: to say it has been worked out would be premature.

Mission, in the Anglican Communion, as in every other denomination in the Christian world (except perhaps some which are remarkably assured of themselves) is impeded by the fact that the Church manifests itself as a divided Church. Anything like general reunion seems to be far in the future. Meanwhile maximum appreciation must be given to co-operation wherever it is possible, and to the kind of ecumenical collaboration in this sphere developed by the World Council of Churches, and such of its programmes as Joint Action for Mission. Mission is indeed one of the more compelling agencies for reunion. The point is made by Pope Paul VI in his Apostolic Exhortation *Evangelii Nuntiandi*, when writing of our witness to the world, he says: "Our divisions hinder this witness, hinder the work of Christ. . ." and calls for "a greater common witness to Christ before the world in the very work of evangelization" (paragraph 77, and quoted in the *Common Declaration* with the Archbishop of Canterbury, Archbishop Coggan, in 1977).

In the Anglican Communion itself such changes in thinking as these have, of course, had their effect, and the missionary societies, which although not identical in their approach, have played an important part. They have been clear that, whatever their differences in style, their existence is as servants of the whole Church.

Although it is not an exact foretelling of what happened, the following passage in the report of the Lambeth Conference of 1920, when it is expressing itself on 'missionary problems' and the Church of England in particular, said:

> It is desirable that the Central Board of Missions should be brought under the control of the National Assembly, from which it should receive its authority. . . . We urge that it is of the utmost importance that this task should be taken up by the National Assembly from its first inception; that it should be assumed as one of its normal and most precious functions; that the Assembly should claim, from the first, and as a whole, to be the supreme missionary authority, superseding none but embracing and co-ordinating all. (*Report, 1920, page 81*)

Over the years the deepening appreciation of the oneness and universality of the Communion, together with a deeper appreciation of the great identity of Church and Mission which underlies the 1920 Report, were studied, developed and applied, especially in the Societies and relevant Boards throughout the Anglican world. Meanwhile, too, the role of the missionary was changing, as we have seen. In due course much of this found expression in the document *Mutual Responsibility and Interdependence in the Body of Christ* in 1963. (The title, while being theologically good, is not alone among Anglican titles in being cumbersome. The document, as well as all that followed from it, is known as "MRI.")

In 1963, immediately before the Anglican Congress in Canada, Bishop Stephen Bayne, as Executive Officer, brought together a gathering of Anglicans from around the world with special interests and responsibilities in mission. The discussion led to the writing, unpredicted, of the MRI document. So important did the document seem to be that it was passed on to the whole Congress where it figured with a prominence that made it, in the opinion of many, the most significant feature of that Congress.

The memorable impact of MRI was that it revised many inadequate assumptions about mission and the relationships of the Provinces of the Anglican Communion, and accomplished this in a way that produced a welcoming response among Anglicans. Basic ideas which had been developing for a long time but not fully appreciated by church members generally began to be taken aboard as an appreciated cargo; but that was not the end of the voyage. With a brevity suitable to this study, the following account is given in *Preparatory Information* for the 1978 Lambeth Conference (page 67).

> The Anglican Congress in Toronto in 1963 said: 'The keynotes of our time are equality, interdependence, mutual responsibility'; and 'Mission is not only a giving to others, it is equally a sharing and receiving.' The Congress proposed a new form for the Anglican Communion — Churches related in partnership in a common missionary task; but this in turn depended upon the transformation of the relationships between the 'older' and 'younger' Churches — in fact 'the birth of entirely new relationships.' The Directory of Projects, which attempted to realize the concept of *Mutual Responsibility and Interdependence in the Body of Christ*, contributed to a new approach to missionary co-operation, but did not overcome the old division between the 'giving' and 'receiving' Churches. MRI came to be identified in the end with the project system and with the creation of the 'shopping-list mentality,' and failed to be a means of transforming relationships and attitudes. (*1978 LC Preparatory Information*, p. 67)

The decline was such that about ten years after Toronto the response to the MRI Projects Lists accounted for little more than 4% of the financial support from one part of the Communion to another. That in itself was not a condemnation, but it was plain evidence that further advance must be made. The vision given initially by MRI was not allowed to fade in obscurity. Analysis of mission and evangelism such as had been given expression in 1971 at the first meeting of the Anglican Consultative Council at Limuru was a principal factor in bringing into being 'Partners in Mission' (PIM) in 1973. PIM was not simply the next set of initials supplied to keep the Churches going, and to persuade them on to the next campaign. It had, and has, a finality: it attempts to say what the New Testament says.

Something of its character and way of working is explained in the continuation of the same article from *Preparatory Information*, thus:

> The Dublin meeting of the A.C.C. in 1973 proposed new styles of co-operative partnership through a process of joint consultation

between Churches. It based its proposals on the idea that: "The responsibility for mission in any place belongs *primarily* to the church in that place. However, the universality of the gospel and the oneness of God's mission mean also that this mission must be shared in each and every place with fellow-Christians from each and every part of the world with their distinctive insights and contributions. If we once acted as though there were only givers who had nothing to receive and receivers who had nothing to give, the oneness of the missionary task must now make us all both givers and receivers." (*Preparatory Information,* p. 67; cf. *ACC-2 Report,* p. 53)

PIM is still feeling its way forward, and by experience, including the discerning of mistakes, slowly discovering how hopes can be realized. Some account of this is presented in two more paragraphs from the same critique (page 68):

A first attempt at evaluation of the Partners in Mission process was made at the A.C.C.'s meeting in Trinidad, 1976, and it was agreed that this process of joint consultation had "proved to be an important co-operative and educational experiment, which is beginning to enrich the life of the local church in its obedient response to Christ in his mission." The positive values of the process were said to be:

"i. For the first time Churches are meeting as equals so that there is a new open-ness between partners, both local and world-wide;

ii. A deepening sense of relationship of autonomous Churches within a world Anglican family has begun to develop where previously in some cases there has been emphasis on relationships with mission agencies;

iii. There has been a growth in self-perception by member Churches, and in the understanding of their local tasks, leading to a realization of resources within as well as without." (*ACC-3 (Trinidad) Report,* pp. 55-56)

. . . However, the objectives of the PIM process have proved easier to grasp in those Provinces which still depend upon the more affluent sister Churches. New relations of partnership and interdependence now seem more attainable. But in the older Churches partnership and interdependence are not so immediately attractive, and the PIM process seems less intelligible, because a surrender of inherited ideas of mission is involved and a transformation of attitudes to 'the Church Overseas'. The missionary societies and mission boards have recognized the PIM process as promoting decision-making in the context of the Anglican Communion as a whole and as an instrument for building mission strategy. Their collaboration with each other through Partners in Mission has opened up the possibility now of working towards new patterns of mission throughout the Anglican Communion which will embody new relationships between Churches and a common understanding of mission and obedience to its call. (1978 LC *Preparatory Information*, p. 68)

When a consultation is held the Province holding it itself chooses which Provinces it would like to come and join in, and suggests who it would like particularly to be its partners. In developing relationships there is no restriction to Churches of the Anglican Communion. Such consultations, in which missionary societies and boards are taking an influential part, tend to be informative to all involved, sometimes to an unexpected degree as the experience and the criticisms of one part of the world are pressed upon another, and eyes are focussed on what the gospel requires of Christians. Where Churches are not wealthy they tend to concentrate on making financial links with those they consider are. That, as an early stage, is understandable, but generally there is not much progress in that direction. Another of the problems that is still with us is the need for dioceses and Provinces to decide in advance of a consultation what are their priorities — what are the most important things for the advancement of mission and gospel in their part of the world. Peoples and cultures are diverse: some do not take easily to planning; others are inclined to do it with vigour and determination for everybody. As is suitable, experience, as much as any other acquisition, is shared. The fact that there are suggested 'Guidelines' (*ACC-2 Report*, p. 56ff) for PIM and for consultations, and advice about subsequent consultations and the preparation for them as well as for the follow-up has, one hopes, the implication that the procedure of PIM is not a cloud of ideals but a down-to-earth attempt to respond to the needs of Christ's Church in every place. The history of PIM, as an expression of past events, is still a small part of the story of what may be accomplished, and in any case this is not the place for histories.

PIM does not have exactly the same emphases everywhere, nor even the same title. In the United States of America there is 'Venture in Mission' (VIM), and the British Isles, principally England, includes 'Partnership for World Mission' (PWM). This is an operation of great potentiality especially in the country where in the past so much missionary activity has begun, which, one might say, has picked up the urgent proposals of the Lambeth Conference of 1920 which we have quoted already (page 180). PWM is bringing into collaboration the several missionary societies and also the General Synod of the Church of England. As its roots extend, and as difficulties are met and overcome, the unity of Christ's mission is increasingly finding its expression in the singleness of Christ's Church.

There is no wish here to say that in the Anglican Communion PIM has achieved its goal. One may contend that in PIM the Communion has perceived its goal more clearly, and that though much has been accomplished in a comparatively few years, the bulk of the potential is yet to be achieved. However, what is taking place is not merely change: it is development.

f. The Anglican Communion and Training

People who write books, give lectures, analyse a state of affairs, frequently, as they lead into a summing up, point out the value of finding the right questions to ask, in the hope that the day may come when answers are found. They imply that they have found the questions, and state that they do not have the answers. But what most people want is some answers. Unfortunately as the subject of Anglicans and training is discussed, as increasingly it is, a lot of questions come to light, but not many answers.

The study or training takes place widely today throughout the Christian world, and so, too, do experiments. The Anglican Church gains some points from a measure of participation in the search, but beyond that its score is modest — there is little that could be called development. Perhaps it will come.

With that hope in mind, it may be worth noting something of the diversity of fields in which training is relevant. It is interesting, and at once depressing, that resources for training are seldom very high up in the priorities which Provinces list for PIM consultations. But here is what we are told by Bishop Henry Okullu (Bishop of Maseno South, Kenya) writing on lay training in a preparatory paper for the fifth meeting of the Anglican Consultative Council (*ACC-5 Preparatory Papers*, p. 301f).

In Africa when we talk about lay training, invariably we mean the training of lay-pastors, and not the educating of the Church itself for mission in the world. This may not be the case in North America or in Europe, for example. Take the case of a diocese such as ours (the Diocese of Maseno South, Kenya) with 600 worshipping communities. We call them churches. These are divided into 40 parishes, which means that each parish has an average of 15 churches. The vicar lives in one of the 15 churches whose congregation does not have any special features about it anymore than the rest of his churches have. It is not, for instance, the largest congregation, nor does it have the largest building.

In a situation of this kind, the vicar or pastor or padre (we use all those titles) is virtually that of a dispenser of the Sacraments, or that of an itinerary evangelist, if he is a talented preacher. He visits a new church to baptize both adults and infants, celebrate the Eucharist, and talk about various instructions, requests, etc., from the diocese, rural dean and archdeacon. He gets on his bicycle and makes for another church, between 7 to 15 miles away. He is not seen again for another two months or so when he comes again for a repeat performance.

If this is the pattern of the ministry existing in the Church in Africa, we may now wish to ask ourselves who is *teaching* the Church.

In every church of the 600 churches referred to before, there is a church teacher. We call them 'evangelists' or catechists. They are 'chosen from among the people,' having demonstrated natural ability for leadership and as godly men or women. Such a person's name is given to the vicar who, having satisfied himself of the person's qualities, recommends to the bishop that the person be licensed to become a church teacher. He then becomes, essentially, the pastor of that church. He leads the worship service on Sunday, he instructs both baptism and confirmation candidates, he preaches every Sunday, he visits the sick and buries the dead. He is the pastor but he is untrained, by any standards. His only qualification is that he can follow, somehow, the Prayer Book.

In some countries, as much in the west as anywhere else, lay training is barely prominent yet, let alone the desire for it which may be quite strong, especially in parts which having abandoned religious commitment in recent years, and then having found how barren life is out there without it, are now turning back. For whatever reason, lay training has found a new life in recent years. Mr. D. Barry Menuez, of the Council for the Development of Ministry, USA, wrote in 1981:

> There are now thirty eight diocesan training schools which are open to persons interested in theological education but not intending to be ordained. Many of these schools were originally created to prepare people locally for the priesthood. Because of the demand by the laity for education, virtually all of them offer courses for the laity and some have shifted completely to lay education. In addition, a survey of major camps and conferences over the past several years would indicate the increasing number of weekend, week-long, two-week programs committed to the development of ministry. Curriculum materials abound, put together by parishes and dioceses, seminaries, publishing houses and private consultants. (op. cit. page 305)

What is appropriate is the consequence both of local culture, experience and approach and of the state of training a country — or part of the country — is at. And this also raises the question of the appropriateness of institutions. Here, in the same set of papers for ACC-5, is the Revd. Dr. Kortright Davis of the West Indies:

> Enough has been hinted at in the foregoing which should serve to de-emphasize the role of institutions, systematic pedagogy, established programmes of training, and hard-and-fast criteria for qualifying for ministry and service. The rapid decline in the ability of churches to sustain traditional theological institutions at increasing levels of proficiency is a fact which is not without its

own significance. When this is placed beside the avid thirst of many lay persons for wider exposure to the practice of theological reflection and discovery, the Church cannot but take careful note of where the Spirit is leading. The mission of the Church today must surely be bound up with the total world process of change, advancement, struggle and search. (op. cit. page 308)

Theological Education by Extension (TEE) is one of the most important additions to the world scene in recent years. It is ecumenical, and various, the variety unfortunately — but perhaps inevitably — extending to the quality. However, although it is widely established and used, these are still early days. Dr. Kortright Davis again:

> Theological Education by Extension would then become more of the servant process for the life of the local Church that it needs to be. TEE is really designed to identify and strengthen the capacities of local congregations and their leaders to become more and more the chief agents of reconciliation, mission and renewal. TEE is best at work when it enables different kinds of church communities, both in rich and poor countries, to develop their own ministries from within. TEE confronts the notion of theological education as being mere 'ministerial formation', and places the congregation in a position to respond creatively, and in living faith, to the spiritual and social dynamics and challenges in their part of the world. (op. cit. page 309)

So far we have just touched on issues concerning training for lay people. The purpose here is to do no more than indicate the extent and diversity of the subject, and tentatively to suggest that experience is leading to the asking of some of the right questions.

Training for the ordained ministry, while inseparable from lay training, has also its own issues for consideration. Here are some notes first on the institutions we Anglicans have; and then some notes on whether we want institutions at all.

In the developed countries seminaries and theological colleges whose purpose or style of curriculum is mainly academic and possibly pastoral have in general a standard that is either quite good, or better. But their relationship to the Church of their Province as a whole still bears limitations. Most were founded by societies or godly individuals for the increase of the ministry as they preferred it. They have a built-in churchmanship approach. It is possible to make a very likely deduction about a priest's ecclesiastical outlook by finding out from a reference book which college he went to.

In other parts of the world the problems are many. A single diocese may have its own college. But it must be remembered that distances are vast. Small colleges do not make good communities, even when it is usual for students residing there to bring their wives and families as custom may demand. Some, nevertheless, do not stay the course but probably, and sooner rather than later, are ordained anyway: the need is great. There are a few places where training now is not expensive, especially if it is to a standard comparable with that in the surrounding environment. This compounds a problem smaller colleges already have, namely, adequate staffing. It may well be that a small staff — sometimes the complement of full-timers may be only one — teaches everything both within and outside any specialized field they may have. There is the chaplaincy and advisory work to be done too. The achievement of such a staff is often remarkable, but is unfair on both staff and students. An inevitable result is that most of the ordained ministry is poorly trained. The list of disadvantages continues: languages — and there may be several in one diocese; expatriate staff members whose familiarity with culture and language is inevitably restricted, and who may not stay long; the whole problem of continuity of staff and of the college itself, and more besides.

The matter of languages involves several complications. Not only may there be need for several languages in one institution, but most students will need the languages which are used in teaching as well. In Anglican colleges this is not necessarily English, though it is likely to be a European one, but a major local official language is increasingly frequent, for example, Malagasy or Swahili. Associated with this is the difficulty of an adequate number of books on Anglican — or other — Christian theology in the place where the teaching is done. Probably more resources of the Communion should go to translating than is the case. But even a few text books still leaves most Christian literature out of reach. Indeed, in rural parishes among the clergy one can still encounter an acute desire for literature that can be read and studied, or even such as will provide news and a spiritual article or two. These restrictions about language and literature have also made academic development more of a problem, though increasingly it is being overcome. The appointment of people to international ecclesiastical commissions is unhappily disproportionate, too, unless the person with suitable prowess and experience is outstandingly fluent in a foreign tongue. Most Anglican conferences are held in English. Increasingly now there is some translation, but undoubtedly difficulties remain — not only for those most conversant with, say, Chichewa, but those whose mother tongue is, say, Japanese or Spanish.

In the developed world, for all purposes a relationship with a university is beneficial and increasingly frequent, but elsewhere there is little possibility of this. That colleges should work in ecumenical collaboration with institutions of other denominations, and consequently in larger institutions, may improve the situation, but it must be recognized that united colleges — even where the arrangement is otherwise a possibility — do not always work. Many factors make for this situation.

One may contend that in the great missionary spread of the 19th century the older Churches of the Anglican Communion, and England in particular, should have provided from among its best scholars for the new and vastly influential colleges. But one has to ask from where, in the newly developing countries, students would have come from who could have benefited from that kind of training. There is a case for saying things turned out better in the slower progression to a time when an indigenous method and theology were asserting themselves. But that is not a case that will carry conviction for everyone. Too many seminaries have been fragile and temporary, and too much training has been haphazard.

The idea of a central Anglican college has appeared at Lambeth Conferences for a long time, and the possible location was thought to be St. Augustine's College at Canterbury. There it came into being in 1952. It was in many ways an admirable and competent college, but outside the richer countries few were able to take advantage of it, though many who did remember it with affection. Inevitably the standard of the intake was uneven to the point of difficulty, and to be a servant promoting cohesiveness in the whole Anglican Communion it had a nigh impossible task. Unless a student (often already ordained) could collect considerable backing he found living away from home, family and work for perhaps a year or two was more expensive than could be managed. To some it had the great disadvantage of being in Canterbury, England. To some, especially if they perceived a touch of glamour, it was a very great advantage indeed. However good the concept may have been it was probably the cost that killed it more than anything. It closed as a college for the Anglican Communion in 1967.

Whether seminaries and similar institutions, traditional in the pattern of training, are needed at all is a question we have already seen raised by Dr. Kortright Davis (pages 186,187 above). Somewhat allied to it is a point about ministry by Bishop Wesley Frensdorf of Nevada which questions the traditional pattern of church congregations structured round a professional priesthood:

> Our customary models for living out the Church's life and carrying out her mission are largely dependent on professional, university-educated, stipendiary clergy or other full-time persons. This, together with other pressures for professionalization, has brought about an incredible clericalizing of ministry. The Church, *in effect* (not in theory), is understood as a community gathered around a minister rather than a ministering community. (op. cit. page 310)

These are questions which it is good to raise: to denigrate them as little more than a manifestation of the temporarily fashionable is a superficial treatment. What one must recognize though is that what may be desirable in one place is not necessarily applicable in another. There are parts of the world, perhaps those where Anglicanism is very thin on the ground, where the life of the Church centres on a growing congregation, its place of worship and teaching, and a trained, full-time priest present at the heart of the activity. Then again the question arises as to where and how that priest should be trained.

A question which adherents to the approach of both Kortright Davis and Wesley Frensdorf may have to consider is what of people who seek training in another country than their own? The cultural, or non-institutionalized ministry that arises from within a culture, is then more difficult to hope for, although 'further study' and 'in-service training' may be less of a problem.

Because much that was customary has been assumed by successive generations any attempt at a radical re-thinking about training has come only very slowly on to the Lambeth Conference agendas until recently. The discussion which did take place at the Conference in 1978 was not outstandingly memorable but did do something to manifest the issues and illustrate the diversities. A rather longer concern, though, has related to training for bishops. This may be because to a conference of bishops the existence of such a subject came as something of a surprise, especially as it was realized it was not particularly new indigenous bishops in foreign parts that were being talked about. The Lambeth Conference 1968 Resolution 39 recommended "that bishops should have opportunities of training for their office" and asked the new Anglican Consultative Council to do something about it. The Council's efforts did not get far (*ACC-1 Preparatory Papers*, page 24). What was clear was that the one place that was active was the Episcopal Church in the USA. That Church has continued to be in the lead, with Bishop David Richards in the van. It was contended in opposition that what might be possible in the USA with its numerous bishoprics not so far apart might be quite unsuitable where there were few dioceses in a vast area. it is encouraging to observe that three conferences held in St. Julian's, Nairobi, and with Bishop Richards asked to take a leading part, have taken place and are appreciated. It will be interesting to see what develops from that. In some places the need has been felt, by bishops in particular, that appointment to episcopal office launches a man into an ocean where a quantity of administration is required of him that extends far beyond any previous experience. One response is to say that therein is displayed a misunderstanding of the bishop's office, with a rider that given half a chance Americans will introduce management into anything. A response is that anywhere in the world of today a bishop's work will necessarily include some amount of organization and management, and that the part of his episcopal training that helps with that enables him to do it more quickly and so to have more time for the pastoral and similar duties. That also sets a measure of limitation on those who maintain that a suitable person to be chosen as a bishop should be the sort of person who does not need special training for the job. So, caricatured a little perhaps, the discussion takes place. The question is raised, and the consideration is serious. What the outcome will be, and to what extent a solution in one place has relevance to another, is yet far from determined. In this context it serves to underline what has been proposed about this whole subject of training, of which we have touched little more than the fringes, that any Anglican contribution is a degree of contribution to the debate, and not a progress as the result of questions being answered.

g. Liturgical Revision and Bible Translating

Within the Anglican Communion the official liturgies have been closely related to those produced in post-Reformation England, in some cases by way of the Episcopal Church in Scotland which more consciously drew on the Fathers and Eastern rites. But all had a family likeness. Such other variants as there were derived, often through a vicar's personal researches, from the Roman Tridentine rite or some other favoured source. Revision that was officially countenanced came, for a long time, very slowly and hesitantly. Permission might be given for a bishop to allow, on an experimental basis, slight variants that had real indications of improvement.

Then the scene changed dramatically over much of the Christian world. Motives bearing upon this were the acceptance of renewal in the Church in a changing world, the desire to bring about increased congregational participation in formal worship, and the wish to single out with recovered emphasis those features of the Eucharist which had their grounding in the apostolic and ancient Church. There was also recognition that a liturgy, in its form of expression, could lose clarity of purpose with age, and effective impact through familiarity. These motives were in general not in conflict one with another. So once change started it continued with a speed that is not frequent in ecclesiastical affairs. Moreover, this was not a form of renewal confined to one Church only, but was widespread in the west. It was ecumenical; and in the very area of Eucharist established a new convergence among the Churches. A major factor was new thinking among liturgical scholars in Rome; and the whole activity gained confidence and impulse when the value of the revisions was recognized in the events of Vatican II.

It is worth recording that at the Lambeth Conference of 1978, following a practice established by the Anglican Consultative Council, the daily eucharist was in turn celebrated by different Provinces of the Communion using their own rites and in their own languages. Although the rites were often revised ones, and the language not understood, all who were present knew what was being done and had no difficulty in participating. In the course of the Conference the death occurred in Rome of Pope Paul VI. The Roman Catholics who were present at the Conference came together in the main hall of the Conference, where all eucharists were celebrated, for their own eucharist for that occasion, and they invited such Anglicans as wished to be present. Nearly all came. But to some it was a happy surprise to find that the eucharist then celebrated was virtually indistinguishable from their own Anglican rites. Renewal had made it plain that for us all — and not only Romans and Anglicans — the God-given bases of the eucharist are in common.

Liturgical revision signifies something wider than eucharistic revision. Revision has followed different patterns in different Churches and in different parts of the Anglican Communion. In some attention is on eucharistic renewal and little else. Some, not least in the Anglican Communion, have revised (or are in the process of revising) other services too — the marriage rite, visiting the sick, Christian initiation, and so forth. With most a process of experiment is followed, and revised forms are first issued 'for use, study and comment' or with some similar qualification. There are instances in which a whole Prayer Book is revised. This too will almost certainly go through provisional and experimental stages, and as likely as not contains permitted alternatives. The end product may continue to be for optional use (like the 'Alternative Service Book'), or may be intended largely to displace and supersede what has gone before (like the 'Book of Common Prayer according to the use of the Episcopal Church' authorized in the USA in 1979).

This is not the place to try to set out the whole intricate story of Anglican liturgical reform. Usefully we can pick it up at the Anglican Congress in 1954 at Minneapolis. Topic II was entitled *Our Worship*. The two principal speakers were eminent liturgiologists: Professor Massey H. Shepherd, Jr., of the USA, and Dean Colin Dunlop of Lincoln, England. One quotation from each will make a valuable contribution to this article. Speaking of the Anglican Prayer Book Dr. Massey Shepherd, an advocate of scholarly and pastoral revision, said:

Our liturgy was compiled with painstaking care. Unlike some of the liturgical reforms in Continental Protestantism, it was not conceived either in a merely negative spirit, or as an occasion for novel experiments. What were considered medieval corruptions in worship were eliminated, to be sure; but the liturgy was not left at that — a mutilated collection of fragments. Into the texture of liturgical prayer retained from the medieval services, Cranmer skilfully interwove phrases drawn from many sources, ancient and contemporary, with occasional touches of his own creation. The result was a fabric conceived as a consistent whole, with an integral blend of old and new threads and colors.(*Anglican Congress 1954 Report*, p. 74)

Dr. Dunlop, in his companion article, said:

The most notable trend in Anglican worship is the deepening of sacramental life and the enrichment of the forms of Eucharistic service. The method of this enrichment is to use not the medieval but the earlier liturgies as the starting-point for development and to this nearly all the recent revisions of the Prayer Book witness. (ibid. page 91)

In the 1958 Lambeth Conference the large committee on Progress in the Anglican Communion had a main section on *The Book of Common Prayer* (*1958 LC Report*, pages 2/78 to 2/98). As the title indicates, the study there is not confined to the Eucharist. A passage of particular interest occurs on page 2/81 where there is a list headed 'Suggested modifications or additions for the further recovery of other elements of the worship of the Primitive Church.'

A review of liturgical developments covering the following ten years, 1958–1968, was compiled in preparation for the Lambeth Conference of 1968, and the review was continued to 1973 by Dr. Ronald Jasper. This report covering 1968–1973 was prepared for the second meeting of the Anglican Consultative Council (1973), and appears as Part 6 of the report of that meeting (*ACC-2 Report*, pp. 70–86). Dr. Jasper's article includes a clear setting out of Anglican liturgical changes in many different parts of the world.

From there the resolutions of synods and liturgical committees may be conveniently followed in the issues of *Anglican Information Service* which comes out from the ACC three times a year, and in which a section is assigned to 'Liturgy'. There is information from virtually every part of the Anglican Communion; an indication of this is that by July 1976 information had been received and circulated from: Australia, Canada, East Asia, England, India, Indian Ocean, Ireland, Japan, Kenya, North India, South Africa, Sri Lanka, U.S.A., USA (province IX), Wales, West Indies. Some of the activities in other Churches were made available, too, thus there is a Lutheran decision in *Anglican Information Service*, No. 8.

Anglican participation in the movement is manifest, and its awareness of continuity with the apostolic Church made the direction taken by much of the best revision appropriate. So, too, did widespread sympathy with the emphasis on renewal. A fault which still remains, but is now less serious than it was a few years ago, is that often there was less communication with other parts of the Anglican Communion than there should or need have been. This was true also in the limited use that has often been made of ecumenical studies in liturgical revision. It has not been unknown for similar researches to be duplicated in different parts of the world where a sharing would have enabled better results to be achieved.

Sometimes, still, it is assumed that the principal purpose of liturgical and biblical revision, and the use of more contemporary language, and of increased participation in worship by a congregation, is to make everything more understandable and participatory, and to reduce an outdated remoteness, so that more people, especially young people, would come to church and fill the pews. This was never the main reason, though no doubt some have hoped earnestly that it would happen. But a measure of sympathy with those who protest at new books is not out of place. There are people who over a lifetime have become accustomed to inherited words and ways and whose appraisal of the revised forms is characterized by regret. That one can understand, even while not being of the same mind.

Finally a word about new translations and versions of the Bible. They are fairly numerous, and some are much better than others. The best are distinctly better translations of the Greek and Hebrew originally written, and on the whole they speak with a clarity suitable to their subject. One example: at the end of the parable of the labourers in the vineyard the King James version says — "Is thine eye evil, because I am good?" (Matthew 20:15) which is not now —

or even, one supposes, for St. Matthew — the clearest way of making the point. The wording in the New English Bible is — "Why be jealous because I am kind?"

This example leads to a point that needs making. Usually the introduction to a new translation explains the purpose for which the translation was done. That is worth reading before the judgment.

Translations are often joint efforts by people of different Churches. The ecumenical factor is large, as well as good in itself. Similarly other new versions, new translations, are most often the work of people of two, or several, denominations working together — probably for years — in the various parts of the world. In this, too, it would seem that the Anglican contribution is substantial, and it is a matter of proper satisfaction that the Anglican Communion has played a notable part in the liturgical and biblical aspects of the renewal of recent years.

VII

Moving with the Stream

Consideration of liturgical revision and of Bible translation has taken us into areas that are less particularly Anglican than most of the subjects we have looked at previously. It is with this wider field that we shall stay in this section.

There is hardly any matter that bears on Christianity about which it is inappropriate to consider whether in recent years there has been some Anglican development. Changes, whether of advance or retreat, are perennial. Some matters in any generation are prominent features of the Christian stream. The cases to which we give attention here, which may well be very important in themselves, are subjects generally related to Christianity as a whole, where the Anglican participation is not one of being particularly creative in its own right but of moving with the stream as it proceeds. If there is any virtue it is because the Communion has not stood on the bank and merely watched while the river flowed on its way.

a. Christianity and Politics

Christianity and politics have a large area of common interest. Both concern people, and both (each in its own way) give attention to destiny. In recent decades it has become increasingly difficult to hold the two in separation. A major cause of this lies in the increased recognition we have observed in the place that justice, liberation and freedom play in Christian response to Jesus and the gospel. The consequences for thought and Christian behaviour are not always welcome, and so while some make efforts to hold religion and politics apart, others are emphatically grateful that there is a more real recognition of the whole gospel message. And so there is conflict. However much one may acknowledge that justice is right or that God does not respect persons, it does not come easy to recognize these things as absolute if one has been used to classifying them as a laudable ideal.

It seemed to me that both the truth and the difficulty were appreciated by a sympathetic and friendly Caribbean priest who in the course of a discussion at a meeting of the Anglican Consultative Council said that he was afraid that what he was about to say could not be properly understood by anyone whose grandfather had not been a slave.

The increased insistence among Christians, including many Anglicans, that politics cannot be taken in separation from religion, has, then, as one of its main constituents, the recognition that both concern the well-being of people — of people in this life. The life to come is another matter, although not an intrinsically different one.

The Christian concern for the poor, the oppressed and the deprived will remain a matter of strife for a long time to come both within and beyond those who adhere to the Christian faith. Power, tyranny, nationalism, are dominant the world over, and all are, at the very least, questionable when weighed in a gospel balance. In the 19th century, in east and west, north and south, Christianity and expression of the Christian faith were often, and not always unfairly, seen as the ally of a dominating power and of imperialism. In strife and slaughter around the world today Christians are likely to be on both sides as they seek national supremacy, and the politics of many governments and the fears of many people become involved. Christianity cannot be unconcerned, and it has standards that are different. It is a cause for thought that in South Africa one has been told by black and coloured Christians that to remain Christian is increasingly difficult when from the older, safer Christian world comparatively little is heard of those protests which arise from the gospel imperative. Sometimes exception is made for the Roman Catholics, especially the Religious Orders, and one honours that, but regrets it is not so everywhere.

Here one has done no more than touch on the issues of Christianity and politics. One hopes it has served to show why there is serious discussion about human dignity, multi-national organizations, individual and national motives, and many other issues which are affairs of both politics and religion. Critical to this whole relationship is the belief or assumption that politics requires ethics. And that is true. The Christian politician aims to think out his politics in terms of Christian ethics, and he has a right to turn to the gospel and the Church to help him there. It is reasonable that the politician should want to include in his calculations what the Christian implication is on, say, democracy, bureaucracy, community. It is also reasonable that underlying every calculation should be concentration on the nature of the purpose of life — life which always ends in death.

b. War and Nuclear War

War has been transformed with the coming of nuclear weapons. The termination of all human life on the earth is now a possibility. This means that in little longer than the twenty-five years of this study human existence has moved into a different world from any before, and there is no return. Total destruction can now happen; some would say that in less than the next fifty years it is a probability. Given this situation, one might suppose that the implications of it would take first place in the Christian evaluations and guidance for this world and for the life to come. It is not from any disregard of the importance of the potential of nuclear destruction that this subject is not given greater prominence in this study but because such Christian re-appraisal as there has been of war and peace contains no especially Anglican development, nor, indeed, significant new thinking by any major denomination of the Christian world. Development, and it is a tragic development, has come with the nuclear potential of destruction, not in the response to it. Anglicanism has not ignored the new situation but, rather, as with other denominations, it does not know what effective guidance to give — assuming that any effective guidance can be given at all.

Christian concern has been strongly expressed, but this voice is generally personal in its origins rather than deriving from any widespread declaration from any one Church or from the Churches as a whole. The procedures urged are various, and are often made at great personal cost; what is in common is the depth of concern. Often the pressure is not directly attributable to a Christian origin at all, but where it is the common concern tends to override denominational separations: the separations take on for many people an irrelevance such as renders the Christian communities incapable of giving adequate voice and guidance in this greatest of human crises. A kind of ecumenism is appearing which apparently no previous efforts towards Christian unity could achieve. That is a cause for thought.

It would be easy to blame the Church for having no agreed policy, but that would be to ignore one of the greatest Christian moral problems. It seems never to have been possible, despite all skill and sincerity, for a clear and universal doctrine of the Christian attitude to war to be arrived at.

The perennial problem that has faced the Church is that whereas Christian principles derived from the gospels give no ground for engaging in wars which aim to kill other people, a Christian is also a citizen of an order which usually employs force when its laws and authority are under threat. In the first Christian centuries some of the Fathers were of the opinion that in all circumstances the gospel principles were alone applicable and must prevail. Thereafter the duties of a Christian as a citizen were increasingly emphasized, but usually with the insistence that for a Christian citizen to engage in war the purpose must be such as would bring benefit to society (so St. Augustine of Hippo), or such as defended the Christian faith. This latter condition developed until it justified the Crusades, and until figuring prominently in battles was part of the qualification appropriate to being a Christian gentleman. Memorials and family histories provide ample evidence of this.

A curb to too assured a view was asserted by St. Thomas Aquinas when he gave a definition of what has come to be called a 'just war' in which it is right and acceptable for a Christian to participate (*Summa Theologica*, ii, q. 40). He gives three conditions as necessary: the war must be authorized by the sovereign power; the cause must be just; and the intention must be to promote good and oppose evil. Often there is added a fourth condition which derives from the Spanish school of theologians associated with Francisco de Vitoria who lectured in the early part of the 16th century. This was the requirement that the war must be waged by 'proper means' (*debito modo*). Recourse is still taken to these conditions, but the character of war being so different from that known to such as Aquinas and Vitoria, the extent often being so much greater, and slaughter including civilian and non-belligerent people in their homes and refuges, the recourse looks like a convenient port in the moral storm. Such conviction as it has carried diminishes, even though no satisfactory alternative has general acknowledgement. Faced by the dilemma inherent in teaching a Christian attitude to war, and feeling that some kind of pacifism is not a wholly acceptable answer, Churches more often made an assertion than they argued the case. Such appears to be the statement in the 39 Articles which were authorized by the Convocations in 1571. Article 37, "Of the Civil Magistrates," in its final paragraph asserts simply that "It is lawful for Christian men, at the commandment of the Magistrate, to wear weapons, and serve in the wars." (The Latin text reads: *"Christianis licet, ex mandato magistratus, arma portare, et justa bella administrare."*)

Also relevant is the growth in the idea of nationhood from the time of the renaissance, and which as basic in the conception of human relationship continues to the present time.

This brief survey is to emphasize how determining a doctrine of an acceptable attitude for Christians to war and violence has varied and never come to rest. As we have moved into the present time the problems have intensified and the need for guidance has increased. The demand, in many countries and cultures, for justice has intensified, and it is not unusual for violence to be seen as the way — often as the only way — of obtaining it. The freedom-fighter and the terrorist can be the same person — often the same Christian person — according to your hopes, politics, morals, history or race. The person who has upheld war and violence in one situation may deplore them when the circumstances of his life change. For the Church to give guidance in such conditions may be possible and is done, but the measure of diversity in the situations, and indeed often in the guidance, impairs the effectiveness.

In this respect the past world and the present are not totally unlike. But with the insertion into such a state of affairs of the power in human hands of nuclear destruction we have moved into a different world. The potential of nuclear bombs is such that the destruction of most, or all, of mankind is possible. If there is any survival from nuclear attack it is doubtful if it is a survival of a kind that is worth hoping for. With the developed nations such as have nuclear armaments, it may well be true that while nuclear bombs may be used to threaten or deter they would never be used for aggression because retaliation, probably triggered by a virtually instantaneous computerized reaction, would totally destroy the attacker as well as the attacked. No one would win. Maybe no one would survive. In such nations there is emphasis on the alternative of 'conventional weapons' as being capable of accomplishing a victory without destroying the aggressor. What is not certain is whether in a conflict with conventional weapons the loser would not find his last resort in the use of nuclear armaments. He might. No one knows. And it is to be hoped that no one will ever find out.

The issues concerning nuclear war which are urgently discussed by the nuclear powers are agreed among them to be important beyond all other factors, and the reactions of ordinary people in those countries, and in those related to them, illustrate the extreme gravity of the condition that has been reached. In the developing countries, or those without nuclear military resources, one hears less of the great nuclear debate. To some minds the situation may be very clear. But it is where this is not so that a great danger may lie. Only recently has it been widely grasped that a nuclear war in the northern hemisphere would not confine itself there. Any nuclear war will be total to the world: some say in hours, some say in months. It does not matter much which is right. The implication is also that the aggressor-nation will not survive, even if the opposition does not have nuclear bombs. It is doubtful if anybody survives *anywhere*. No one wins.

There is before us the possibility not merely of suffering, but of death, on a gigantic scale; even of the termination of all human life on earth, and therefore to God's creation as we have known it. What has Christianity to say to the prospect of death on this scale? One answer is that as the danger comes near no nation, power or government will allow such destruction to occur. That is reasonable, and to ensure such prevention is the motive underlying all protests and anti-nuclear activities — civil, military and moral.

A crucial assumption in a belief that nuclear destruction need never happen is that human beings are in the end reasonable. Of the vast majority this is true, but it does not include the maverick and the fanatic. The making of crude nuclear bombs by individuals or small groups is not impossible. A mechanism can be devised. Plutonium can be stolen by one means or another. While such a device may be of limited effect the possibility may not be dismissed that the detecting of one nuclear explosion might, perhaps almost instantaneously, start the train by which civilization and humanity is brought to a total end. To some a happening of this kind before the end of time —

more probably within the coming century — is considered the likely course that events will take. Annihilation by nuclear disaster must be seen as an undoubted possibility.

Christianity today is, then, confronted with two huge responsibilities in our world of nuclear power which carries with it the possibility of a nuclear destruction that is ultimate. One is to give as effective moral guidance as possible, and to foster all non-violent and acceptable moral pressures which aim to ensure that nuclear war never occurs. The second is to face the possibility that nuclear destruction will occur and to give careful thought to what the consequences may be for creation, redemption and eternal life.

At the beginning of this section the assertion was made that the implications of the possibilities now of nuclear destruction have not been ignored by Anglicanism, but that 'as with other denominations, it does not know what effective guidance to give' (see page 199). The brief and limited review in the paragraphs that follow that passage has been given to examine that assertion again. The appropriate form of the question is whether the Anglican Communion has made the kind of significant contribution in this field which could be considered a development. The answer seems to be that, as with other Churches, it has not. The subject has not been neglected, but, in general, previous attitudes and doctrines have been re-asserted. If there is a new factor it is an increase in emphasis. Perhaps more than that should not be expected, and even may not be possible. A recent Anglican international meeting which discussed these things is not necessarily to be dismissed as incapable or inadequate because its concluding statement was not a trite pronouncement but a call to prayer.

c. The Holy Spirit, Charismatics, Healing

Recent decades have seen an emphasis among Christians on the activity of God the Holy Spirit, particularly personal and communal response to His power and presence. Characteristic of the presence is joyfulness and of the power an experience with a transforming quality. Among the many varieties of this religious phenomenon a large number may be associated with charismatic experience, and with acts of healing which are public and in the presence of a supportive congregation. These movements of the Holy Spirit are not par-ticularly or predominantly an Anglican thing. It is suitable, though, to refer to them here, not in order to give a history but to consider whether they have a special significance in Anglicanism.

That they play a part in recent Anglican experience is not disputed, but it is not particularly an Anglican phenomenon. For example, charismatic characteristics are not uncommon in Roman Catholic congregations. There, as with Anglicans, and some of the long-standing Protestant Churches, manifestations of particular movements of the Spirit relate more to particular congregations than to wider Christian areas such as dioceses. Some of the movements, however, are very wide indeed. This would be true of aspects of the 'Revival Movement' in East Africa. Often, whether local or much wider, an individual plays a dominant part. The influence in some parts of the world is closely associated with 'Prophets' and the 'Pro-phet Movement.' The manifestations are not identical though they have features in common; moreover the 'Prophet Movement' is almost certainly on the decline now.

Healings are abundant in the gospels, and there is ground for expressing surprise that they have not played a more prominent part in Christian life. Certainly they are no new thing. It is no surprise that the ministry of healing was a subject in the discussions of the Lambeth Conference of 1930, and that the relevant resolution (No. 73) says in section (d):

> Seeing that the ministry of the Church is a ministry for the whole man, it is of the utmost importance that the clergy should equip themselves for a fuller understanding of the intimate connexion between moral and spiritual disorders and mental and physical ills.

Ministries which concentrate on healing and have official support and encouragement are widespread in the Anglican Communion as elsewhere. Among Christians there are different approaches and practices, but this is not a field in which one would contend that some particular or outstanding development has taken place in the Anglican world.

One could wish to see a revived concentration on the theology of the Holy Spirit. The traditional theologies of Christendom are pro-found and fundamental to the Christian faith, but one feels that the full depth of this subject as it appears in the New Testament, and as

Christian experience has sometimes encountered it, has not yet been plumbed and explored to the full. But that exploration, one must allow, is not a requirement of this study. Here it is appropriate to say that in matters pertaining to movements of the Holy Spirit there has been, and is, Anglican participation.

d. The World of Christian Scholarship

In proceeding with this study of developments in the Anglican Communion no decision has been more difficult than deciding what place in it, if any, should be allotted to the role and performance of academic theologians. One has been tempted to omit it altogether, but their role is far too important for that. Anything like a comprehensive study of the subject would, however, be a major undertaking in itself, and would need a fund of information that this writer does not have. So here a limited selection of points is made by which it is hoped a reasonable conclusion may be drawn.

First an elimination. On either side of the turn of the century it was the custom with some publishers to advertise at the back of their books all their other available publications on similar subjects. The proportion of these that are quite forgotten is fascinating. Academic competitiveness and contemporary minor controversies produce books that have but a short time to live. This is true of all Churches.

On the other hand there is academic theology — again in all the Churches — which has a permanent importance. It may have a smaller immediate readership, but it has a lasting significance. Broadly it is of three kinds. One is of biblical studies, and while making use of all available thought is also concerned to reject bad thinking. The second is focussed on some part of the whole history of Christian traditions and theologies: it has its Denzingers and Binghams, as well as its Gregories and Barths, and its students of the Fathers and the ecclesiastical affairs of nations. The third is concerned to interpret the faith in the light of contemporary attitudes of thought — of evolution, secularism and internationalism, for example. It cannot be said that any one of the three is more important than the others, though each in turn may seem to be so while attention is centred on it.

One of the things they have in common today is the essential element of ecumenism. The scholars whose preoccupation they are, and who are often personally related in their work, are not of one denomination, and the objects of their study in most cases have a universal character. This element of universality or catholicism gives substance and hope to the endeavour for unity which can no longer exist in separation from it.

The question for this study is whether the Anglican Communion is an integral part of what is going on. To contend that it plays the leading role would be difficult to sustain. The significance of roles and achievements attached to particular names is not a fruitful debate or one that is of much concern. There is Anglican participation of value throughout the field. One is thankful that there has been Anglican participation in the studies of the relation of Christianity to secularism, and to the 'Death of God' debate. The point is not that a particular view was contended for, or is thought to be prevailing, but that our Communion has participated significantly in a very real debate on a major contemporary issue. It is not necessarily bad scholarship which asserts that a mould may have to be broken. To assess in terms of 'development' in the Anglican Communion does not commend itself, if it is possible at all. Any satisfaction that is appropriate arises only because the Communion has not stood on the bank and merely watched while the river flowed on its way.

VIII

Degrees of Development
in the Anglican Communion

in the last twenty to twenty-five years

John Henry Newman's book *Development of Christian Doctrine* ends with the words "My eyes have seen your salvation." The book is beyond doubt the work of a great and very Christian mind. It was written in years when Newman himself was in a troubled search to discern what relationship there might be between the faith of the apostolic Church and the faith and doctrine he encountered in his own life. They were the years that included his departure from his own Anglican allegiance for obedience to the Roman Catholic Church in 1845, the year with which the Preface is dated. They were years when he was seeking a peace that could satisfy his sensitive mind. He does not in that book examine the gospel and its revelation of God's salvation: the apostolic faith is assumed. His thought is occupied with logic and with the history of the centuries that followed. He found the link he sought in the evolution of Christian doctrine, in the increasing realization, through the centuries, of what was implicit from the beginning. Through all the vagaries and passing conflicts of human agents the necessary contents of Christian doctrine became more explicit. There was nothing essentially new.

To a reader today the minuteness of much of the historical study and the application of logic can seem almost excessive, and more than the subject requires — that is until the date of Newman's study is recalled. Darwin's *The Origin of Species* was published in 1859, fourteen years after Newman's book. It is largely because of Darwin's work that our minds are ingrained with the tenets of evolution, and that concepts of development are so widely applied. Newman had to work it out for himself, in a way that would satisfy his critical and unpeaceful mind. The deepening understanding of Christian doctrine, which owes so much to him for its inauguration, continues in theological thought. Nothing is more significant for any study of Christian development than that phrase of his from *Nunc Dimittis* with which he ends. The foundation of all that has come after is the gospel of salvation. Development, as he discovered, is not to be explained, as is too often the case, by what seemed progressive at the time. It is something that must be implicit in the apostolic gospel.

As one has worked on this study it has become increasingly apparent that the tendency to assume that one knows what 'development' means and involves must be an assumption surrounded by caution. Of course the profundity of Newman's examination has an approach which is not for every occasion. Certainly a use of the word in the plural, which is what we have — 'a study of developments in the Anglican Communion' — has a more ready meaning, especially in the decades of virtually universal post-Darwinian assumptions, but one has learned that the fundamental must never be lost sight of: that at the heart of the matter is the apostolic gospel.

Perhaps in some parts of this study recognition of that requirement will be apparent. Simply to have listed what may be thought (at any rate by me) as developments in the Anglican Communion in recent years would not have been satisfactory. We have ranged fairly widely, not only in the interests of compiling a list, but more especially to help us to awareness of an impression that is both significant and worthwhile. What Newman has taught us is to suspect any Christian impression that does not have its foundations in the gospel of salvation.

An area in which Anglican development has been particularly apparent is the maturing of internationalism and universality. The great growth that has been observed in Provinces and their autonomy has stressed the extension of God's universal work of redemption throughout the Church in which we have our being. The Anglican Communion has established its own relationship as that of a family that is also a family of equals. Authority is characterized, as in the early days of the Church, by free association, discussion, and mutual esteem of the whole. Limited interpretations, which may have served a purpose in their day, are fading. For centuries the

Church has respected persons, and the developing appreciation of the universality that typifies God's outlook is serving to emphasize that there is no future in that. The divine universality which the Church is in process of re-expressing in its life and structure is inseparable from the biblical condemnation of oppression and poverty, of a disregard of justice or of community.

Structures and organization are necessary and acceptable in a world-wide Church; the requirement is that on the godward side they shall be an expression of Christian obedience, and that on the human side they shall embody the response of faith to Christ.

Christian doctrine, of course, has its foundation in the gospel of salvation, and because that is of universal relevance its expression is limited when the experience on which theology and faith are built is restricted to one tradition or culture or national history. 'The International Theological and Doctrinal Commission' which the Churches recently brought into being through the Anglican Consultative Council is significant in the impression of Anglican development that it gives. In several ways it is still immature, but it is international in thought and membership, and while honouring the dictums of past conferences, and theological skills that are national and may assume a national norm, it turns essentially to what is felt to be the universal and the apostolic.

In that area of development the impression is that fundamentals have been established, and that building on them proceeds, not without hesitations and qualms, but without basic fears for the future impetus of the development. In some areas of development there is little fear that all may not be well.

Repeatedly this study has had cause to refer to 'the whole people of God,' that is, to the understanding that Christ's Church is composed of all the faithful, and that its present activity is based in Christ himself and all the living members of his Body. Distinctions of function within the Church are appropriate and necessary, but secondary. A form by which in practice this understanding of Christian membership tends to find expression is the assertion of the full role of the laity, and perhaps of the clergy or presbyterate too, in the life of the Church. The whole Body of Christ has a common ministry of service and obedience. This does not mean that there is not a specially ordained ministry, but this does not constitute the Church but is constituted by it and within it.

Seldom in Christian history is there denial of the belief in the whole People of God, rather it has suffered from being eclipsed or ignored, not least by laity themselves who see themselves as the people who follow, and the hierarchy — which in addition to bishops may include clergy and accepted scholars — as those designated to lead. This is a different concept from the apostolic teaching that there is the one body although within it all do not have identical office. We have noted that the oneness of the People of God has from time to time been explicitly re-asserted, and that such re-assertions were not unusual occurrences in Lambeth Conferences. The more adequate Anglican expression of this concept is one of the great features of the period covered by this study.

We have seen how the effects of the second World War and of the Lambeth Conferences in 1948 and 1958 led to the appointment of the first Anglican Executive Officer, Bishop Bayne, who saw the responsibility to the entire Anglican Communion to which he was called as being distorted if he should think of that Communion as the hierarchy only. The next step was the forming by the Churches of an organization to follow and extend his work. This was the Anglican Consultative Council, with its membership not only extending world-wide to all the Provinces, but composed of bishops, clergy and lay persons — equal in membership and voting power — that is, of the whole People of God. It remains one of the great Anglican developments of the last twenty-five years. It consolidated on a world basis what for a long time — albeit unevenly — had been establishing itself in the dioceses and Provinces, that is, the synods, in which bishops, clergy and laity combined as one body in finding the expression of their response to Christ. The bishop represented his diocese — not himself — to the Church at large; and he was responsible for representing the Church at large — the whole People of God — to his diocese.

One would expect development towards the full working of this concept to have a ride that was not smooth all the way, but the question now is whether development worthy of the name will continue, at any rate for some time to come. There is a tendency for bishops to become oracles again, or with a pre-eminence that identifies more with the functions of chiefs and high executives than with the presidential servants of the People of God. We are in an age of hierarchies: not all of them episcopal, or even ecclesiastical. In the

Anglican world it is an age in which meetings confined to principal Archbishops — Primates' Meetings — have come into being for an undefined purpose, though not, it is fair to say, without some questioning about their significance and purpose.

One can argue, however, that all too often the laity have not been diligent in fulfilling, or sometimes even in understanding the responsibilities and privileges which are theirs as the People of God, of which in fact they are the great majority. (To avoid a lengthy consideration which is not wholly essential here the clergy are not made a subject of separate discussion. For present purposes let it suffice to say that sometimes they are more readily seen as included with hierarchy, sometimes as included with the majority of the People of God.) Too often the voice of the laity is not heard because it is not raised. Too often they seem content to act as spectators. It may not be easy for a bishop to learn what the people of his diocese think. Representation is then not a simple accomplishment, nevertheless he must speak for his diocese when it is required. One cannot be surprised if he and his colleagues come to see themselves as a force in their own right.

There has developed in the Anglican Communion a better understanding of being the People of God. A basic belief of the Church is being better understood and acted upon. It will be a tragedy, not to Anglicanism alone, but to the whole Church, if this appreciation of the Apostolic Church ceases to move out of distortions that have so often plagued it in the past. One of the greatest hopes that this study of developments has stimulated is by no means wholly separated from doubts as to its future.

Another prospect in which a significant horizon has come into view but then remains distant concerns grandeur and pomp. This study has at times left the impression that current and accustomed ecclesiastical ways are less than emphatic about the humility and simplicity which are presented in the gospel. This impression was apparent, for example, in reference to such matters as nationalism and prestige, and to status, and to property, but it does not belong to those things alone. Disquiet about these matters is patchy and spasmodic, and it is far from unusual for higher offices in the Church to be attractive for that reason, among others. At the Lambeth Conference of 1968 the following resolution (No. 41) was proposed by a member with experience of witnessing to the faith in Africa:

The Conference recommends that the bishops, as leaders and representatives of a servant Church, should radically examine the honours paid to them in the course of divine worship, in titles and customary address, and in style of living, while having the necessary facilities for the efficient carrying on of their work.

The Conference, with its world representation passed the resolution with sincerity, but not a great deal has been heard of it since. One felt there was a reaction which agreed that the resolution was right in its theory, but expressed rather more than could be expected in fact; that its merit was that it had planted a good marker which might become suitable for further consideration at some future date.

Considerations such as this have brought us into areas which some would designate as failure areas as far as development is concerned. But the prospects may be a little brighter if we maintain the notion of markers which could provide for future work for developments — that is of the near future, not some distant horizon.

Two which concern changes which are coming in the world are the vast increase in world population (especially in Asia) by the turn of this century; and the rapidly approaching effects of computers on the ways of civilization.

Two which have a much longer Anglican history, but which are probably more amenable now to changes that development would bring, concern diversities within Anglicanism which are less out of place than is sometimes asserted but which can be excessive; and akin to this, but more injurious to universal witness to the gospel, diversities and addictions relating to churchmanship and party. An impression which this analysis seems to urge is that convergence is increasingly appreciated, and mutual understanding valued. With that sort of groundwork procedure towards developments that are worthy of the name are possible.

Convergence marks a more positive development in the field of ecumenics and Christian unity. Progress in the Anglican Communion and in most other Churches is slow: one cannot envisage realistically major unions of Churches happening in this century, but one can envisage them. It is not so very long since efforts towards unity either assumed a disproportionate amount of change in the party, or a measure of pluralism that was unlikely ever to be acceptable very widely — which, in short, defeated the object of the exercise from the outset. Schemes for unions have almost invariably failed in the end among the participants and have lacked allure with most of the non-participants in other Churches (but not necessarily so) who were watching. More recent development has been a change from beginning with the purpose of sorting out classical differences to proceeding by locating common ground and seeing how much can be built together from there. As we have observed, whether one is considering Roman Catholics, Orthodox, Protestants or Anglicans, their common ground with other Churches is bigger than most expected. Moreover churchmen are apt to discover, sometimes to their temporary discomfort, that they have not quite so much in common with the Churches they favour more than with those they favour less. For example, in the Anglican area, despite the notable progress with Rome it seems probable that common ground there may be less than the Anglicans have with the Lutherans. The concept of convergence underlies a more hopeful ecumenical procedure than the period that preceded it. One must doubt whether a study like the World Council of Churches' *Baptism, Eucharist and Ministry* could have been compiled and studied far and wide with hopefulness and seriousness a decade ago. The transition does reveal a measure of ecumenical development, and the participation in it of the Anglican Communion implies a sharing in a work of development, slow though it may be.

The Church's involvement in politics has become a more frequent subject of discussion, and not infrequently of criticism. The implication of this is that the Church is indeed more involved than it used to be and the change cannot be ignored. In noting this change earlier in this study — and of course it is not Anglican alone — we have asserted that this is a proper Christian manifestation of concern about what is happening to people. So it is right to classify the more overt involvement in politics, and particularly in political justice, as more than a change: it is a development. To many good people, particularly in the older countries, there is criticism of the involvement often on the basis that the cobbler, in this case the Christian Church, should stick to his last, and that means sticking to religion and not becoming involved in politics. To an increasing number of Christians active expression of concern about people, and justice and freedom is a Christian principle. Development occurs, but not without turbulence. In appraising the Anglican development a fair description might be "Slow ahead".

Factors influencing events there include the increase of travel by individuals so that they see more of what their fellows in other countries are confronted with, and what powers are most influential: they may approve or disapprove of what they see, but the broadening which their thinking undergoes becomes an element in the thinking of their own community and relationships. There is also influence from a slow increase in the consideration of what life is for, and what makes living and dying worthwhile. This may be discounted by some as a religious and not a political factor. In fact it is fundamental to both; and so further serves to emphasize that the one cannot be separated from the other. It is because religion and the Church on the one hand, and politics and power on the other, dispute rights in the same area that people like Archbishop Janani Luwum are put to death. Perhaps the greatest influence affecting the Anglican Church's making its voice heard in political affairs relates to the growth in awareness of its universality. We have previously observed how the greater realization of, for example, justice and liberation from oppression, or of the unity of all people in the eyes of the Creator, derives from that understanding of the gospel message which experience of divine universality attests as nothing else does. The Anglican involvement is justifiably concerned equally with people in Chile, or South Africa, or England, or USA or Japan or Uganda.

There are areas in which, while the Anglican Communion has not stood still it has nevertheless made no notable general contribution. The impression we have used when weighing some of these subjects is that, roughly speaking, Anglicanism has moved with the stream. Subjects we looked at related principally to teaching concerning the Holy Spirit, and related matters concerning charismatic beliefs and healing. To these one might add the use of facilities for information and communication. There are much greater facilities than a few years ago, though a good use of them is a complicated procedure. Many Christian bodies are involved and making progress in one way or another. Among these is the Anglican Communion, but compared with the achievements of others it is not outstanding. If one is going to speak of an Anglican Communion development here it would not be to indicate a notable Anglican progress among the Churches, but that in its own information activities the Anglican Communion is doing better than it was.

The ordination of women to the priesthood is an outstanding change in the behaviour of the Anglican Communion. That is not in doubt. Whether that change constitutes a development is a controversial matter. Accounts of how the subject has proceeded are not always accurate, and because the decisive events are mostly too recent to have received normal historical treatment an attempt has been made in this study to give an objective record of what has taken place. From that basis an analysis asserting development could seem premature, though many would not agree. A timely assertion at this stage may be to say that without doubt and for better or worse a mould has been broken which concerns the Anglican Communion and some other Churches, and that there is no likelihood that the Anglican Communion will return to the former state. What may well be considered commendable is that on an issue about which there is a deep diversity of feeling, and in a Communion where there is at present diversity of action concerning ordaining women, there is so much patience with other people's points of view, and that at the Lambeth Conference of 1978 a *modus operandi*, a way of living together in the one Communion, was acceptable to the vast majority.

An assessment of developments in the Anglican Communion in the past twenty-five years is inseparable from an assessment of spirituality in that period. All through the writing of this study the need has been recurring in one's mind, and yet only here, as the very end is approached is a direct reference made to the course that Anglican spirituality has taken. The reason for this is that spiritual things, the sincerity of the search for Christ, the commitment in prayer and worship, are too hidden and personal to be a subject for comparisons. An impression, for any worth it has, may well be rejected, and there must be no complaint. My own impression, which is fragile and subject to those limitations, is that the last quarter century has not been a great spiritual age in the Anglican Communion. There has been continuation of the spiritual element in the common life; there have been some outstanding spiritual figures, men and women, in various parts of the Communion, but not a Saint John of the Cross, or even perhaps an Evelyn Underhill. There has been a growth in esteem for quietness, but not a great deal of it. The Religious Orders generally seem fewer in numbers and less in influence than had been hoped. But many people, including the clergy, in a world of problems, have their problems too. The turbulence and frustration that often press upon their lives, when placed in a setting of prayer, may involve no less spiritual effort than in the past became associated with George Herbert and the response his gentle devotion encountered. In any age we can be unwise in deducing more than a little about a person's struggle or neglect for the things of God. We do not know enough in this life for contentions about developments: the most that one might do is to register a tentative impression — the impression already given that the last quarter century has not been a great spiritual age in the Anglican Communion. One hesitates to suppose that much that the master asked for in the highways and hedges has been achieved.

The collecting together of information in this study, and particularly in this last section, has produced an assessment that in a moderate way asserts developments more than it glooms at the lack of them.

Beyond any valuations extracted from particular performances it is appropriate to repeat what was said earlier about the basic factor against which any change must be measured. It was said then (page 22), and it will always remain true, that the "basic factor is the purposes of Jesus Christ — the gospel and what he said. Development is to progress in fulfilling the Father's intention of salvation through Jesus. The Church through the ages, and any part of it, exists for that reason." To that may be added that such development as there may have been is the Father's own accomplishment and not the achievement of even the most devoted agents. As Saint Paul underlined for us, it is not the gardeners who cause things to grow. The gardeners do not count:

> After all, what is Apollos? What is Paul? We are simply God's agents in bringing you to the faith. Each of us performed the task which the Lord allotted to him: I planted the seed, and Apollos watered it; but God made it grow. Thus it is not the gardeners with their planting and watering who count, but God, who makes it grow.
>
> (*I Corinthians 3:5-7; N E B*)

Appendices
I

Dates and Events since the Second World War

Year	Anglican	Other Ecclesiastical Affairs	Political and Social Affairs, etc.
(before 1945)			
1928–42	Lang: Abp of Canterbury		1933 FD Roosevelt: Pres. of USA
1942–44	Wm Temple: Abp of Canterbury		1934–36 China: the Long March
		1542 BCC.	1936 George VI to throne
			1940 Churchill: Prime Minister Coalition Government
1945	Fisher: Abp of Canterbury		Hiroshima: first atom bomb
			Churchill: PM
			Attlee: PM
			Truman: President of USA
1947	Sherrill: Pres. Bp USA	Ch. of S. India formed	Burma: Political independence
1948	Lambeth Conference	WCC founded, Amsterdam Athenagoras I: Ecumenical Patriarch (1948–72)	

Year	Anglican	Other Ecclesiastical Affairs	Political and Social Affairs, etc.
1949			People's Republic of China declared
1950	West Africa Province created		Korean War began
1951			Churchill: PM
1952			Queen Elizabeth II
1953			Korean War ended
			Eisenhower: President of USA
			Stalin died
			Khruschev: Party Secy
1954	Ang. Congress, Minneapolis	WCC Assembly, Evanston	
1955	Central Africa Province created		Eden: PM
1956	*Naught for your Comfort* published		Suez affair
			Transistor developed
1957			MacMillan: PM
			Ghana: Pol. independence
			Sputnik I
1958	Lambeth Conference	Pope Pius XII died	
	Lichtenberger: Pres. Bp	Pope John XXIII elected	
1960	Bp Bayne: first Executive Officer		Nigeria: Pol. independence
	East Africa Province created (Kenya & Tanzania)		

Year			
1961	Abp Fisher visited Rome (Dec.) Ramsey: Abp of Canterbury Uganda, Rwanda, Burundi & Boga-Zaire Prov. created	WCC Assembly, New Delhi	John F. Kennedy: Pres. of USA Sierra Leone: Pol. independence Tanzania: Pol. independence
1962	*Compasrose No. 1*	Vatican II began (Oct.)	
1963	Anglican Congress, Toronto	Pope John XXIII died Paul VI elected	Uganda: Pol. independence Kenya: Pol. independence John F. Kennedy assassinated Lyndon Johnson: Pres. of USA Douglas – Home: PM
1964	Bp Dean: second Executive Officer		Malawi: Pol. independence Zambia: Pol. independence Wilson: PM UDI Rhodesia
1965	Hines: Pres. Bp	Vatican II ended (Dec)	
1966	Abp Ramsey to Rome; *Common Declaration* with Pope Paul VI LCB meeting: Jerusalem Advisory Cte to Ex. Off. met in Nairobi	WCC: Blake succeeded Visser t'Hooft as General Secretary *Anglican – Methodist Conversations.*	
1967		Commission with RC's met (Jan.)	Arusha Declaration (Nyerere)
1968	Lambeth Conference Anglican Consultative Council	Comm. with RC's: *Malta Report*	

Year	Anglican	Other Ecclesiastical Affairs	Political and Social Affairs, etc.
	proposed	WCC Assembly: Uppsala WCC: MM Thomas elected Mod. of Central Committee Humanae Vitae published by Pope Paul VI	
1969	Bp Howe: third Executive Officer Churches agreed Anglican Consultative Council		Nixon: Pres. of USA First man on the moon (July)
1970	Kenya Province created Tanzania Prov. created Burma Province created General Synod of Ch. of England inaugurated	Ch. of N.India formed Ch. of Pakistan formed Anglican/Lutheran Commission first met	Heath: PM
1971	ACC-1 met (Limuru) ACC: Bp Howe first Sec.Gen. Anglican Information No. 1 First women priests (Hong Kong)	Demetrios I: Ecumenical Patriarch	Uganda: Amin to power
1972		WCC: Blake succeeded by Potter	

	Anglican Communion	Church/Ecumenical	World
1973	ACC-2 (Dublin) Indian Ocean Prov. created	Anglican/Orthodox Joint Doctrinal Discussions – first meeting	Wilson: PM
1974	Coggan: Abp of Canterbury Allin: Pres. Bp Consejo Anglicano Sud Americano Prov. created	Watergate Ford: Pres. of USA	
1975	Melanesia Prov. created	WCC Assembly: Nairobi Abp Scott (Canada) elected Moderator of Central Cte	Papua New Guinea: Political independence Fall of Saigon (Vietnam War) President Mao died (China) Callaghan: PM
1976	ACC-3 (Trinidad) Jerusalem and Middle East Province created Sudan Province created	Anglican/Orthodox: Moscow Agreement	Carter: Pres. of USA
1977	Abp Coggan to Rome/ Istanbul/Geneva Abp Janani Luwum killed (Uganda) Papua New Guinea Province created		
1978	Lambeth Conference	Pope Paul VI died Pope John Paul II elected	
1979	ACC-4 (Canada) Primates' Meeting (Ely, Eng)		Thatcher: PM Iran Revolution

Year	Anglican	Other Ecclesiastical Affairs	Political and Social Affairs, etc.
1980	Nigeria became separate Province from West Africa Province Runcie: Abp. of Canterbury	Council of Ch. of China formed	
1981	Burundi, Rwanda, Zaire Province created Uganda: separate Province ACC-5 (Newcastle, England) Primates' Meeting (Washington, DC)	Non-Whites became a majority of all Christians (probable date)	Reagan: Pres. of USA
1982	Liberia to West Africa Province	Ang/RC Commission (ARCIC) Report published	
1983	Dr. S. Van Culin: second Sec. Gen. of ACC Primates' Mtg (Nairobi) ARCIC-2: first meeting	WCC Assembly: Vancouver Dr. Held elected Moderator of Central Committee Ang/Lutheran Commission: second phase RC Canon Law published	*Current kingdom [?] not mentioned.*

II

Lambeth Conference Committee Subjects
since the Second World War

1948   I(A)   The Christian Doctrine of Man
        II   The Church and the Modern World
        I(B)   The Christian Way of Life
        III   The Unity of the Church
        IV   The Anglican Communion
        V(A)   The Church's Discipline in Marriage
        V(B)   Baptism and Confirmation
        V(C)   Proposed Chinese Canon on Ordination of
                a Deaconness to the Priesthood

1958   1.   The Holy Bible: Its Authority and Message
        2.   Church Unity and the Church Universal
        3.   Progress in the Anglican Communion
                A.   Missionary Appeal and Strategy
                B.   The Book of Common Prayer
                C.   Ministries and Manpower
        4.   The Reconciling of Conflicts between and within
                Nations
        5.   The Family in Contemporary Society

1968   I   The Renewal of the Church in Faith
                Affirmations
                The Contemporary Scene
                The Church's Approach to the World
                International Morality Today
                The Thirty-Nine Articles and the Anglican
                  Tradition
        II   The Renewal of the Church in Ministry
                Laymen and Laywomen
                Priesthood

III

Anglican Consultative Council
Main Subjects of Meetings

1971 ACC-1 Unity and Ecumenical Affairs
Renewal: Church and Society
Renewal: Order and Organization in the Anglican
    Church
Mission and Evangelism
Financial and Other Matters

1973 ACC-2 Unity and Ecumenical Affairs
Church and Society
Order and Organization in the Anglican
    Communion
Mission and Evangelism
Finance, Membership, and Other Matters
    A. Finance
    B. Membership of the Council
    C. Officers of the Council
    D. Legal Status for the Council in the United
        Kingdom
    E. Communication in the Anglican
        Communion
    F. St. George's College, Jerusalem
    G. Conference for the Abolition of Torture

1976 ACC-3 Unity and Ecumenical Affairs
Church and Society
Ministry
Mission and Evangelism
Lambeth Conference
    Explanatory Introduction
    The Debate by the Council
    The Archbishop of Canterbury's Statement

1979   ACC-4   Unity
Anglican-Lutheran Relations
Anglican-Reformed Relations
Anglican-Orthodox Relations
The *Filioque* Clause
Anglican-Oriental Orthodox Relations
Anglican-Roman Catholic Relations
New Zealand Proposals for a Covenant and
Unification of Ministries
The World Council of Churches
World Confessional Families
Ecumenical Consequences of the Ordination
of Women
Mission
Part A — Mission: The Purpose of Partnership
Part B — Evangelism: The Heart of Mission
A Theological Basis of Human Rights
The Anglican Communion *which includes*
Guidelines for Service in the world-wide
Church
Inter-Anglican Theological and Doctrinal
Commission
Inter-Anglican Dialogue on Women in the
Priesthood
Guidelines for Provincial Constitutions and
Metropolitical Authority
Criteria for New Dioceses
The Anglican Consultative Council
Inter-Anglican Budget
Anglican Centre in Rome
Contributions from united Churches
Miscellanea *which includes*
Anglican Clergy in Exile
The Anglican Cycle of Prayer
Independent Churches
A Summary of the Review Address on Affairs
of the A.C.C.

1981   ACC-5   Review Address by the Secretary General
The Gospel and People

Unity and Ecumenical Affairs
Growing in our Ministries
Anglican Affairs

IV

The Ordination of Women to the Priesthood

Material gathered from the Anglican Churches, mostly in preparation for the Lambeth Conference 1978 (see above page 157)

I. Churches which have Ordained Women

Diocese of Hong Kong

The first ordinations took place on Advent Sunday, 1971.

Anglican Church of Canada

General Synod in June 1975 passed the following resolutions:

Act 63: That this General Synod recommend to diocesan authorities that all types of lay ministries, stipendiary and non-stipendiary, within the Anglican Church of Canada, be open to all qualified persons without regard to sex.

Act 64: That this General Synod re-affirm the principle of the ordination of women to the priesthood

	In favour	Against
Laity	88	18
Clergy	75	30
Bishops	26	8
Total	189	56

Act 65: That this General Synod further affirm that it would be appropriate for women qualified for the priesthood to be ordained at the discretion of diocesan bishops acting within the normal procedures of their own jurisdiction and in consultation with the House of Bishops.

	In favour	Against
Laity	95	9
Clergy	86	19

Bishops	27	7
Total	208	35

The first ordinations took place on 30th November, 1976.

Episcopal Church, U.S.A.

In November 1972 the House of Bishops voted that it was the mind of the House that women should be ordained to the priesthood and episcopate (in favour 74, against 61, abstentions 5). In the House of Deputies of General Convention in October 1973 a resolution in favour of ordaining women to the priesthood was defeated. Voting, by dioceses, was as follows:

	Yes	No	Divided
Clergy	50	43	20
Laity	49	37	26

Where the voting in a diocese is equally divided, it counts as a vote against the motion. The resolution, having failed in the House of Deputies, was not debated in the House of Bishops. On July 29, 1974, there was a service of ordination of eleven women at the Church of the Advocate, Philadelphia. This was not authorized by the Diocese or the Presiding Bishop. Three retired bishops and the Bishop of Costa Rica officiated. A special meeting of the House of Bishops in August declared the Philadelphia ordinations invalid by 129 votes to 9, with 8 abstentions. The House of Bishops in July 1974 re-affirmed by a three to one majority the principle of the ordination of women.

At the General Convention in September 1976 approval was given to the ordination of women to the priesthood. The House of Bishops voted 95 to 61 in favour of the canonical change which makes ordination canons equally applicable to men and women. By a narrow margin the House of Deputies concurred with the Bishops' decision. The voting was as follows:

	Yes	No	Divided
Clergy	60	39	15
Laity	64	36	13

Since 58 clerical votes and 57 lay votes (the Haiti lay deputation did not vote) were needed for the canonical change to be made, the margin of affirmative votes was 2 clergy and 7 lay votes.

The House of Bishops after a long debate agreed to advise two optional procedures for regularizing the orders of 15 women irregularly ordained in 1974–75:

a. A public event conducted by the bishop involved and an affirmation that the ordinations were now regular, or
b. A conditional ordination.

The first ordinations took place on 1 January 1977.

Province of New Zealand

The Bill allowing the ordination of women was passed by General Synod in March 1974. The procedure required that it should be submitted again to the dioceses and brought to the next General Synod for final decision. General Synod in May 1976 passed the Bill, but a year has to elapse before it can be implemented. During this period appeals may be made to a Tribunal set up under a Parliamentary Act of 1928. An appeal was made to the Tribunal, and was heard in November 1977, and dismissed. For the appeal to be dismissed it is necessary for at least two-thirds of those present to concur in such dismissal. This means that there remains no impediment in the Church of the Province of New Zealand to the ordination of women to the priesthood.

By 31st December, 1977, five women had been ordained to the priesthood.

II. Position in Other Anglican Churches (1977 unless otherwise indicated)

Anglican Church of Australia

A Report prepared by the Commission on Doctrine was referred by General Synod in May 1973 to the dioceses for study. The Commission published a further Report entitled *The Ministry of Women*, recommending the ordination of women as deacons and priests. This Report was debated by General Synod in August 1977, and the following resolution was passed:

> That this General Synod having taken note of the report of its commission on doctrine entitled *The Ministry of Women* believes that the theological objections raised do not constitute a barrier to

the ordination of women to the priesthood and the consecration of women to the episcopate in this Church.

	In favour	Against
Bishops	13	6
Clergy	50	33
Laity	44	33
Total	107	72

The legislation necessary to implement this decision is likely to take some years to complete.

Episcopal Church of Brazil

The General Synod in 1980 rejected a motion to permit the ordination of women. A two-thirds majority in favour in each order was required. Voting was:

	In favour	Against	Abstentions
Bishops	5	1	—
Clergy	7	5	—
Laity	5	5	2
Total	17	11	2

Church of the Province of Burma

The Provincial Council in January 1972 passed the following motion:

> This Council accepts on principle the ordination of women to the priesthood and agrees to its introduction when circumstances so require it.

Church of the Province of Central Africa

The following actions were taken at the Provincial Synod 1976:

i. Episcopal Synod put before Synod the question 'Should the CPCA permit the taking of steps to provide training for women for ordination to the priesthood?' An informal vote was taken by houses, resulting in the following:

	In favour	Against
Laity	7	16
Clergy	5	18
Bishops	2	6
Total	14	40

ii. This Synod affirms the request of Episcopal Synod to the Church of the Province of Canada not to act in the matter of ordination of women to the priesthood, at least until the Lambeth Conference has given some clear lead to the Churches.

iii. Synod agreed overwhelmingly that it should remain in full communion with any other Province which canonically ordains women to the priesthood.

iv. In reply to the question 'Should a diocesan bishop in the CPCA, at his discretion, in consultation with his synodical authorities, be permitted to allow women canonically ordained elsewhere to the priesthood to exercise their ministry in his diocese?', the Synod answered overwhelmingly in the negative.

Church of Ceylon

A majority of the clergy of the Dioceses of Colombo and Kurunagala have voted to take no action at present because this matter is not an issue of importance or urgency in Sri Lanka.

Council of the Church of East Asia: Diocese of Singapore

The Synod in December 1974 voted against the ordination of women to the priesthood.

Church of England

The General Synod on 10 July 1975 passed the following resolutions:

That this Synod considers that there are no fundamental objections to the ordination of women to the priesthood.

	For	*Against*	*Abstentions*
Bishops	28	10	0
Clergy	110	96	2
Laity	117	74	3
Total	255	180	5

That this Synod invites the House of Bishops, when, in light of developments in the Anglican Communion generally as well in this country, they judge the time for action to be right, to bring before the Synod a proposal to admit women to the priesthood.

That this Synod, not wishing to prejudice improving relationships with the Roman Catholic and Orthodox Churches by removing without consultation with them the legal and other barriers to the ordination of women in the Church of England, requests the Presidents to

1. inform the appropriate authorities in those Churches of its belief that there are no fundamental objections to such ordination; and

2. invite those authorities to share in an urgent re-examination of the theological grounds for including women in the Order of Priesthood, with particular attention to the doctrine of Man and the doctrine of Creation.

At the November 1976 General Synod it was stated that:

The House of Bishops has been advised that, as the law stands, a woman ordained abroad cannot lawfully be invited to officiate as a bishop or priest.

At the General Synod of November 1978 the following resolution was defeated:

That this Synod asks the Standing Committee to prepare and bring forward legislation to remove the barriers to the ordination of women to the priesthood and their consecration to the episcopate.

	In favour	Against	Abstentions
Bishops	32	17	1
Clergy	94	149	1
Laity	120	106	1
Total	246	272	3

The General Synod of July 1979 received a report of the position of women lawfully ordained abroad and considered a motion proposing that the Standing Committee should prepare legislation to permit such women to minister in England as priests on special occasions with the permission of the Archbishop and the Bishop of the Diocese and the goodwill of the incumbent and parochial council. The motion failed, having been rejected by the House of Clergy:

	In favour	Against
Bishops	26	10
Clergy	87	113

Laity	110	65
Total	223	188

At the General Synod in July 1982 a private member's motion instructing the Synod's Standing Committee to introduce legislation enabling women lawfully ordained in other Provinces to be given permission to exercise their ministry on particular occasions during temporary visits to England was accepted. The voting was as follows:

	In favour	Against
Bishops	24	4
Clergy	106	68
Laity	103	60
Total	233	132

When the legislation is finally voted on in the Synod, majorities of two-thirds will be required in all three houses.

At the General Synod in November 1983 the Synod gave general approval to the Draft Women Ordained Abroad Measure which seeks to enable, under strict conditions, women ordained in other Provinces to minister in the Church of England. The voting was by houses, as follows:

	In favour	Against
Bishops	24	9
Clergy	122	73
Laity	130	71
Total	276	153

There were 19 abstentions.

The Measure next goes to a Revision Committee.

Before the debate it was announced that the officers of the House of Laity had designated the measure as Article 8 business. The effect of this designation is (i) that before the Measure can finally be approved it will have to be remitted to the diocesan synods, and (ii) that a two-thirds majority will be required in each house at the Final Approval stage.

On Thursday, 15th November, 1984, the following motion was passed:

That this Synod ask the Standing Committee to bring forward legislation to permit the ordination of women to the priesthood in the Provinces of Canterbury and York.

Voting was:

	In favour	*Against*
Bishops	41	6
Clergy	131	98
Laity	135	91

There were 5 abstentions.

It is understood that the earliest date at which draft legislation can come before the General Synod is February, 1986; and before the dioceses is November, 1986; and if, as is probable, dioceses refer it to the deaneries, the legislation is unlikely to reach the Final Approval stage before 1988-1989.

Church of the Province of the Indian Ocean

In November 1974 the Provincial Synod passed the following resolution:

That the Provincial Synod of the Church of the Province of the Indian Ocean approves in principle of the ordination of women to the priesthood and leaves it to each diocese to put this into practice, which decision shall be communicated to the other dioceses of the Province.

Church of Ireland

In May, 1976, the General Synod resolved "that this House approves in principle the ordination of women subject to the enactment of any necessary legislation."

General Synod, in 1979, debated the question of the ordination of women, and referred the question back to the diocesan synods prior to deciding in 1980 what its next step should be.

In 1980 a motion that leave be granted for a bill to be introduced in the 1981 session of the General Synod for the ordination of women failed to achieve the necessary two-thirds majority in the Synod's 1980 sessions. Voting was as follows:

	In favour	Against
Bishops and Clergy	92	57
Laity	136	41
Total	228	98

Japan Holy Catholic Church (Nippon Sei Ko Kai)

The bishops meeting in 1976 agreed that there is no fundamental objection to the ordination of women to the priesthood from the aspect of biblical theology. But the bishops said that the necessary steps for ordaining women could not be taken until there was sufficient understanding of the issue at the parochial, diocesan and provincial level. "While acknowledging the need for a free exchange of opinion, we must guard against the danger of division and schism within the Anglican Communion arising from disagreement." "Further, in view of our relationship with other Churches, the discussion should also proceed on the ecumenical plane."

Church of the Province of Kenya

The House of Bishops in November 1976 "accepted in principle the ordination of women to the priesthood but felt the need for further discussion on diocesan and provincial levels." The Standing Committee of Provincial Synod, meeting shortly after, decided in favour of the ordination of women and said: "If and when any woman is called by God to this office, the bishop will be open to put her through the normal process as all other candidates for training and ordination." But the Province "would not rush women into ordination simply because other Churches are doing the same."

The Episcopal Church in Scotland

The Provincial Synod in October 1979 passed the following motion by one vote:

> That this Synod encourages the fullest use of the ministry of women but, desirous also to preserve the unity of the Church, notes that their ministry in the Episcopate and Presbyterate would not command that degree of acceptance we deem to be an essential mark of such ministry.

In November 1981 the following resolutions were passed in the second chamber but defeated in the first chamber (bishops) by 4 in favour to 3 against — a two-thirds majority being required in each chamber for a resolution to pass:

That the Provincial Synod accepts the advice of the Lambeth Conference to permit the Ordination of Women to the Order of Deacons.

and a resolution to change the wording of a Canon from 'The Order of Deaconesses is the one order of ministry to which women are admitted by prayer and the laying on of hands. . . .' to 'The Order of Deaconesses is an order of ministry to which women are admitted by prayer and the laying on of hands. . . .'

The resolutions therefore failed.

The Church of the Province of South Africa

The Provincial Synod in November 1976 carried a motion that the debate and vote on the ordination of women to the priesthood should be deferred until the relevant report, *Patterns of Ministry*, which recommends the ordination of women, had been translated into some of the other languages used by the Anglican Church in South Africa. The matter would be proceeded with at the next Provincial Synod due in 1979.

South Pacific Anglican Council (SPAC)

The bishops deeply regretted the division in the Church caused by the ordination of women priests and resolved 'that we believe we cannot find in the Bible arguments for or against the admission of women to Holy Orders. Nevertheless we cannot recommend such a step to the Church in our region at this time'; and 'that if any women priests visit the SPAC region, they will not be permitted to exercise priestly functions in our SPAC dioceses' (February 1977).

Church of the Province of Tanzania

In 1976 the Provincial Synod passed the following resolution:

This Synod of the Church of Tanzania is not ready to ordain women to be priests.

The voting was 32 in favour and 7 against.

Church in Wales

Debate took place in the six dioceses before the Governing Body voted in April 1975. The Governing Body decided that 'there are no fundamental objections to the ordination of women to the priesthood', but that 'it would be inexpedient for the Church in Wales to take unilateral action in this matter at the present time.'

Church of the Province of West Africa

The bishops of West Africa have discussed the issue since 1972, but as it 'affects theological, cultural and sociological matters, we feel that it requires further careful study of the Office and Work of the Priesthood so as to educate our people against the background of their own locality. Until this is done, we do not consider the subject as urgent.'

Church of the Province of the West Indies

The Provincial Synod in February 1975 requested all dioceses 'to address and educate themselves to the importance and implications of the Ordination of Women.' This is to include 'the encouragement of informal discussion among the laity' and 'the building up of the role of women in the Church and the creation of opportunities of leadership roles in the Church for women, and the encouragement of such roles.'

BISHOP JOHN HOWE was born in Essex, England, in 1920. He received his theological education at St Chad's College, Durham, and was ordained in 1943 for the Diocese of York.

From 1946–50 he was chaplain of Adisadel College, Ghana, and then moved to Edinburgh Theological College, Scotland, as vice-principal. In 1955 he was consecrated Bishop of St Andrews, Dunkeld, and Dunblane. He succeeded Bishop Ralph Dean (Canada) as executive officer to the Anglican Communion in 1969. His immediate major task was the implementation of the 1968 Lambeth Conference Resolution which proposed to the provinces of the communion the establishment of the Anglican Consultative Council. By October 1969 the formation of the Council was approved by all the provinces, and at its first meeting in Limuru, Kenya, in 1971, Bishop Howe was appointed secretary general, a position he held until December 1982. He was chairman of the council for the Anglican Centre in Rome (1974–78), and president of the annual meeting of Secretaries of the Christian World Communions (1974–78). Since 1982 he has been engaged in research and writing, and in lecturing in many parts of the Anglican world.

Bishop Howe includes in his recreations hill-walking, geology, and growing alpine plants.